The Language of
TATTOOS
130 Symbols & What They Mean

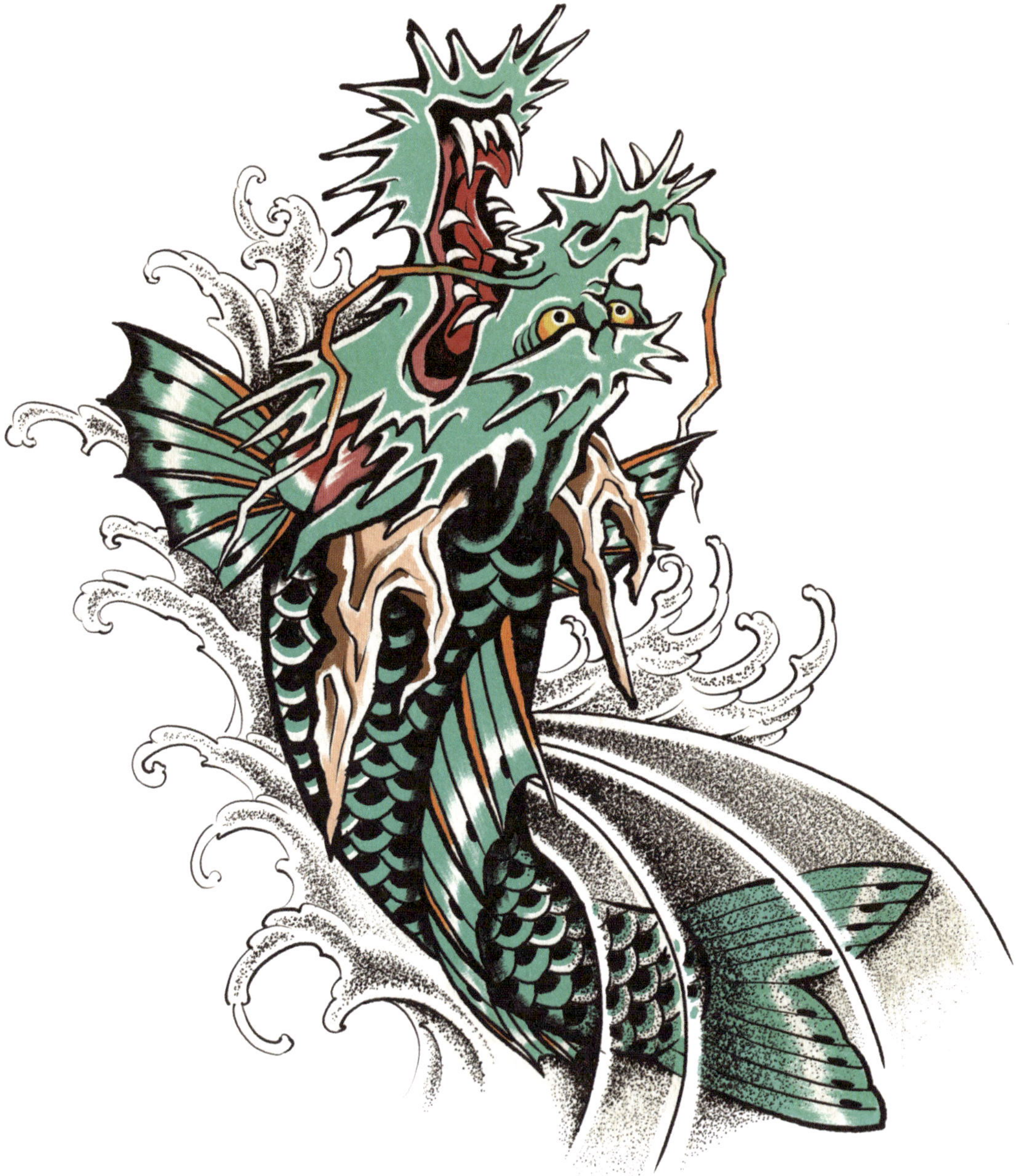

The Language of

TATTOOS

130 Symbols & What They Mean

Oliver Munden & Nick Schonberger

FRANCES
LINCOLN

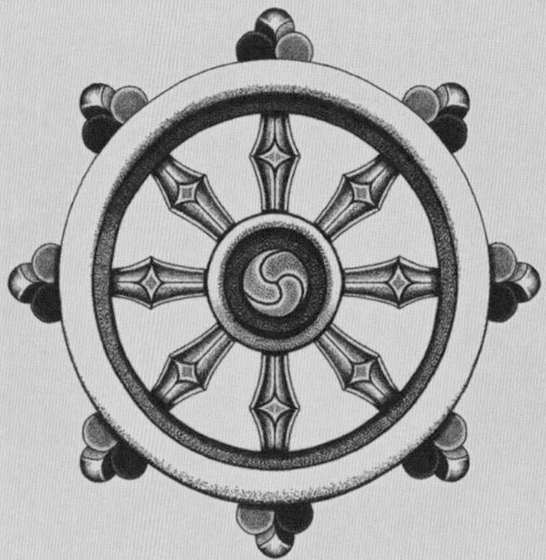

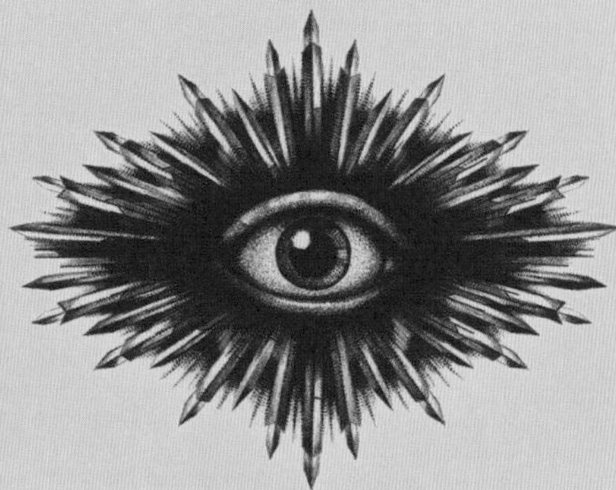

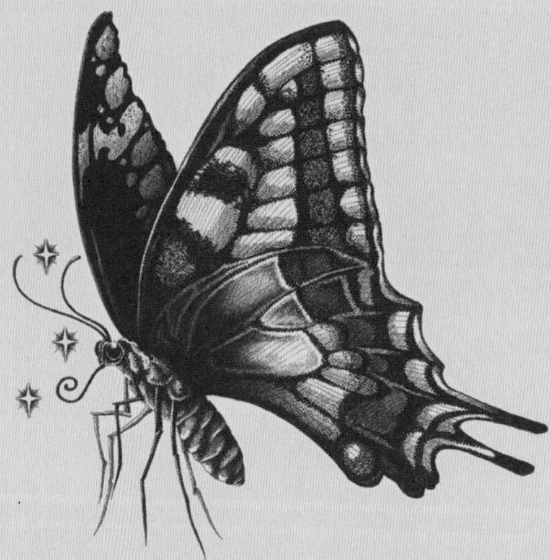

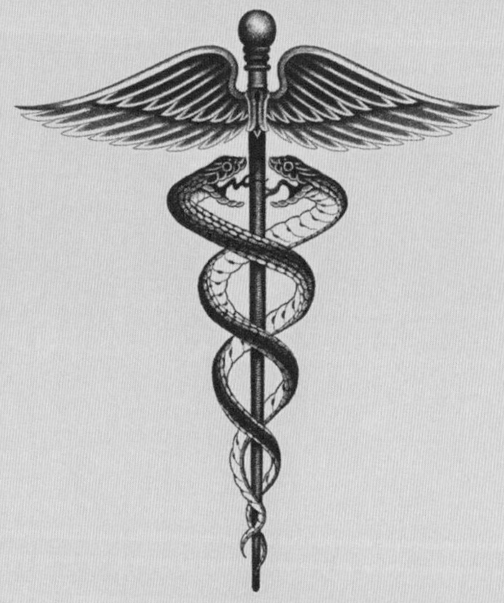

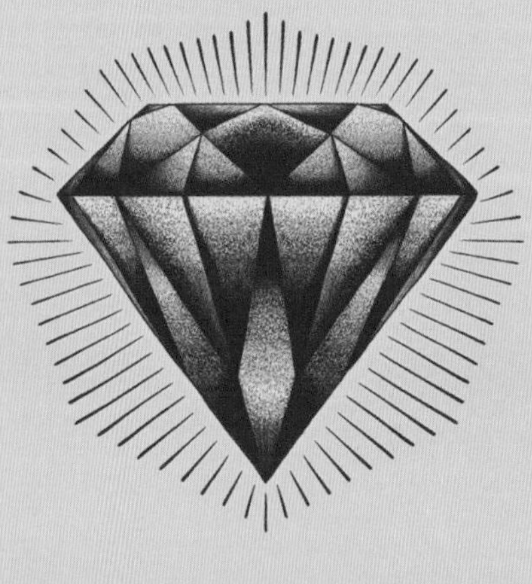

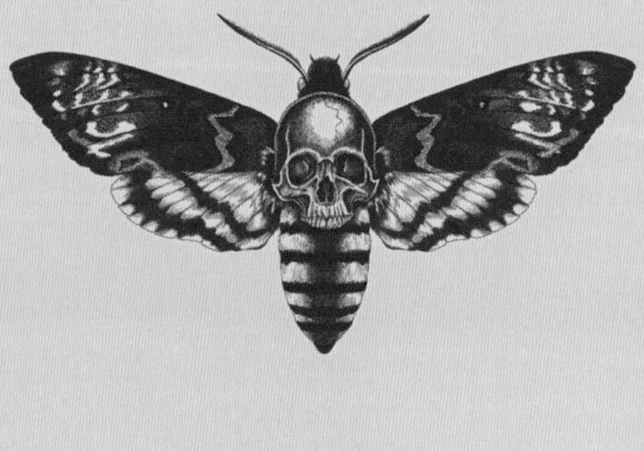

Contents

Introduction

It is not possible to discuss the language of tattoos without first acknowledging appropriation. Many of the images that represent and inform what we generally accept as standard in tattooing have been taken from a diverse range of places and cultures and granted new life as adornments for the body.

The rapid rise of popular print during the 19th century created a wealth of material ranging from dynamic visual interpretations of popular Christian hymns to the robust graphic language of Victorian funeral tradition. In swift turn, such images became motifs for tattoos and, over time, their tattoo forms became more widely recognized than the original designs. Images derived from military insignia, nation building, brand building, the thrills of the carnival, the blur of the locomotive era, the allure of Hollywood and the power of fast fashion enjoyed a similar fate.

Of course, this is the exciting thing about the language of tattoos. Pictures traverse time and environment, layering tones from prior generations with those of new generations to create an ever-deepening shared culture. The varied, and sometimes conflicting, channels for some images reflect the truly multifaceted flow of information – and of visual culture – that is seen on countless pages, web browsers, bodies and more.

A second acknowledgement within the context of this book, is that the images described fall within a particular history of tattooing, specifically, the European/North American tradition. It is in this tradition that tattooing is at once an art and a craft, but also a codified business complete with an intoxicating mythology and the vibrant scene that prevails today.

A long-standing interconnection between American, European and Japanese tattoo traditions realizes another subset of tattooing's language. American and European tattooists have drawn inspiration from Japanese aesthetic and craft ever since the opening of Japan to the West in the 1850s. Despite this reverence, the studied relationship between mythology, woodblock print (*ukiyo-e*) and body-focused composition that informs Japanese tattooing is juxtaposed with remnants of artistic liberty taken with pan-Asian aesthetic.

Polarities of the academic and the base underly a tension inherent to the language of tattoos, at once a celebratory amalgam of global influences and a painful reminder of brazen cultural theft. This notion stands in a third subset of tattooing, the fine-line style. Emerging from predominantly Chicano communities in Southern California, the style now enjoys worldwide demand. Aside from the look, which produces a glorious textural depth via subtle black-to-skin gradation, the style helped popularize a series of images now synonymous with contemporary tattooing. Furthermore, it is imbued with cultural codes and informs a certain cool.

When Oliver Munden began his career, the three dominant tattoo styles of fine line, Irezumi (traditional Japanese tattooing) and western traditional had become firmly rooted as choices for anyone stepping inside a studio, shop or parlour. It is with these styles, appropriated slowly into the widening tattoo business, that today's language of tattoos finds its core. In the early 20th century, it would not be uncommon to see an image of a dragon sharing wall (and body) space with the venerable Rock of Ages. This, and the fact that an image derived from a Japanese tradition might accompany one swiped from a short-lived lithographic phenomenon demonstrates brilliantly how tattooing's vocabulary takes, evolves and standardizes. Today, these stalwarts sit among many hundreds of other symbols committed to the cannon.

In cataloguing the symbols for this book, we are indebted to generations of tattooists who have passed images across cities and decades, documented on bodies and in books. Some of their names are noted in the descriptions that follow, particularly those with historic 'flash' origins, for 'flash' sheets (pages covered with tattoo designs) help determine when a symbol first became a popular tattoo.

The 130 symbols, depicted in fine line, western traditional and Japanese styles offer a snapshot of tattoo choice and tattoo history. Each became an element of the language at a particular moment in time and carries with it an aesthetic and cultural origin. With that, each also holds a specificity and power that helps us find the perfect way to tell our own individual tales. After all, the true story of any tattoo is claimed when the history of both the design and the wearer meet.

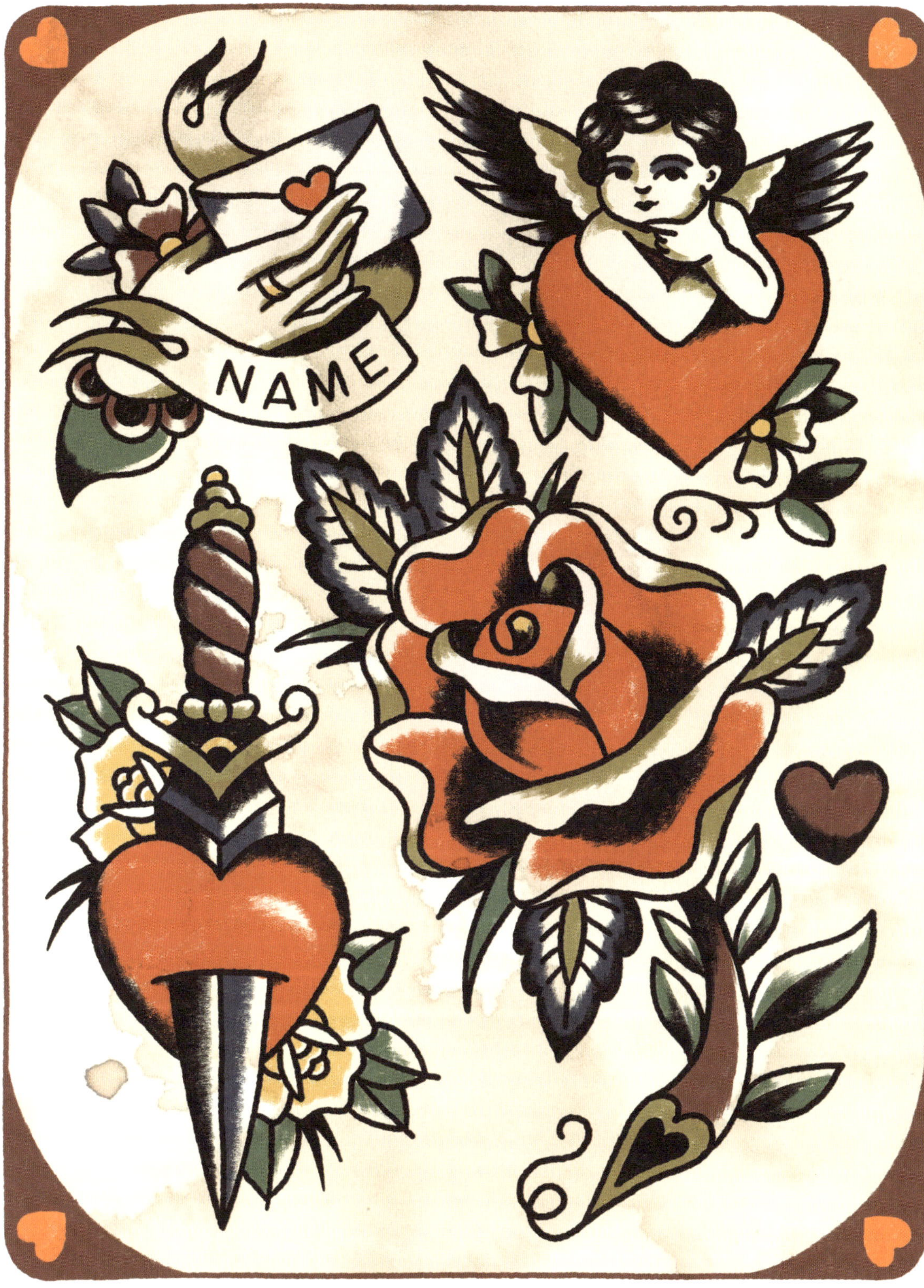
NAME

1

LOVE

The acknowledgement of love is, perhaps, the truest theme in modern tattooing. That said, the disclosure of the sentiment runs the gamut – from overt declaration to subtle attestation – with one's choice of symbol reflecting confidence in one end of the spectrum or the other. And, naturally, given the breadth of romantic feeling, there are countless ways to commemorate union.

Some of the best-known love tattoos are based in the western traditional style. A simple name, alone or in banner, is almost a cliché – played up by Norman Rockwell's 1944 painting, *Tattoo Artist*. A heart festooned with a nameplate banner has timeless appeal, while the mythological figure, Cupid, frequently takes centre stage in tattoo compositions relaying love. Flora and fauna also provide countless sources for inspiration and include the crane, the rose, the tulip and more.

The breadth of symbols tied to love allows for diverse stylistic consideration. Western traditional, as noted, serves for bold, direct disclosure. More precise symbols are beautifully articulated in black and grey or contemporary Japanese styles. Regardless of rendering, love-themed tattoos carry unwavering clarity of meaning for the wearer.

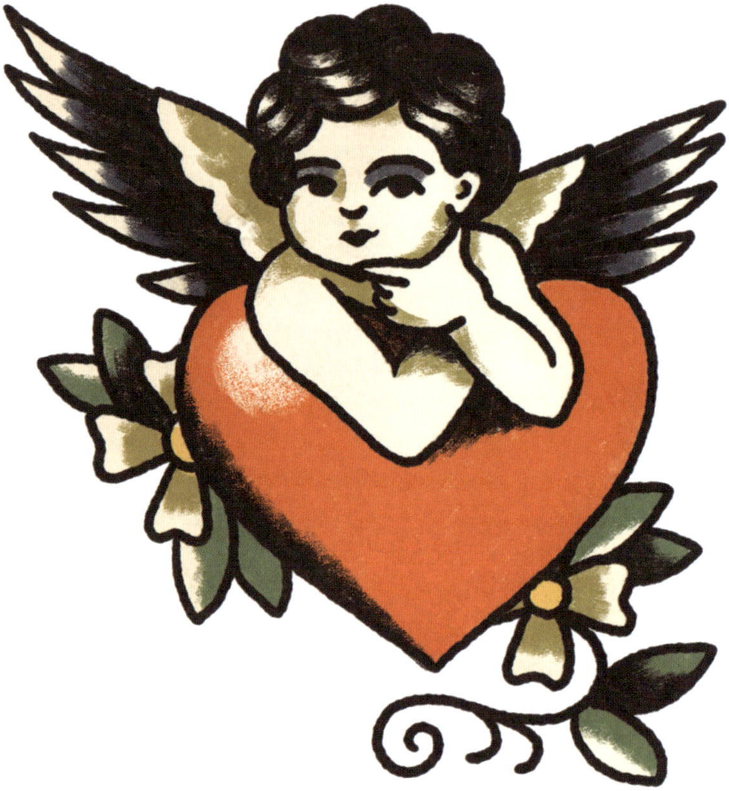

Cherub

Not to be confused with Christian cherubim, which are assigned several different roles, the figure detailed here references desire, lust and love. Stemming from ancient Greek and Roman mythology (as Eros in Greek and Cupid, son of Venus, in Roman), the character often appears as a winged child or young man, with bow and arrow.

This image has persisted for centuries, exploited by everyone from Renaissance painters to opportunistic greeting-card companies. By the 1900s, the image of Cupid benefited from the widespread adoption of Valentine's Day as a holiday. While ancient forms were, at times, moderately mischievous (spreading lust with little regard for the consequences), the later, more secular visions of the boy helped express ideas of love or togetherness.

As a tattoo, the cupid serves a variety of styles, including black and grey (as seen here) and western traditional. The former promises an elegant rendering, while the latter allows easy incorporation with a variety of associated love symbols – heart, rose and more.

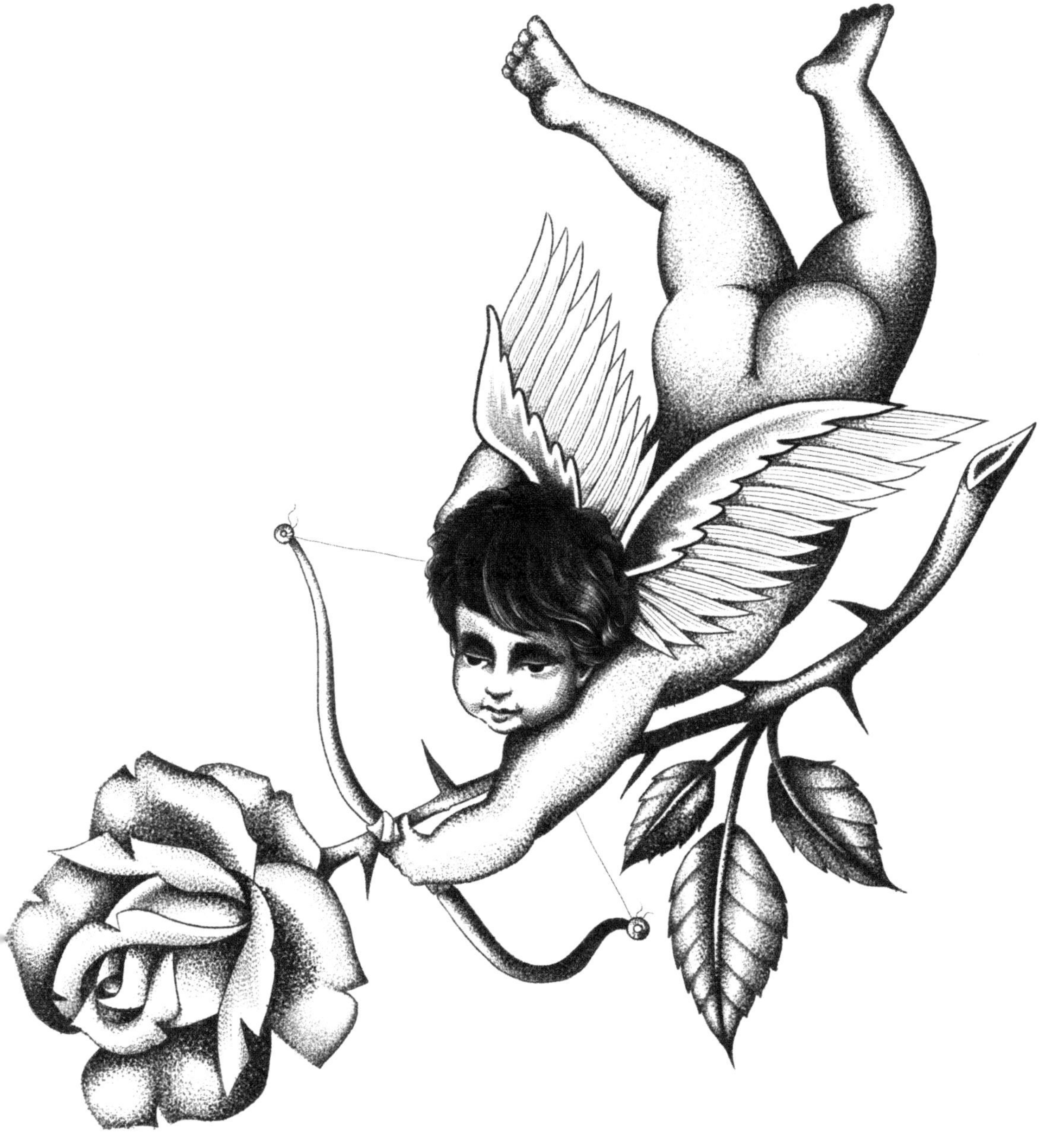

Dove

Positivity abounds in tattoo designs anchored by doves. The bird, with its broad mythological associations (from Aztec to ancient Greek), represents enduring love and peace. Many tattoos featuring the dove are connected to Christian ritual, with the bird appearing in faith-based spaces since the 200s CE.

Doves appear in depictions of the Father, the Son and the Holy Spirit, and in images of the Annunciation. Biblical reference also connects the bird to the story of Noah's Ark, where a dove brings Noah an olive branch marking the end of the storms and floods.

Purity of spirit and a deep compassionate love also permeate symbolism relating to the dove. In this, the historic connections amalgamate in universal feeling, making the dove an appropriate choice for anyone wishing to venerate familial relationships, a deep bond or lifelong commitment.

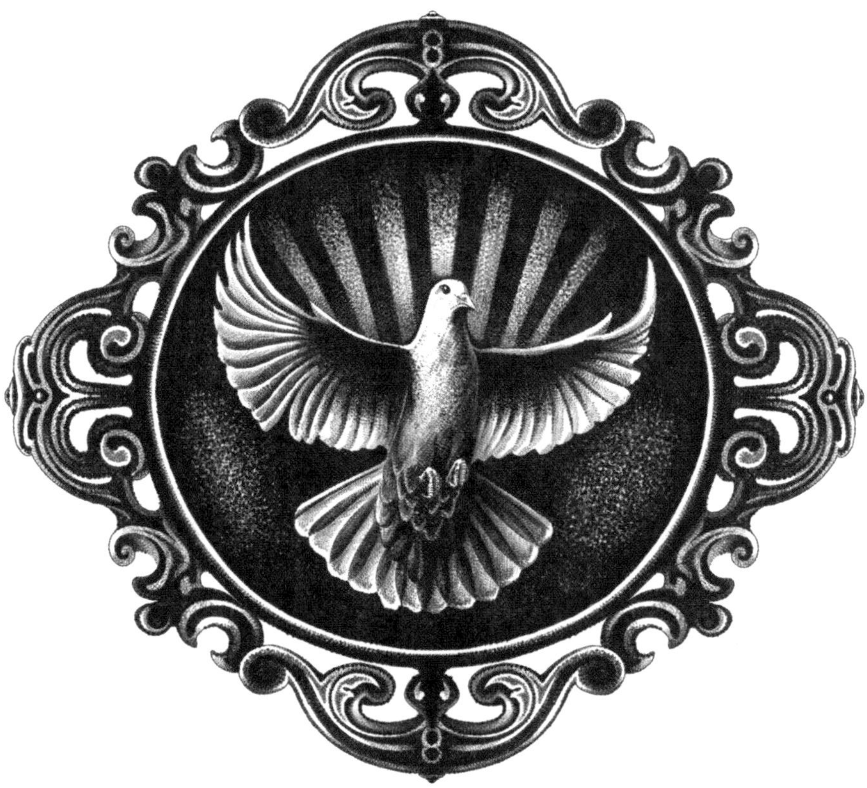

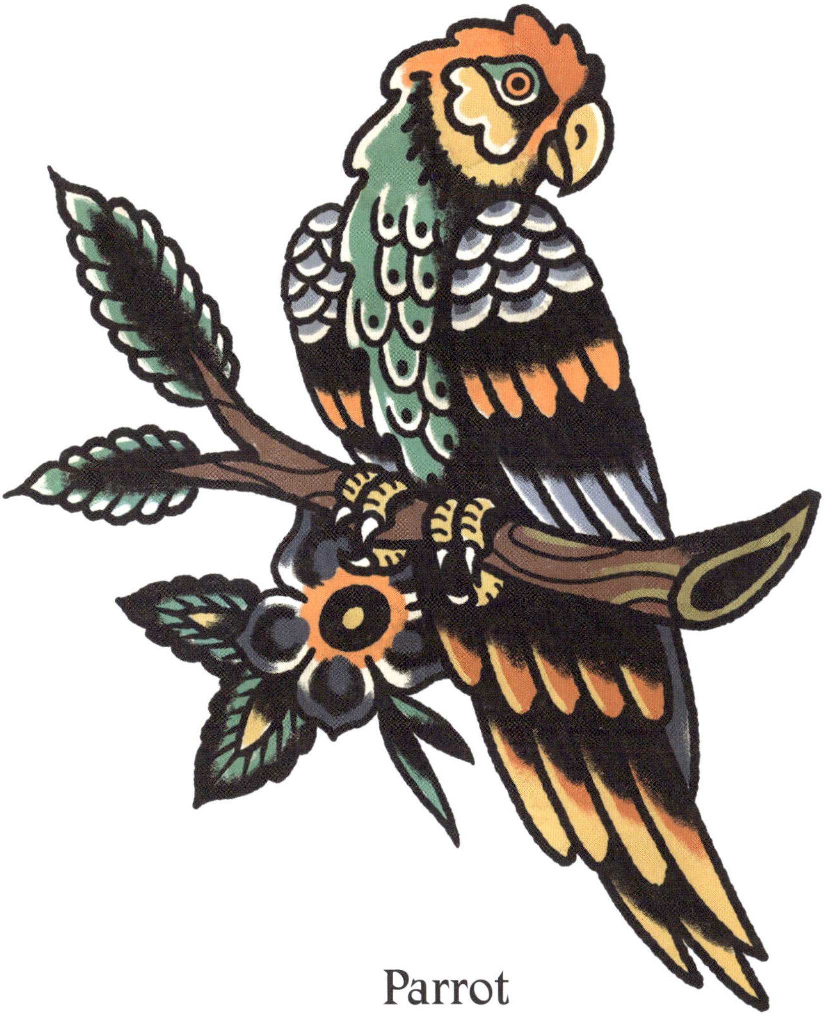

Parrot

Cast aside any preconceptions that a parrot must be linked to a pirate. Instead, this bird's symbolism conveys deep devotion and endearing love. The meaning derives from inarguable characteristics of the species: parrots are affectionate and empathetic. These traits make the birds terrific companions, as they build tight bonds complete with demonstrative displays of devotion.

In tattooing, the association between parrots and love is most common. Depicted singly, a parrot serves as a beautiful reminder of companionship. Paired with a heart in the background, twin parrots overtly relay strength of relationship and perseverance.

Stylistically, parrots are adaptable. One can choose anything from western traditional to hyperrealistic depiction. The natural breadth of colour also allows for innumerable choices in composition.

Crane

When associated with love, the crane stands for fidelity – specifically a long, loyal marriage. The birds themselves are monogamous, initiating long-term breeding pairings that can last a lifetime.

In the broader context, the crane carries associations with happiness, good fortune, peace and longevity. The crane is a common motif in Japanese art, finding expression in many disciplines from Edo-period woodblock prints to Irezumi (traditional Japanese tattooing). The symbol is also deeply tied to traditions of origami, where legend suggests wishes are granted to anyone who folds one thousand cranes.

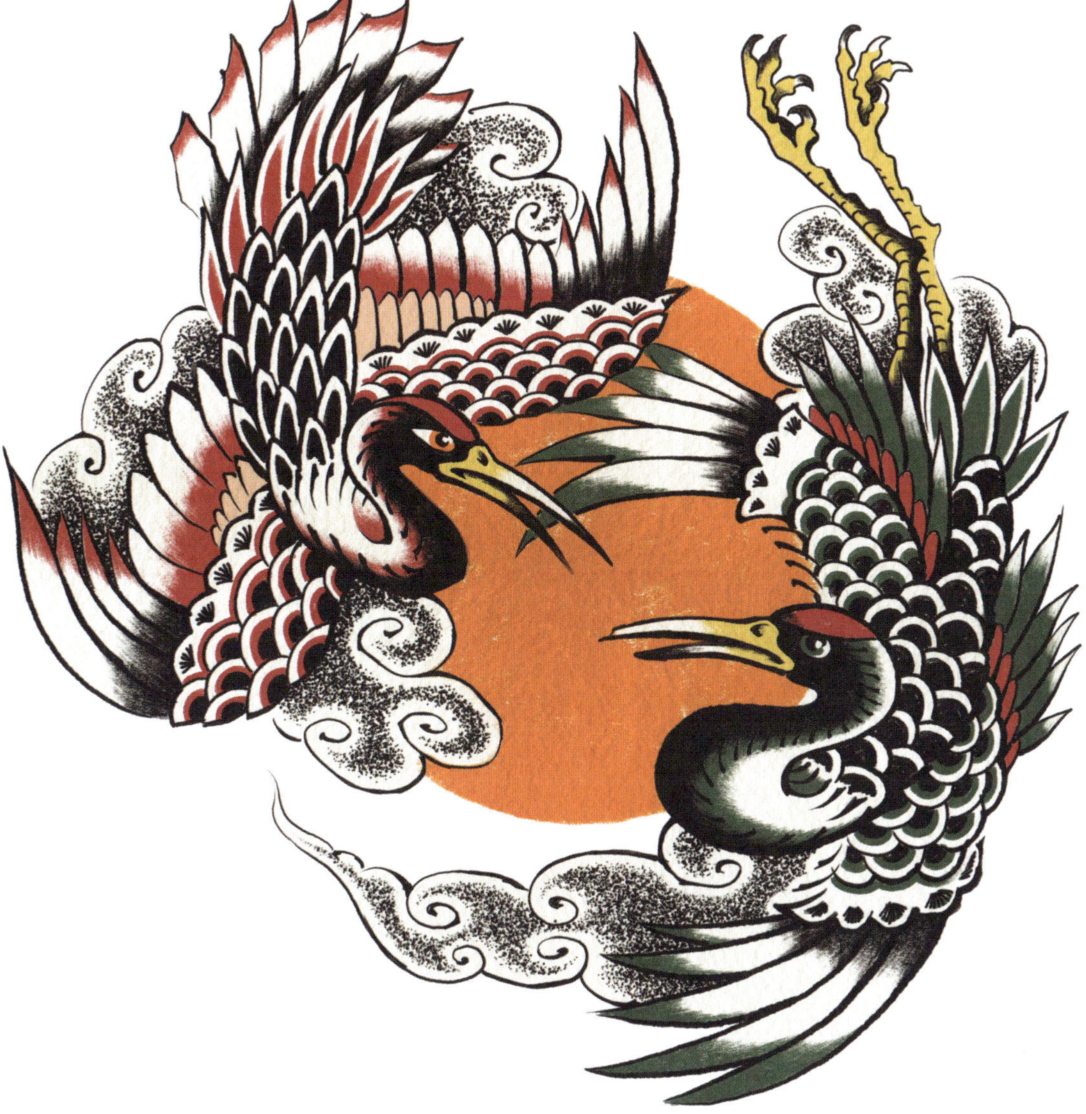

Heart

Pierced by arrow or dagger, adorned with nameplate banner, or broken through the middle, traditional heart tattoos relay the full emotional scope of love.

The now familiar scallop-topped heart shape emerged during the 13th century, appearing as a heraldic symbol and standardized through repetition in various manuscripts (including a collection of Danish love ballads) and on playing cards through the 15th and 16th centuries. In the 19th century, popular use of the symbol exploded, naturally tied to revolutions in mass printing. The heart's association with romance, love, lust and heartbreak became ubiquitous. The rise of the heart symbol in tattooing coincided with this uptick in popular use – tied as the modernization of the trade was to the burgeoning visual culture of the late 1800s. The 1995 exhibition, 'Pierced Hearts and True Love: A Century of Drawing for Tattoos', held at The Drawing Center in New York, showed just how widely recognized the heart has become as a tattoo icon.

In articulation, the heart tattoo can serve several purposes: pierced with an arrow, it signals the wearer is love-struck; ripped through, the heart shares pain; stabbed with a dagger, and betrayal rings clear. With the soft addition of a name in-banner, there's declaration of pure affection. All of these options offer a certain simplicity: while love is complicated, illustrating its nuances is relatively straightforward.

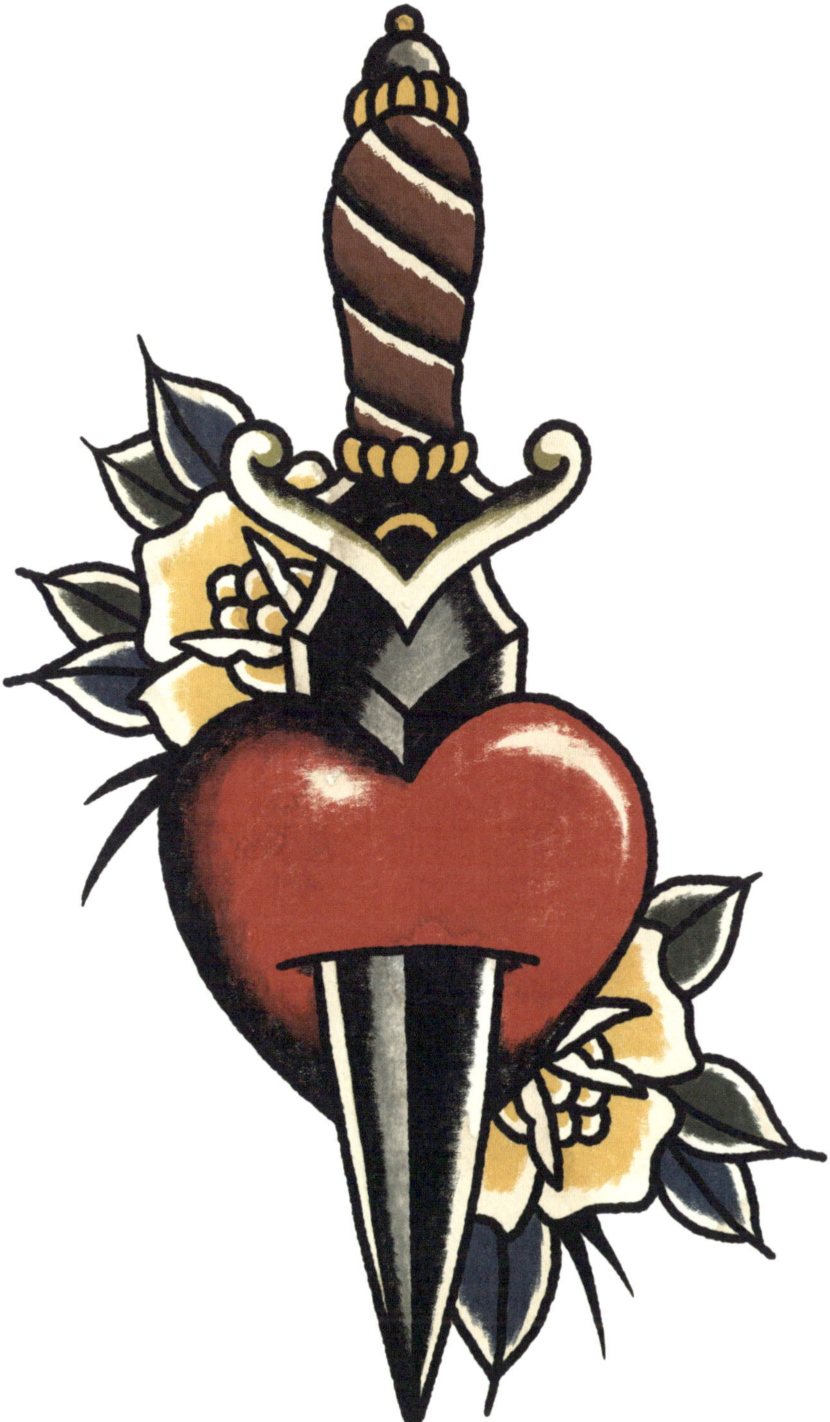

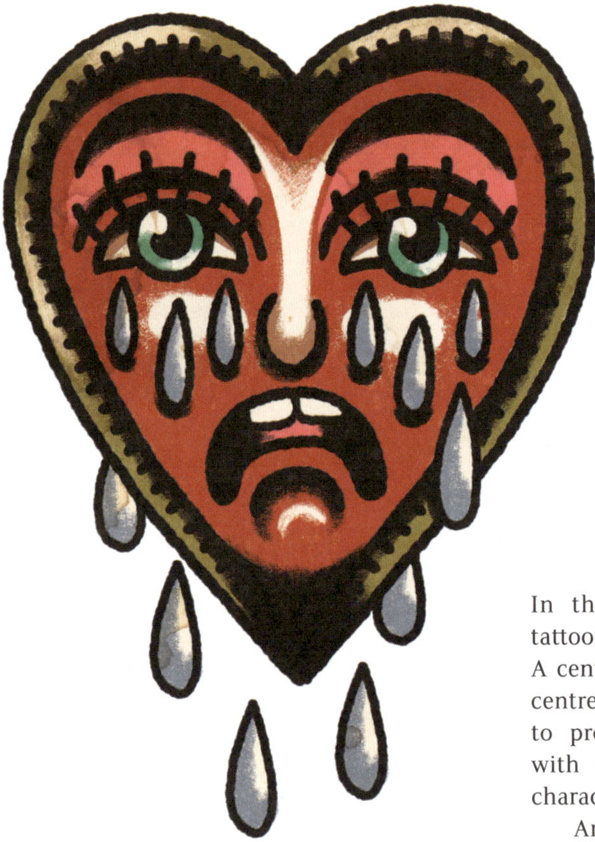

Crying Heart

In the mid-20th century, few American tattooists were as influential as Bert Grimm. A central figure of The Pike, an amusement centre in Long Beach, California, he helped to progress the western traditional style with his instinct for adding emotional character to his designs.

Among the symbols attributed to Grimm, the crying (or weeping) heart is one of the most iconic. It conveys love lost and heartbreak. In its figuring, there are clear connections to cartoon animation styles that gained prominence in the 1930s. Of course, it has much in common with other heart-related tattoos (think pierced heart or prisoner of love), adding a new layer of meaning to a tried-and-true icon.

Today, Grimm's design is applied in myriad variation. Most commonly, the shifts are subtle, manifesting as an homage to mid-century tattooing.

Clasped Hands

The communicative power of hands clasped together defines several tattoos. There is, of course, the ubiquity of the prayer hands. Equally symbolic is the handshake, an image with a variety of subtle meanings but always rooted in bond, love and fraternity.

The roots of the design are centuries old. It features heavily in jewellery – for example, in the fedé and gimmel symbol (derived from the idea of hands in faith) used to finish the loop of a ring. Rings featuring the symbol were popular from 200 BCE onwards, serving to commemorate both betrothal and friendship. Adoption of such symbols in tattooing gained force during the 19th century.

By the early 20th century most Western tattoo flash books contained a range of intersected hands with distinct details. Those extending to the cuffs flanking the hands give each a clear gender designation – denoting engagement or marriage. Sometimes, a finger might even be decorated with a ring of its own. Other articulations find the hands paired with national symbols. In the United States, for example, designs featuring a flag or eagle link to military tattooing traditions. The varied application of the clasped, or shaking, hands design allows for personal tweaks and makes it a popular addition to many traditional-style tattoos today.

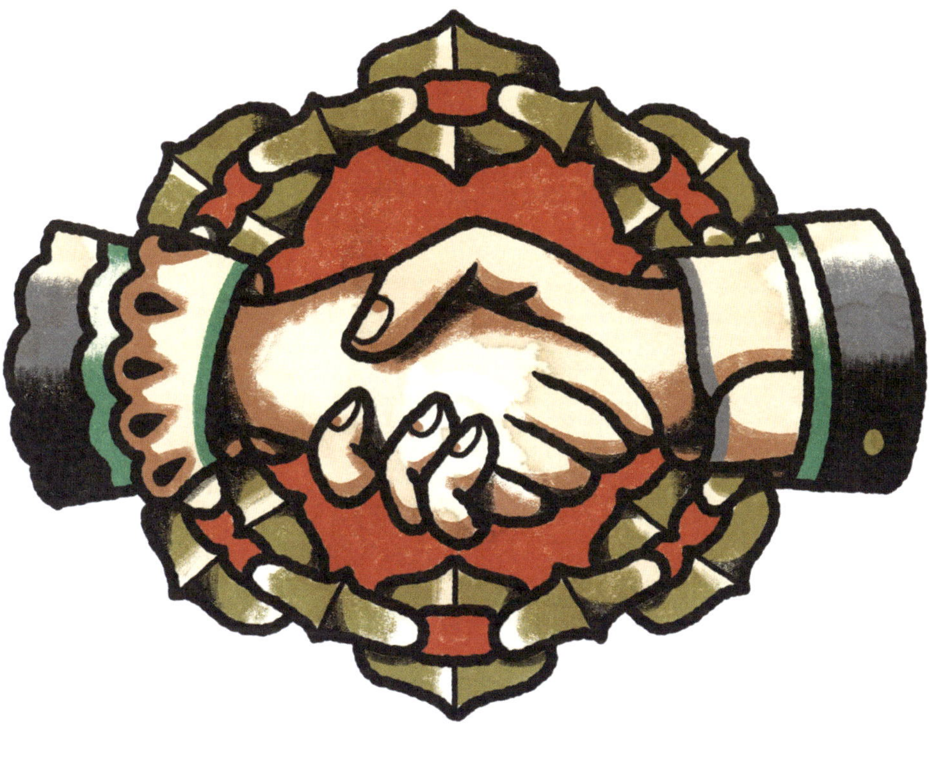

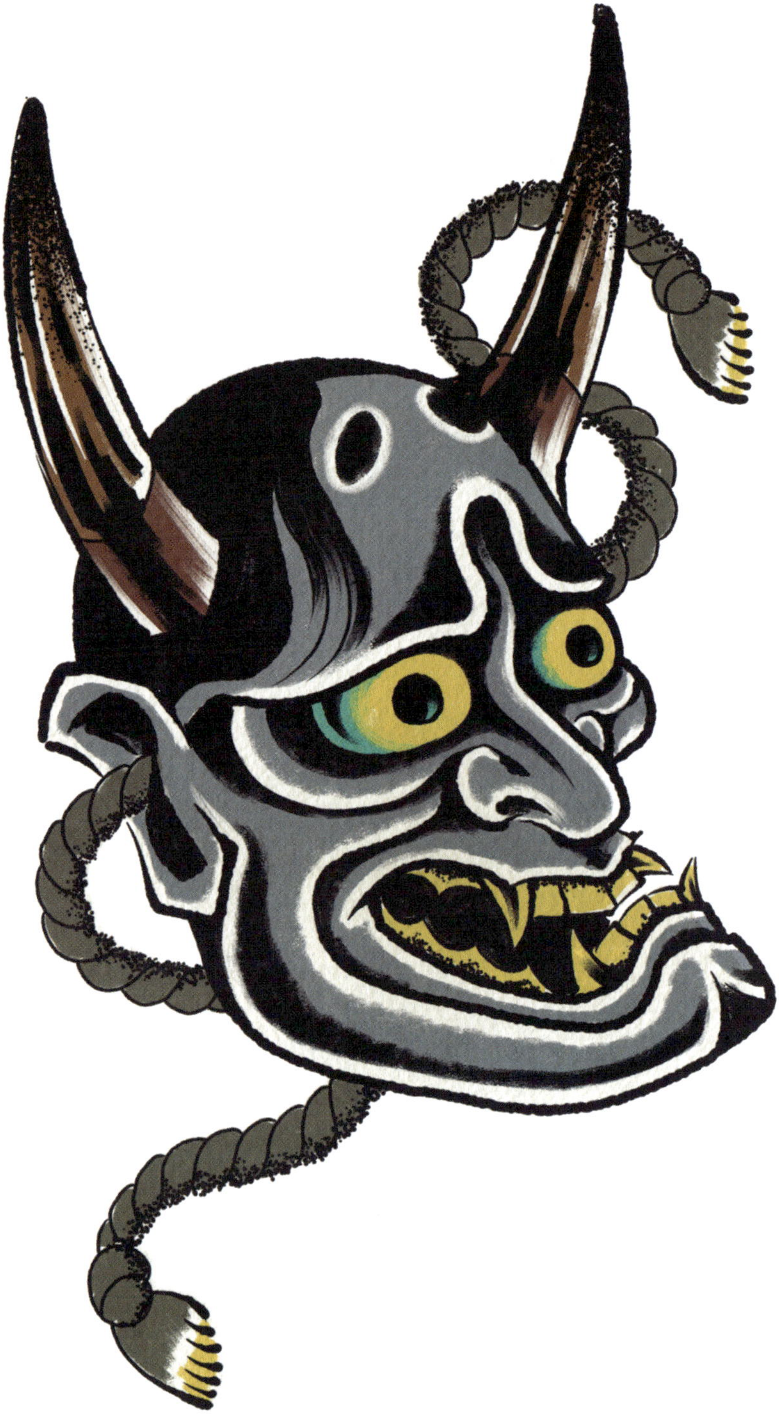

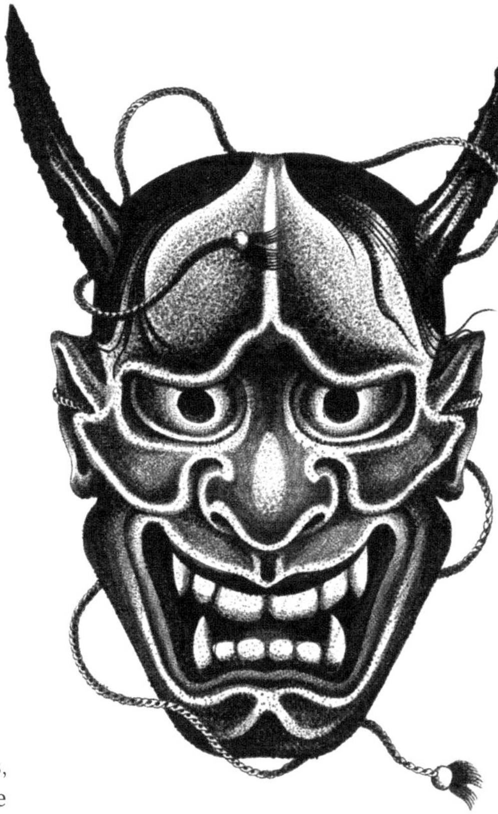

Hannya Mask

Recognizable for its sharp, bull-like horns, the hannya mask is employed in Japanese Noh theatre to represent a jealous female demon. The character arises from a dramatic event: being spurned by a lover. Distraught, the rejected woman – overwhelmed by hurt, sadness and even rage – becomes a demon.

While this origin can give the hannya mask a frightening appearance, its meanings vary. *Hannya* means 'wisdom', and in terms of love this definition allows the mask to be read as a reminder to keep clear judgement in a relationship. The strength of passion behind the mask's origin also allows conveyance of an 'all-or-nothing' attitude to love. The symbol also serves as a shield to ward off evil and is thus considered lucky.

The depth of meaning makes the hannya mask both a complicated symbol and the perfect choice for those who wish to embrace the intense emotional range of love.

Rose

Roses are an almost perfect tattoo subject. The flower itself grows in more than 150 distinct species and thousands of hybrids, each forming a unique shape and dimension to bloom and petals. As a symbol, the rose also holds true as a document of immortal love, through its association with the ancient Greek goddess, Aphrodite. From the goddess's tears and the blood of Adonis, her gorged lover, a rose bush grew – and from this myth, centuries of connection between love and the flower blossomed, too.

One will, of course, find roses within Shakespearean quotes and Victorian codes. Across the gamut, roses embody love in all its harsh varieties. Just as there are myriad types in nature, so the rose tattoo can take endless forms. Western traditional style privileges bold reds. The flowers' undulating blooms make them particularly suited to black and grey renditions, allowing exploration of volume through contrasting light and shadow. Simple black articulations also sharply convey the flowers' power. Such versatility will no doubt assure that the rose remains a popular subject for tattoos for centuries to come.

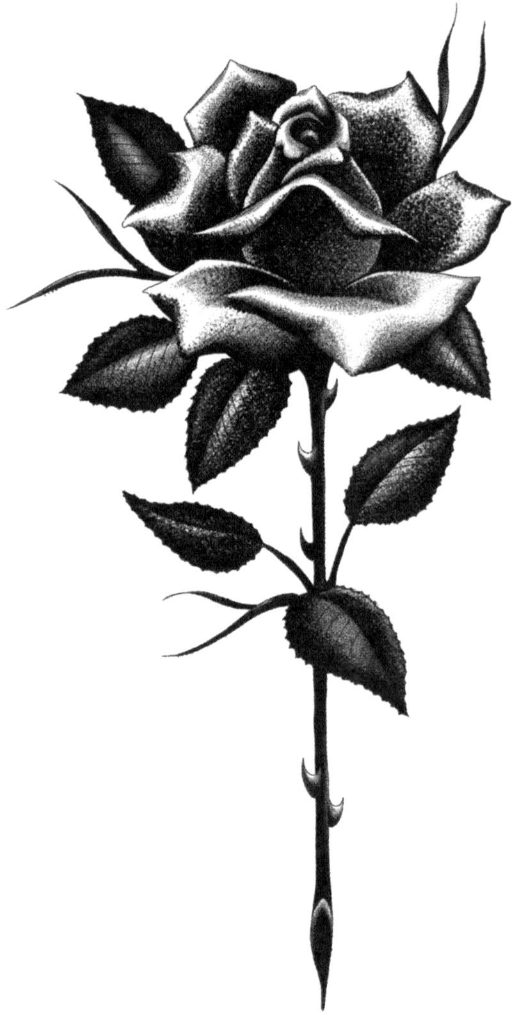

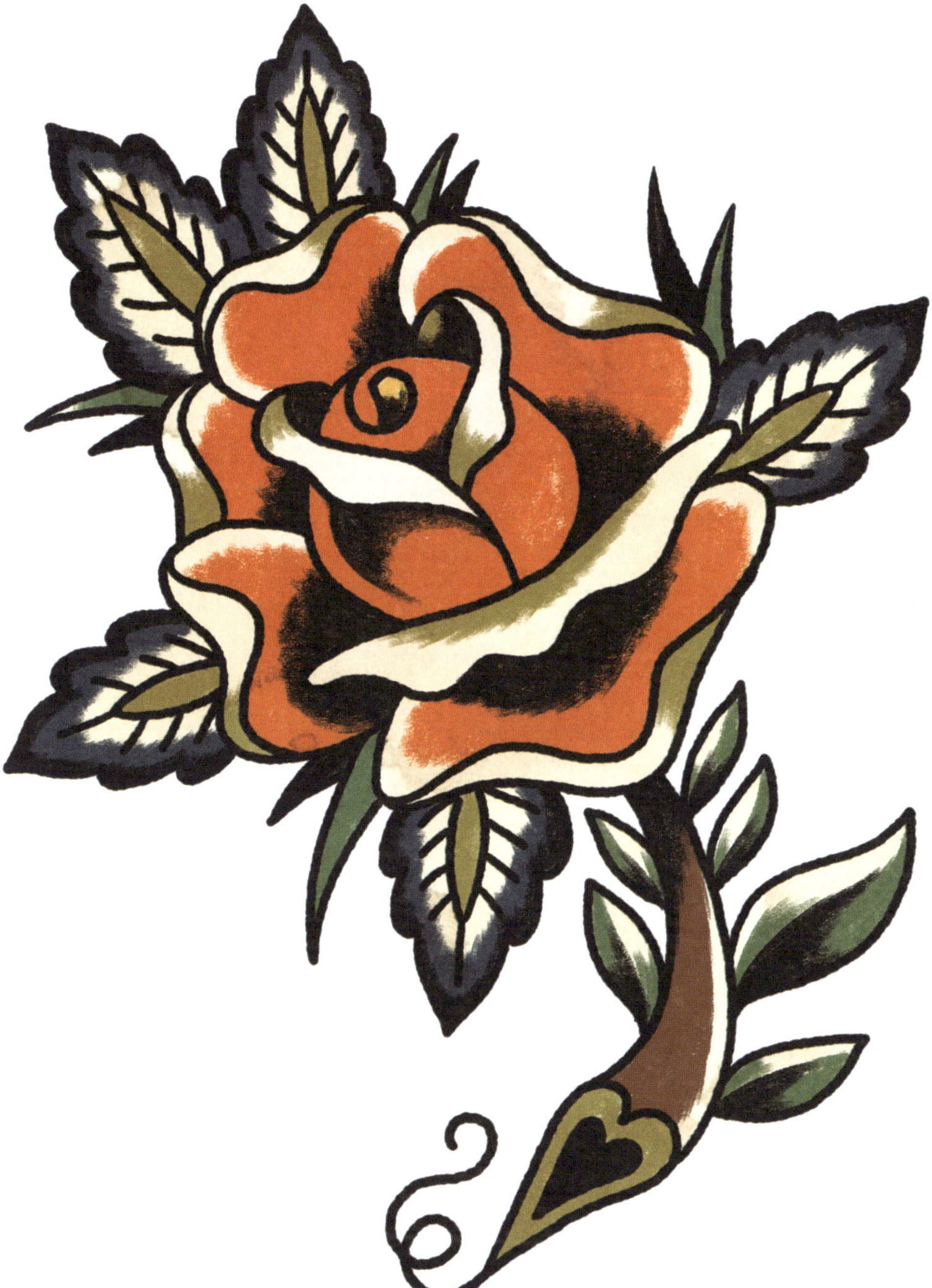

Love Letter

Like the prisoner of love, the love letter tattoo draws on the Victorian decorative arts tradition. The disembodied hand, conveyed here as a soft, feminine form, holds a heart-emblazoned envelope, a banner prepared to carry the name of its recipient. Tattoos like this came into favour in the 21st century, influenced by renewed interest in Victorian print culture.

Letter-writing itself was in vogue during the late 19th century. In fact, there were numerous guidebooks advising suitors on appropriate phasing and composition. These encompassed strict proclamations of love, as well as more tactful modes of initiating courtship. Naturally, hands and printed matter came together in a variety of media, too.

The love letter tattoo simultaneously embodies the quaint peculiarities of a bygone era. Its elements – hand, banner, letter – all serve the western traditional style well. And its meaning, while unique enough to the wearer, also reads as clearly as it would have done more than 100 years ago.

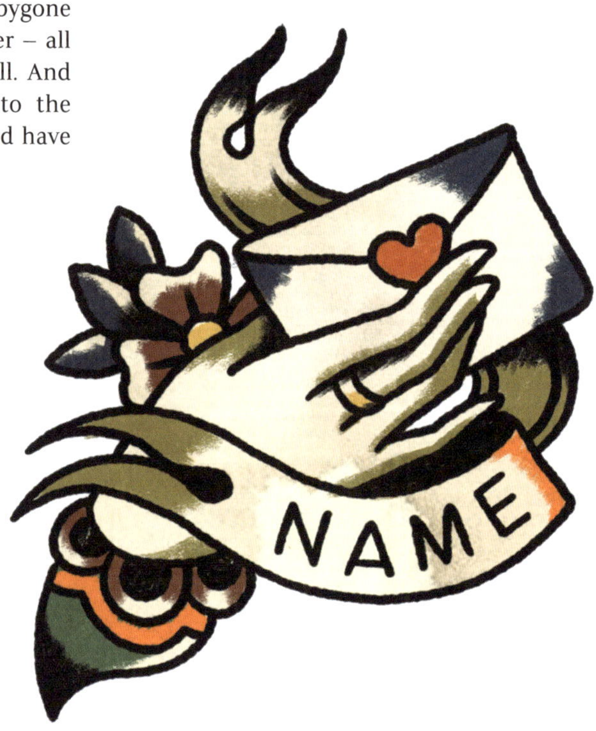

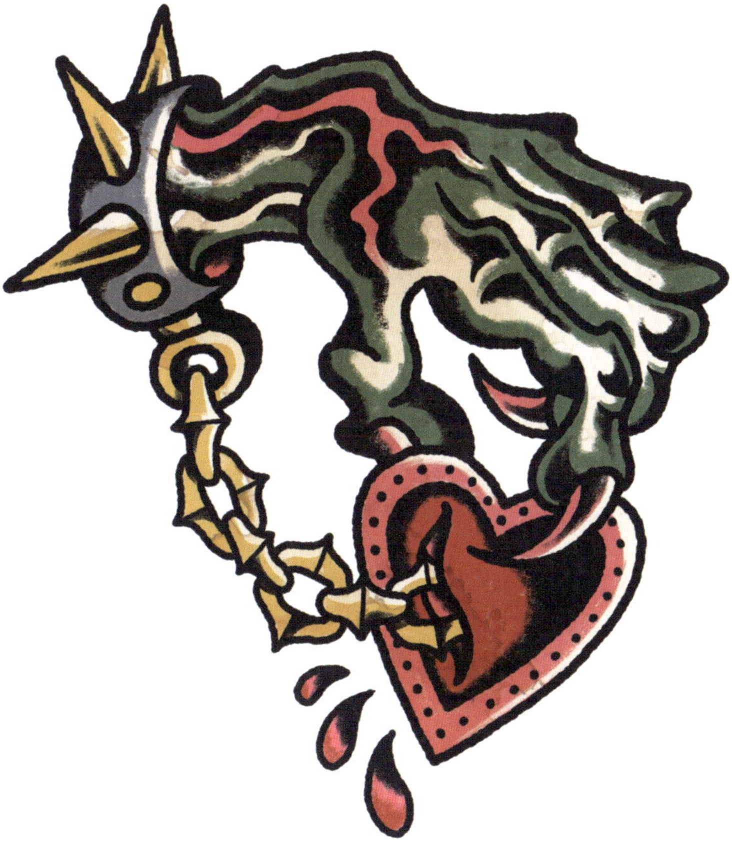

Prisoner of Love

A design that suits a range of western traditional articulations, the prisoner of love comprises a hand shackled and chained to a heart. Belief in love, or reflection on the strength of a romantic entanglement, is inherent to the symbol's meaning. However, the visual elements also offer some intriguing connection to a fascination with disembodied hands that arose during the Victorian era. At the time, hands were considered conduits of deep meaning – from idealized gender to emblems of status, from lust to support for social justice. This led to a vast array of artistic hand motifs in everything from glasswork to sign painting.

In the early 21st century, tattoo trends saw a rise in whimsical compositions influenced by Victorian sign-painting and print culture. As such, disembodied hands asserted a fresh, contemporary graphic sensibility in the western traditional style. And, as seen here, the stylizing of the hand can underscore the grip of love.

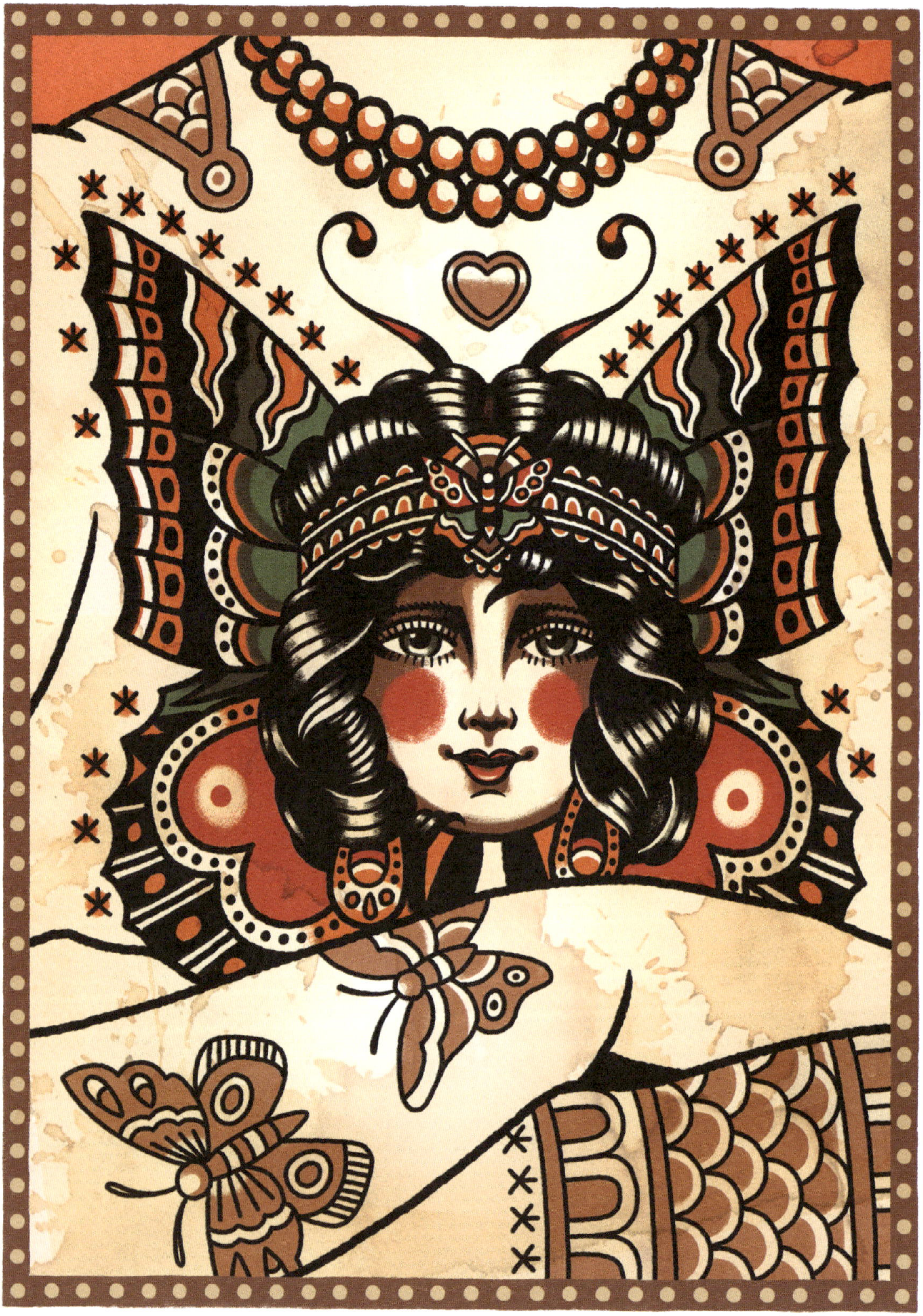

Butterfly Girl

Undoubtedly beautiful, compositions including a female head backed with butterfly wings gained popularity in the 1940s. From American Bert Grimm to the Englishman Rich Mingins (and more), the design is featured on extant flash sheets of the period and has been reborn and reworked by countless tattoo artists since that time. The design's meaning relies on association with beauty, joy and eternal love.

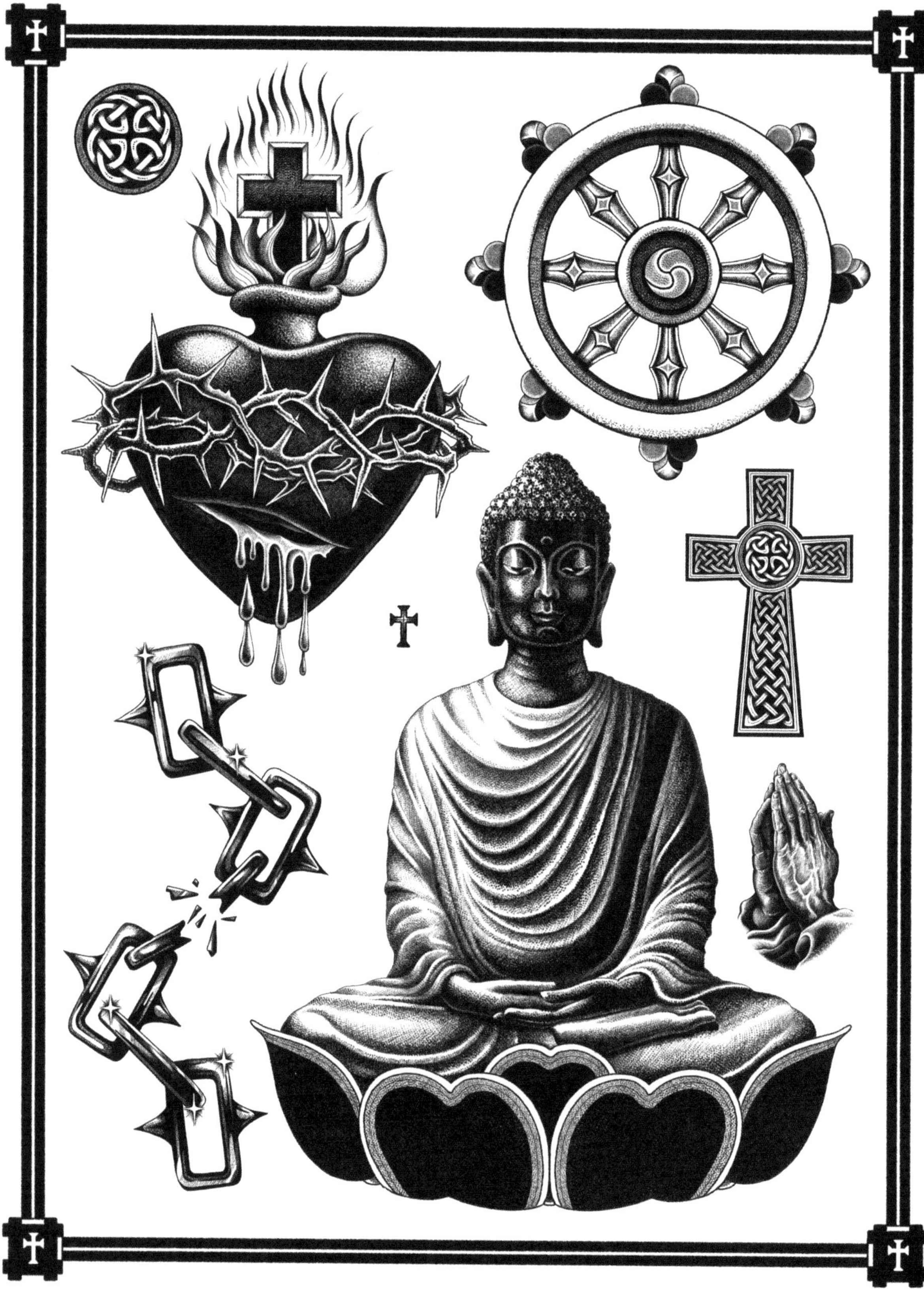

2

FAITH AND SPIRITUALITY

Declarations of faith and spirituality take several forms in tattooing. Notably, there are precise replications of visual motifs from Christian culture, such as the Sacred Heart and the Immaculate Heart, as well as direct references to Buddhist and Hindu traditions. In addition, there are symbols that may once have had specific religious overtones, but now have much wider interpretations – the praying hands are a good example of this.

The employment of religious iconography has a long history in tattooing. Royal pilgrimage to Jerusalem in the 19th century led to several British princes taking tattoos to mark the event, as was the tradition. And as tattooing has standardized over the years, emblems of faith and spirituality have served as outward celebrations of community, but also as statements of a personal, often internal, journey.

As with other thematic selections in the book, the following symbols reflect cultural origins through stylistic association. However, several of the symbols are adaptable between fine line and western traditional.

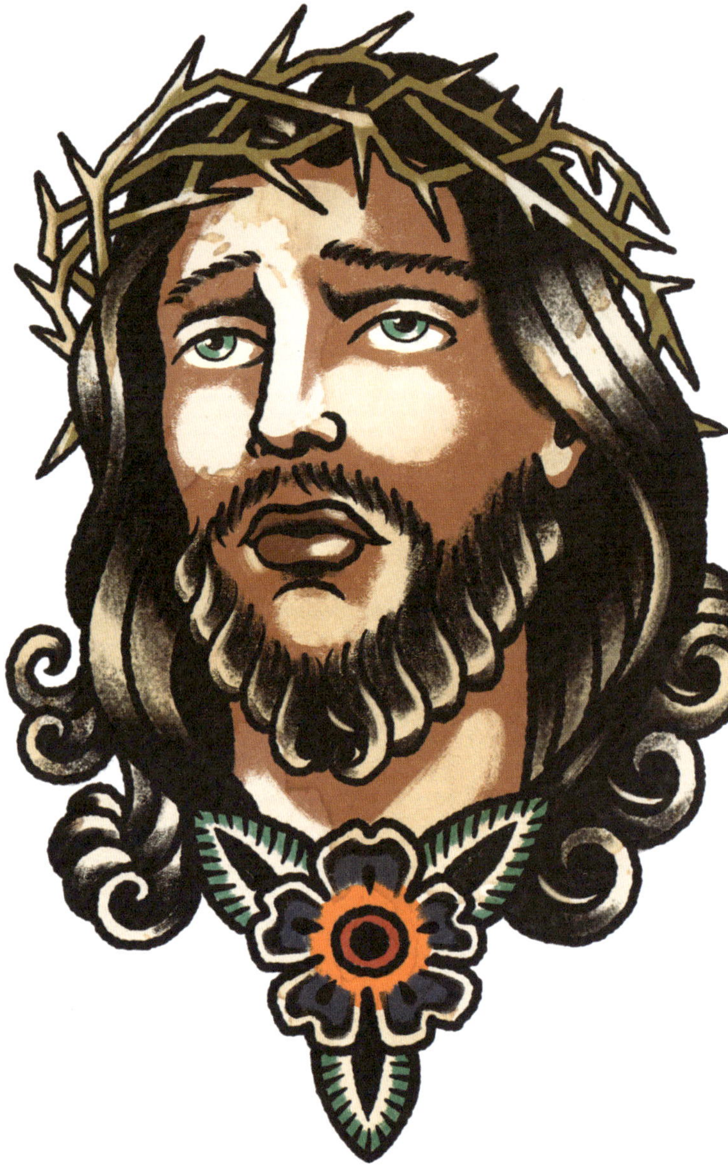

Jesus

Designed with a crown of thorns, a reminder of the pain faced on the cross, the popular head of Jesus tattoo gained popularity in the early 20th century. Christian imagery was already rooting in the 19th century, connected to an ever-broadening funeral culture and articulating ritual ranging from the celebration of birth to the mourning of a loved one.

Early use of the head of Jesus introduced a more universal sense of protection that continues to this day. A sailor, for example, might carry the image to ward off the threat of drowning. Meanwhile, those more closely connected to their faith may employ the icon as protection from general hardship.

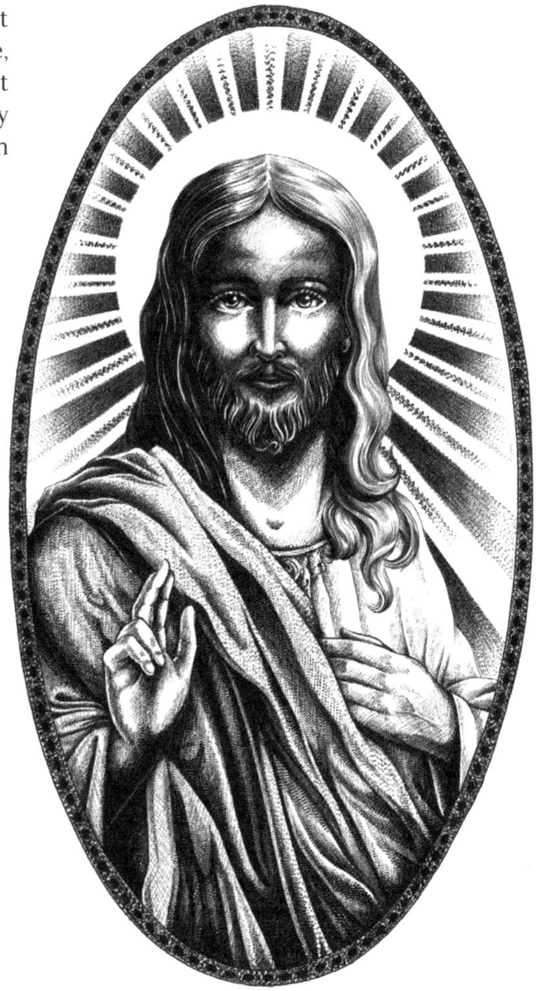

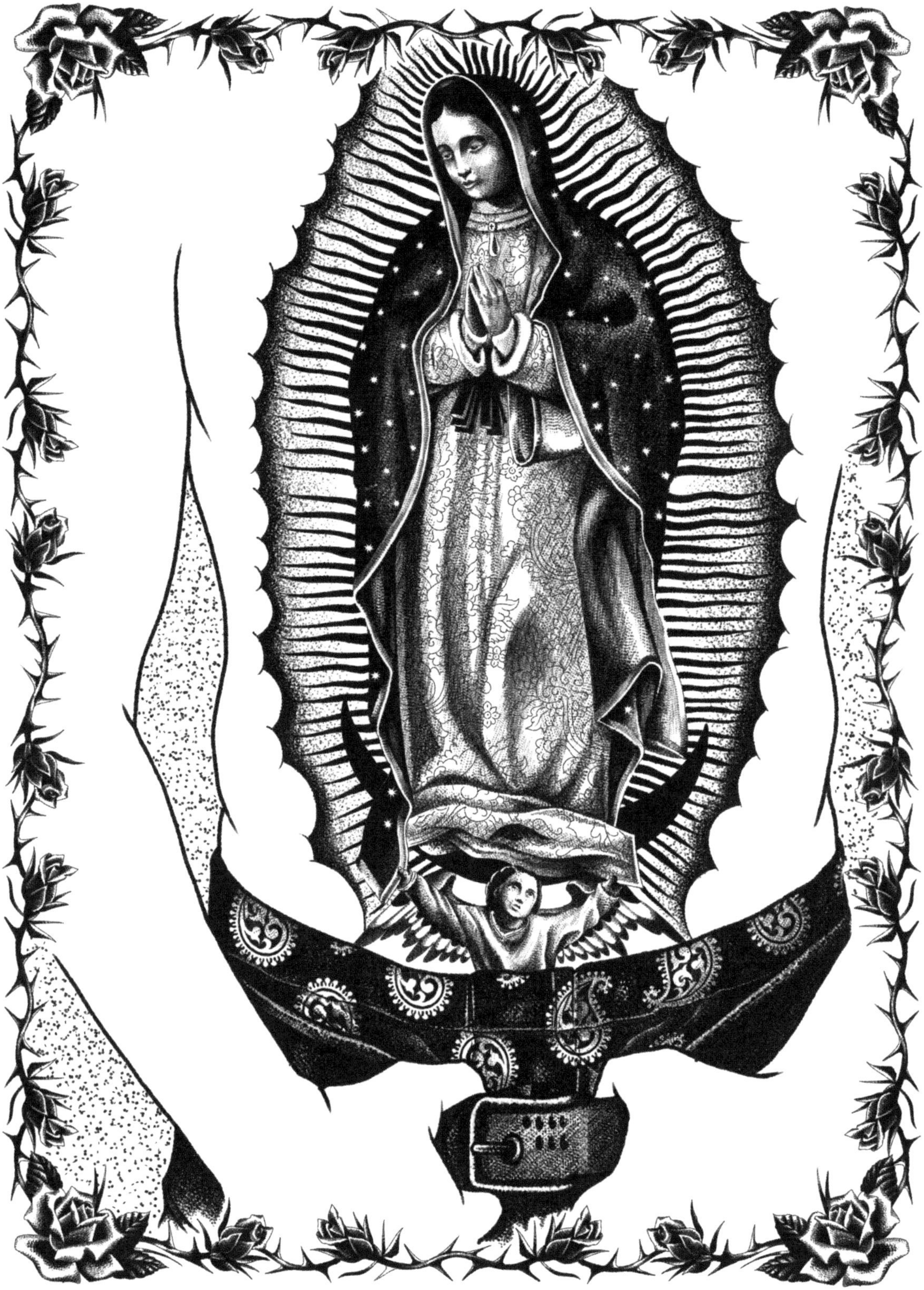

Our Lady of Guadalupe

Deeply rooted in both Mexican and Mexican–American identity, tattoos featuring Our Lady of Guadalupe draw on religious iconography for their composition. However, the image, also rich in societal symbolism, conveys protection and guidance.

Our Lady of Guadalupe is deeply rooted in Mexican religious life and nationalism, and has been since the 1530s, when she appeared to Juan Diego and rose as patron saint. Her image dots the Mexican landscape, where a network of shrines has spread countrywide in her name over the centuries. In 1810, she was held up as patroness for Miguel Hidalgo y Costilla's rebellion against the Spanish, and later, during the religious revival of the 19th century, she was heralded for uniting people in common devotion. Images of the Virgin were displayed on banners carried by Emiliano Zapata's peasant rebels during the Mexican Revolution of 1910–1920 and again during the Cristero Rebellion, which lasted from 1926–1929. In the 1970s, her image was again evoked, this time by American civil rights activist Cesar Chavez, linking her to 20th-century social justice reform.

Praying Hands

Tattooing has a beautiful and cross-generational relationship with art history, and the famous praying hands design remains one of the most tangible examples of this.

The composition derives from a 1508 sketch by German artist Albrecht Dürer, an exploratory study for an altarpiece for a church in Frankfurt. Hundreds of years later, Dürer's work, a depiction of his own brother's hands, resonates not only for its ubiquity – it's one of the most famous images in popular culture – but also its universality. While ties to Catholic symbolism, such as the rosary, are common in composition, alone the praying hands embody a non-denominational piety.

For those purely inspired by art history, added meaning builds from association to Andy Warhol. The pop art icon reworked Dürer's sketch during his career, and it decorates his tombstone in Pittsburg, Pennsylvania.

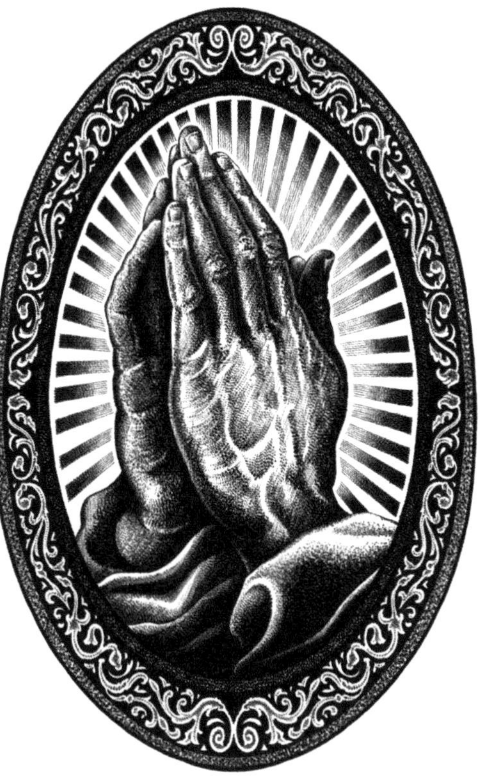

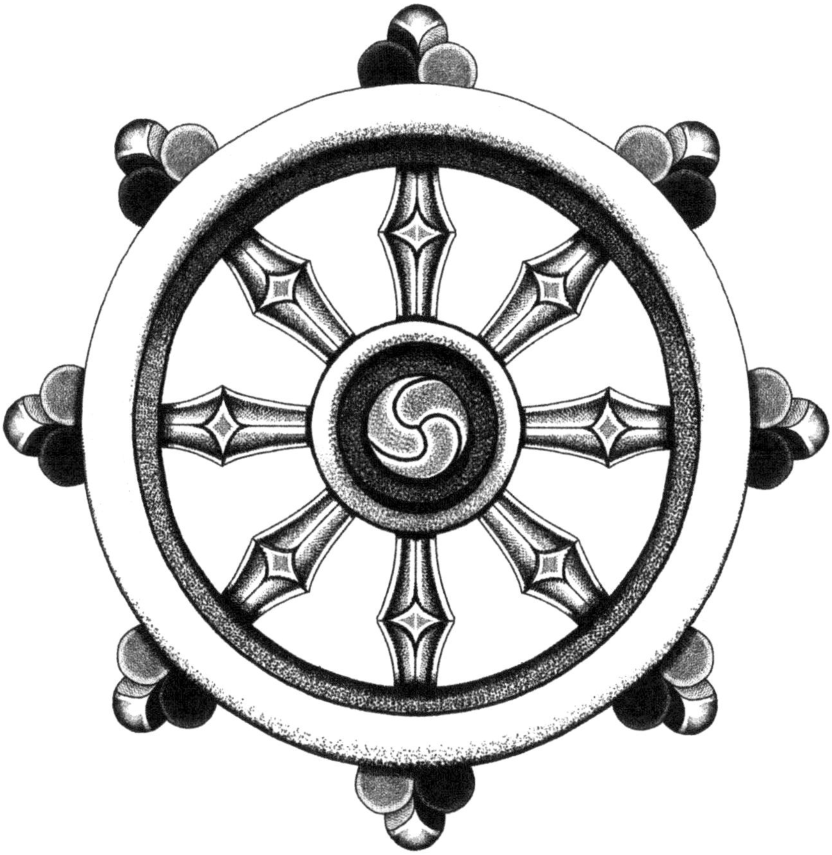

Wheel of Dharma

Symbolic of reincarnation, the wheel of dharma originates in the Hindu faith and is characterized by its eight distinct spokes (more precisely, the Eightfold Path). While the eight-spoke wheel is most common, the wheel may also have four (each reflecting one of the four noble truths), 10, 12, 24 or 31 spokes, depending on specific Buddhist teachings.

The wheel has three distinct parts: the circular rim, the hub and the spokes. The circle conveys perfection of the dharma, its centre a reminder of the stability that comes with practising Buddhism.

Wheel of dharma tattoos are often prepared as guidance to healing and setting intention for a new path.

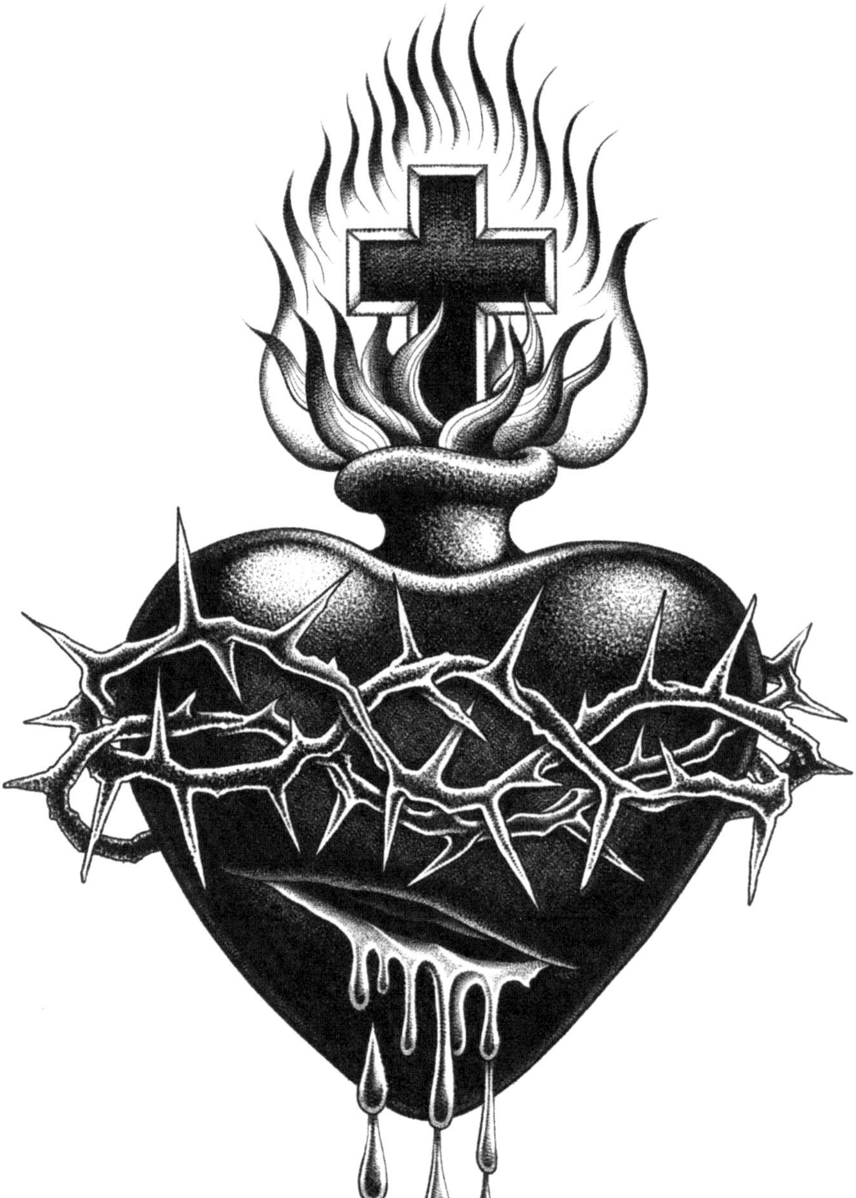

Sacred Heart

The Sacred Heart benefits from an unflinchingly powerful composition. The piercing knife, surrounding thorns and burning flame demonstrate the power of divine love. It is both a symbol of devotion and a reminder of redemption. As an image, the Sacred Heart emerged during the 18th century and spread throughout the 19th century, eventually launching into the tattoo vernacular from popular prints.

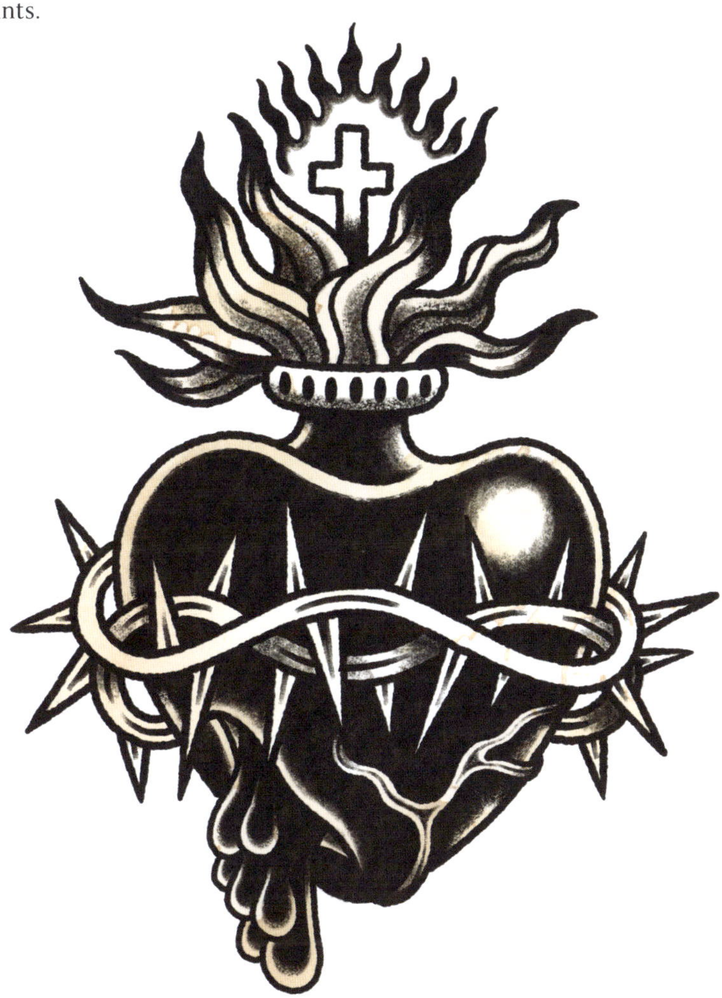

Ganesha

One of the best-known Hindu deities, Ganesha is easily identifiable by his striking elephant head. Images of the figure have circulated since the sixth century. While depictions vary, most deliver a few common characteristics, including a protruding belly, four arms, a broken tusk and a third eye at the forehead.

Ganesha identifies as bringing luck and removing obstacles. The figure's characteristics correspond to unwaveringly positive qualities such as being able to think big, discard bad thoughts, retain positive force and peacefully absorb the good in the world. As such, Ganesha is associated with intellect, particularly in connection to the arts and sciences. Ganesha is also interconnected to the Hindu mantra *Om* and, at times, to the *muladhara* (first chakra), as a guide to the wheel of life.

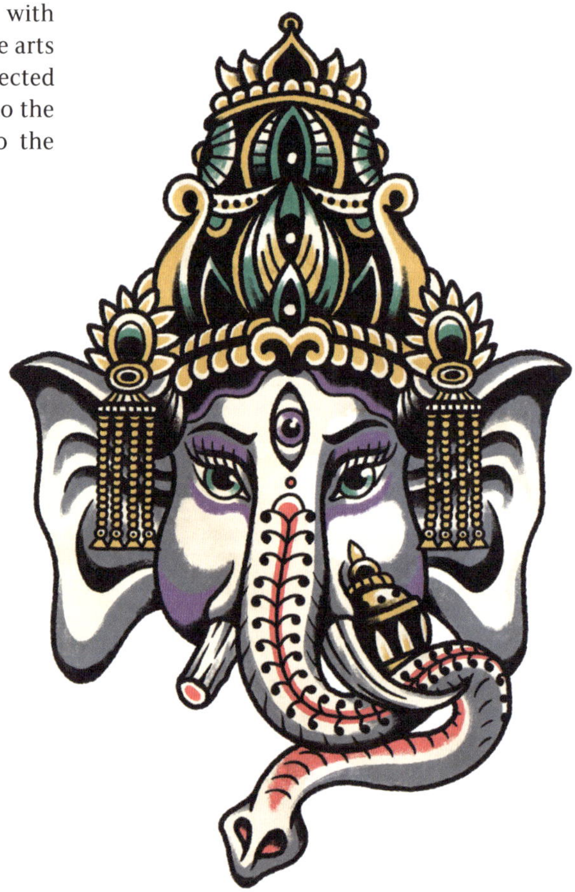

Buddha

The iconic image of Buddha, seated in a lotus position, with open-palmed hands in lap, entered the public imagination centuries after Siddhartha Gautama himself died in the 4th century BCE. It was not until the 1st century CE that this now familiar image appeared, bestowing human form to Buddha – a reflection, in some respects, of the cultural mingling spurred by trade along the great Silk Road.

Sitting in a meditative pose, or depicted in face alone, the physical form of Buddha is rendered in tattooing in much the same ways as it is in art history: some articulations have a round belly, others are of smaller build; some convey a jolly demeanour, while others have a more serious disposition. These stylistic differences reflect Buddhism in its different forms – inclusive of Theravada, Mahayana and Shakyamuni.

As a tattoo, an image of the Buddha,at its most basic level, reflects the path to enlightenment. It is suited to black and grey, or fine line, rendered both simply and ornately. But, like many tattoos sharing ideas of faith and spirituality, the Buddha is often a choice of fashion or trend rather than one of religious conviction.

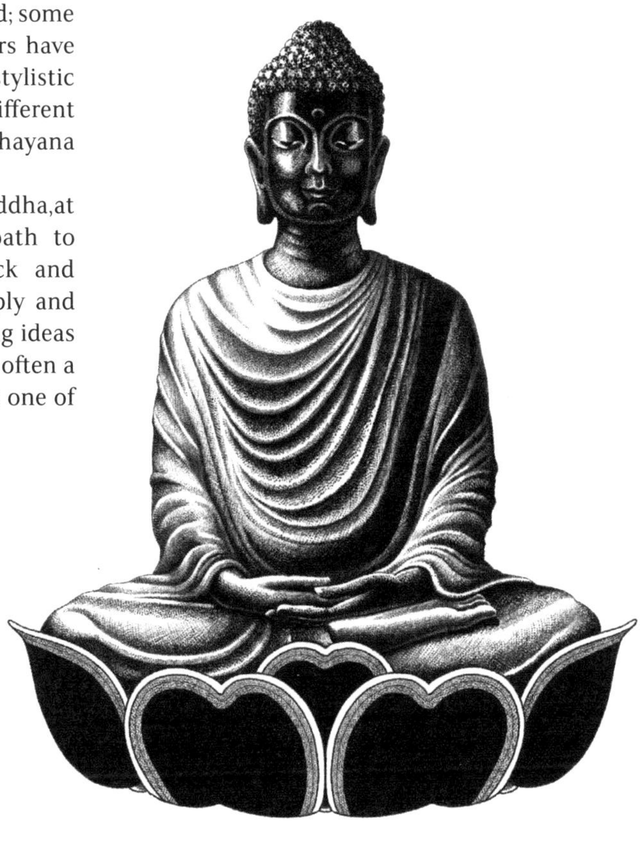

Immaculate Heart

Similar in tone to the Sacred Heart, the Immaculate Heart commemorates the virtues of Mary, Mother of God. The symbol conveys her joys and sorrows, as well as her compassion and love for mankind. Within the composition, the heart is often adorned with roses and pierced with a sword. As with the Sacred Heart, the Immaculate Heart was absorbed into tattoo culture through the blooming of religious print culture during the 19th century.

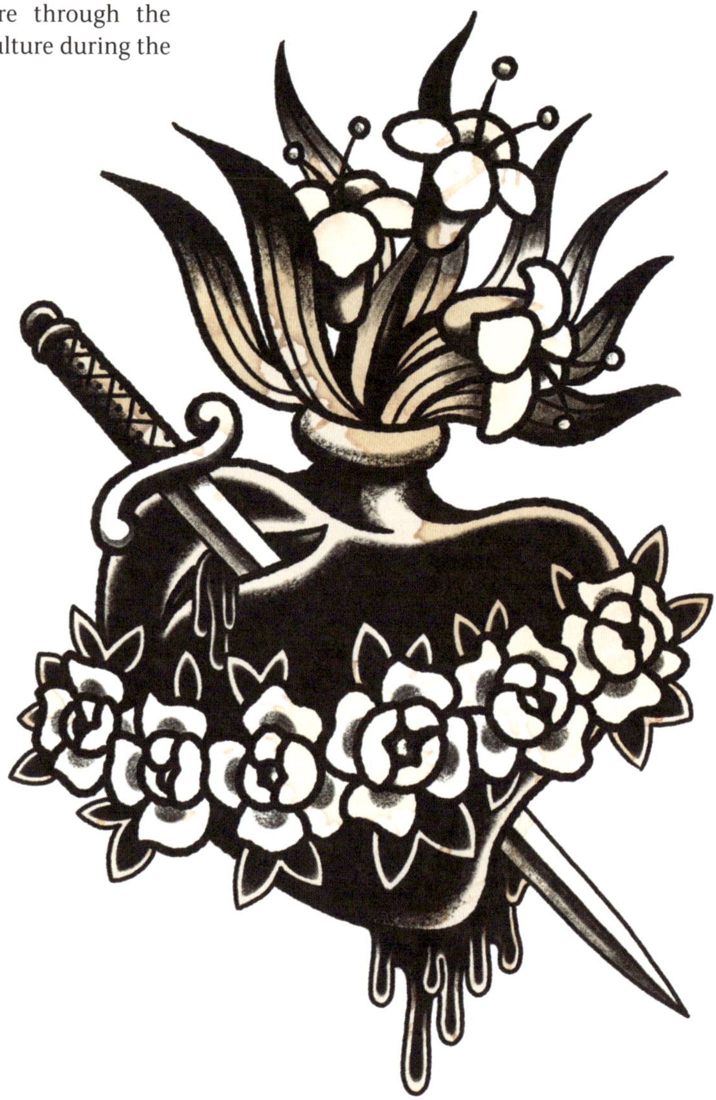

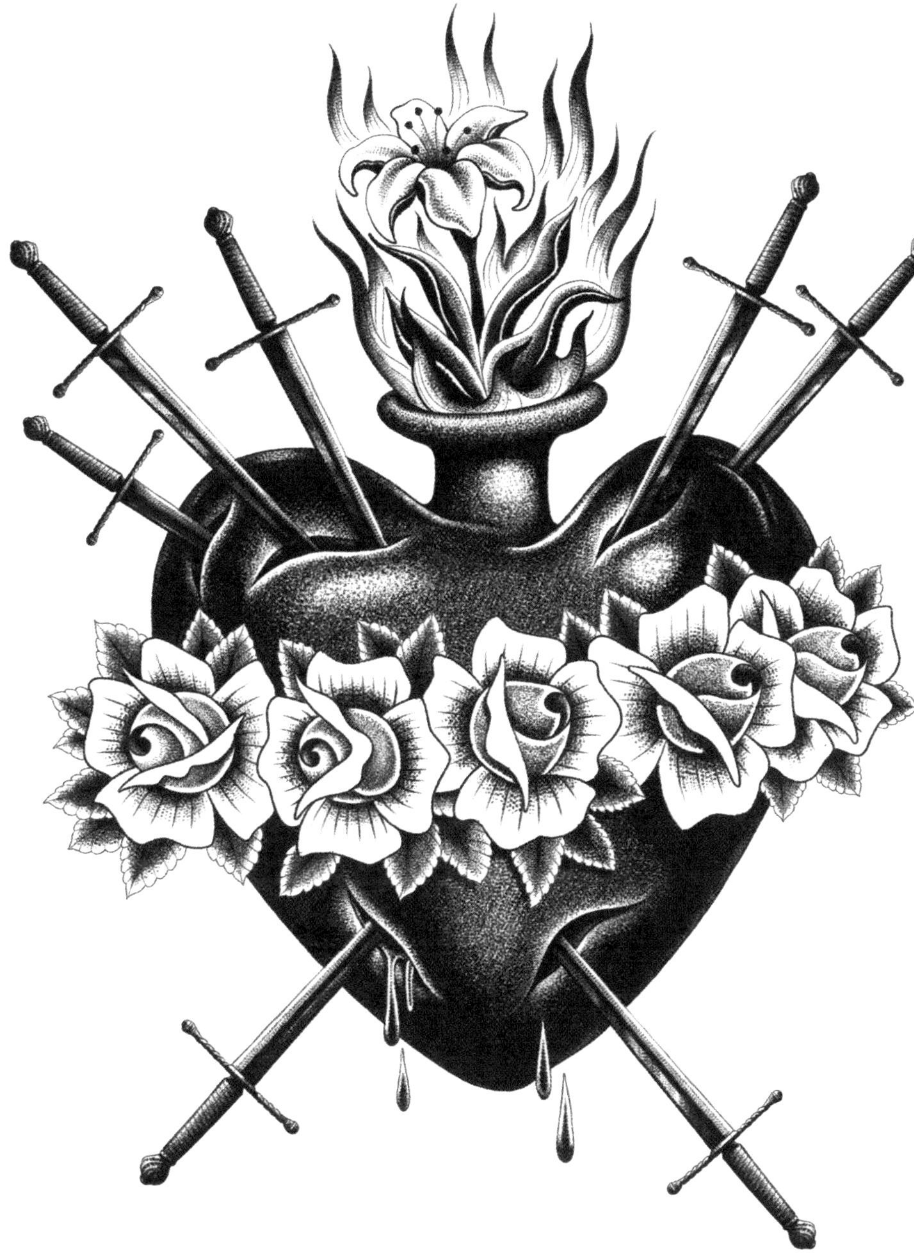

Celtic Cross

Emerging in the British Isles during the post-Roman era (roughly 600 to 900 CE), the Celtic cross combines Christian and pagan symbolism (a common conceit during transitional to formalized religion). Its composition thus incorporates the Latin cross with an interlacing of knots, spirals and other circular patters from the centre across the arms and stem. These patterns reference compassion and knowledge in understanding life's journey.

Popularity of the Celtic cross in tattooing and, as a more abstract design, the Celtic knot, evolved from nascent neo-tribal styles established in the late 1960s and 1970s on the American West Coast to become a standard of both contemporary blackwork and traditional styles. Associated designs convey heritage (often Irish), but also the spiritual associations of eternal life and everlasting bonds. Additionally, the choice of knot – trinity, spiral, triskele – can add depth of meaning. For example, the triskele, associates with earth, water and sky, while the trinity speaks to Catholicism and the centrality of the father, son and Holy Spirit.

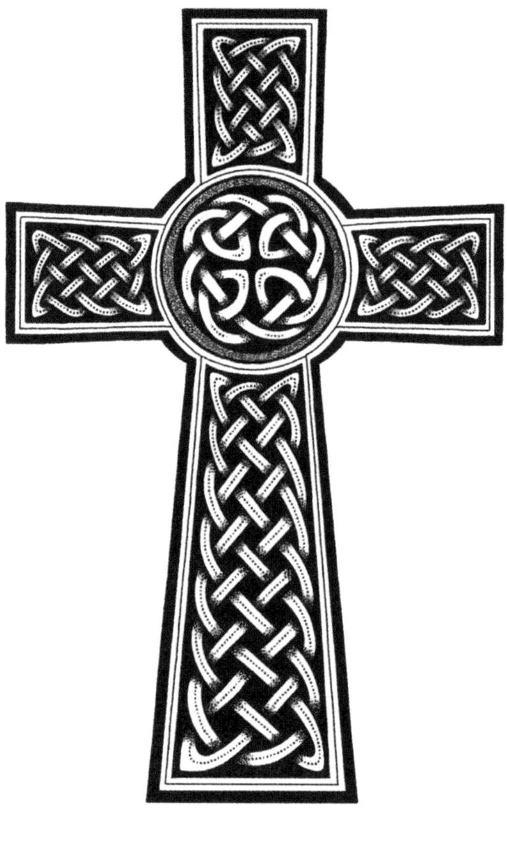

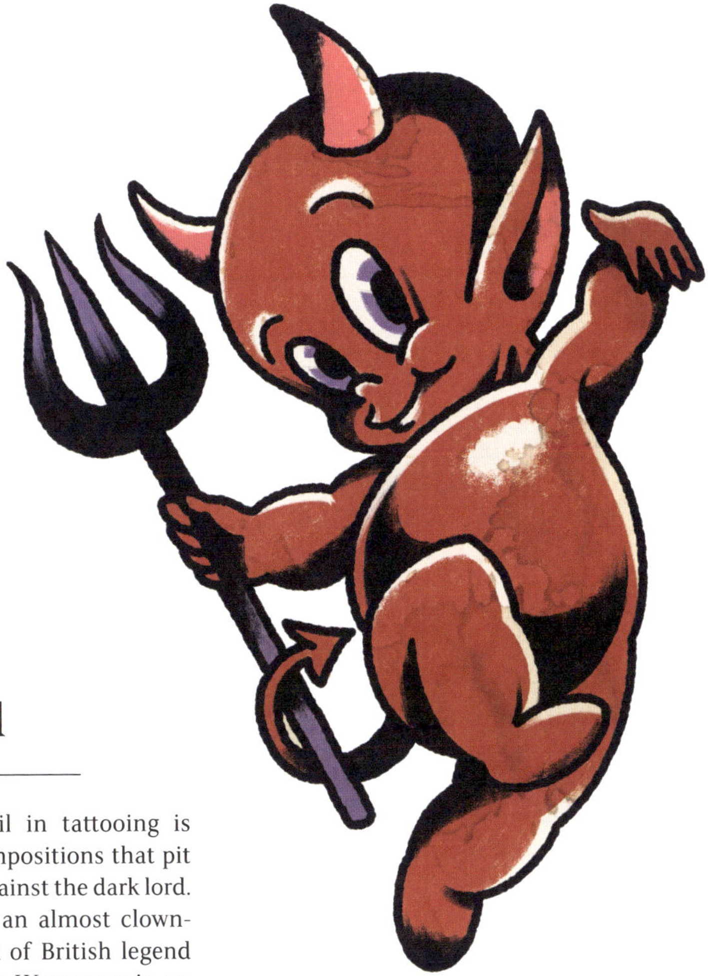

Devil

Consideration of the devil in tattooing is broad. Some feature in compositions that pit a femme fatale (or angel) against the dark lord. Others bend his face into an almost clown-like visage (as in the work of British legend George Burchett), putting a Western spin on Japanese oni masks. Regardless of look, the transmission is clear: protection from evil.

There's also a whimsical link with the devil and mischief. This is best articulated through playful reinterpretation of Kewpie, an invention of commerical illustrator Rose O'Neill, which became fodder for the likes of Percy Waters, Milton Zeis, Lyle Tuttle, among others during the 20th century. O'Neill's initial drawings were comic depictions of cupid. Flipping the tone, but keeping the fun, turning Kewpie into the devil created an icon of playful hell-raising.

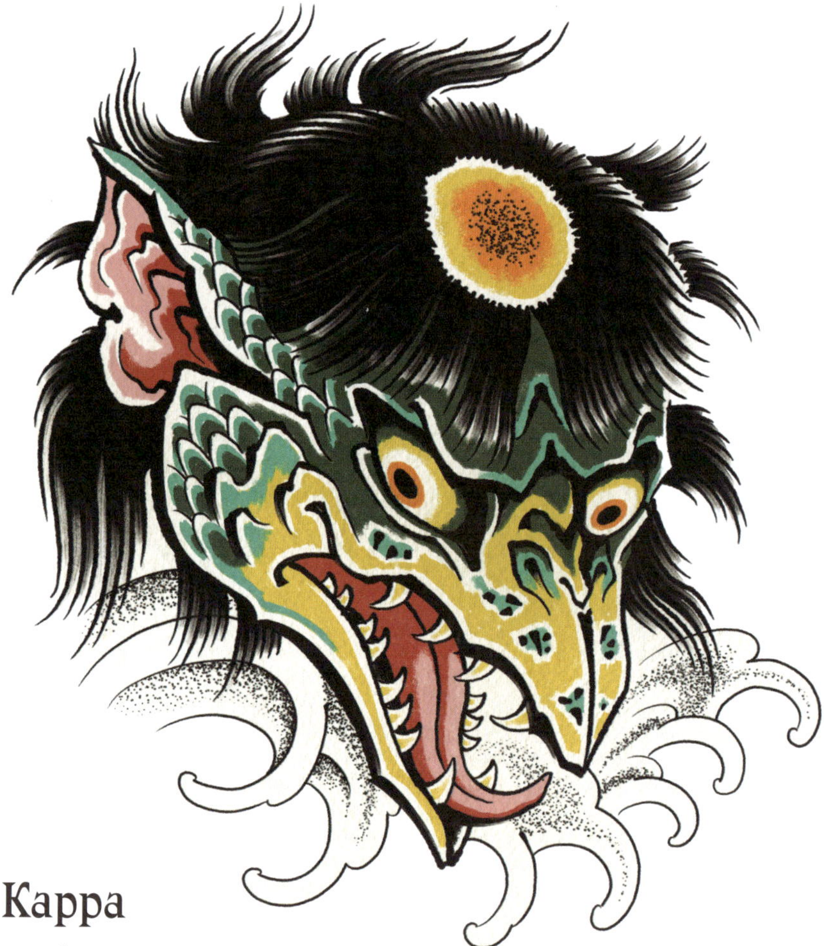

Kappa

One of the most common, and frightening, *yōkai* (Japanese folkloric goblin) in tattooing, the kappa (river child) has a humanoid shape and scaly skin. The mythical creature lives, naturally, in rivers where it aims to devour any child who strays near the banks. Despite this outwardly aggressive behaviour, the kappa is also known to be exceedingly polite. This quirk reflects a fundamental need to balance feelings of subservience and power. Thus, the kappa serves symbolically as a reminder of life's duality.

Saru

The Japanese monkey, or saru, is commonly represented in tattooing as a noh mask. As a character, the monkey is noted for its charisma (it can be a little trickster), and within performances it served as comic relief. Yet, a more powerful association comes from a spiritual association with Shinto and Buddhist tradition. The saru is a reminder to tame distraction and follow divine teaching.

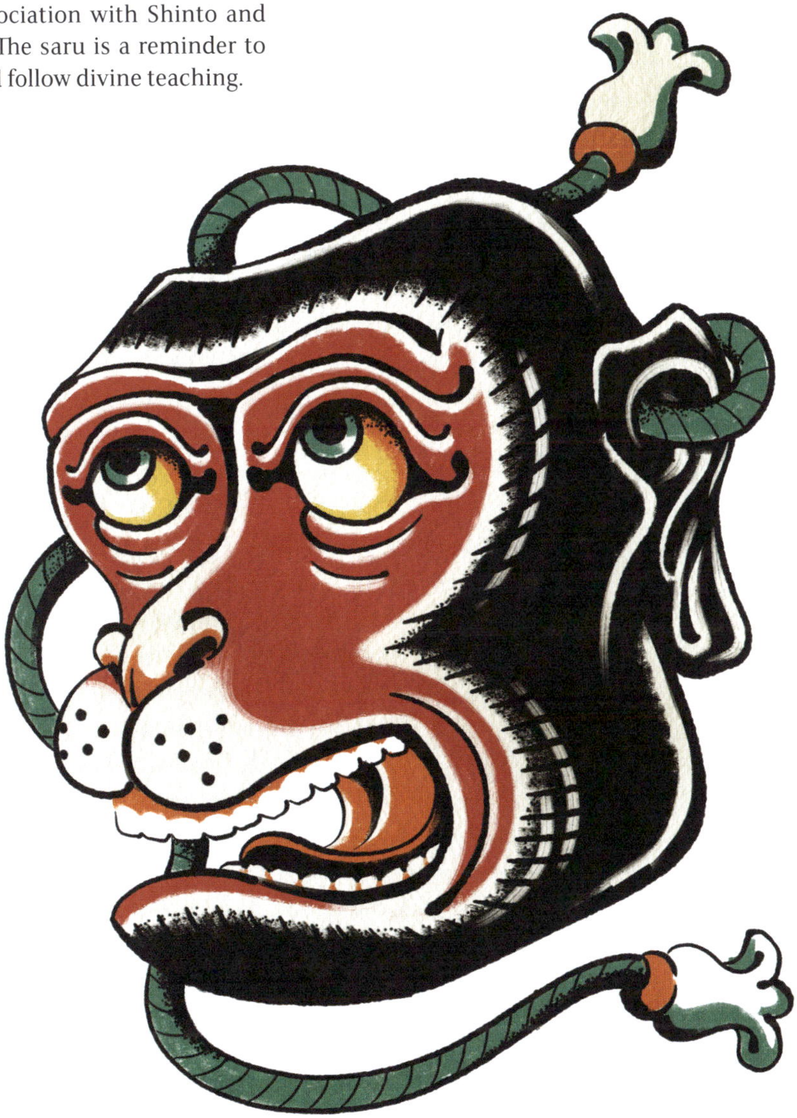

Raijin

The Japanese god of thunder and lightning, Raijin is recognizable for his reddish skin and a three-fingered hand. Raijin is depicted surrounded by drums, which he bangs with mallets during a storm – three bursts at a time – to create thunder. Association with rain makes Raijin an important god in relation to the assurance of an abundance of crops.

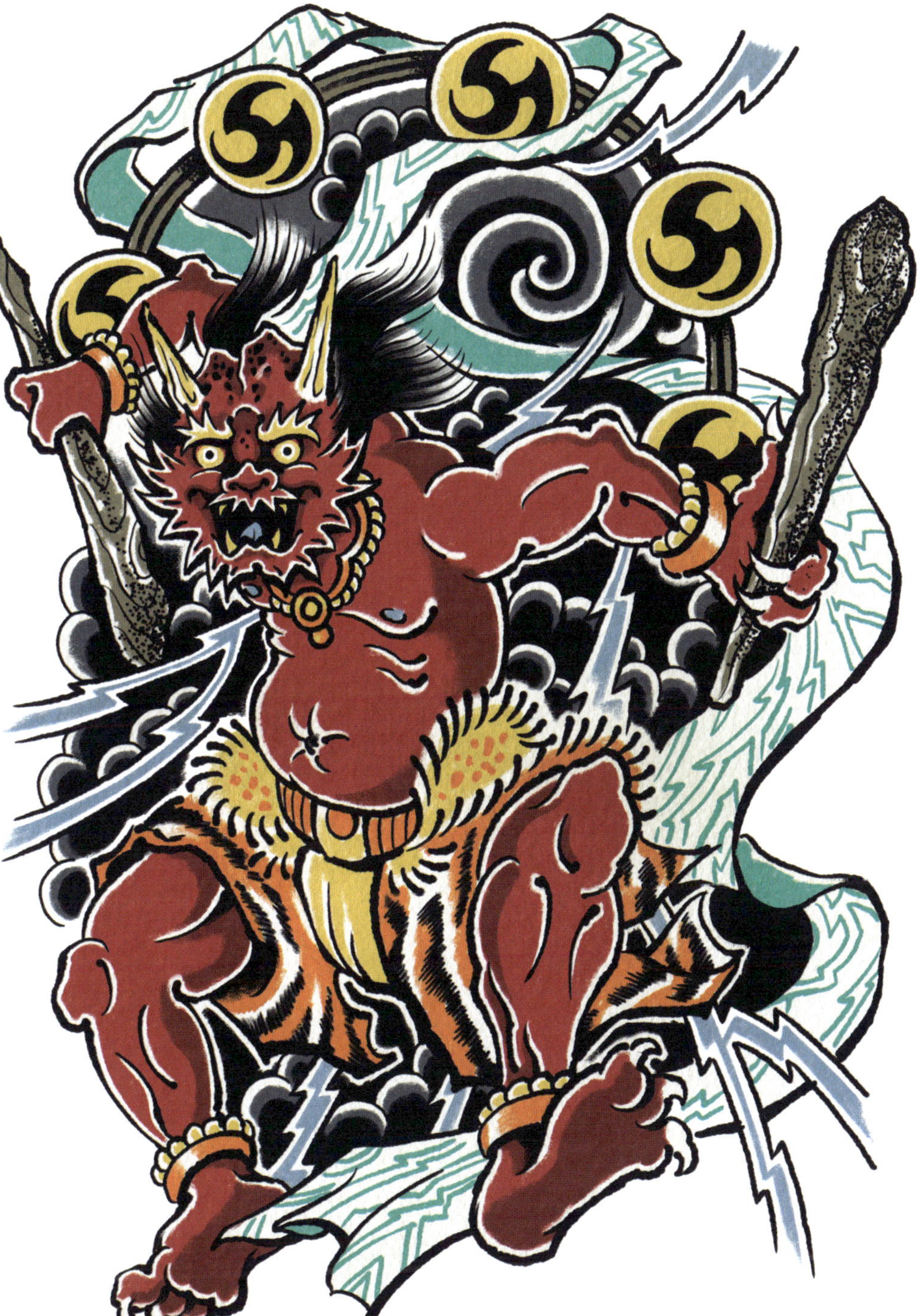

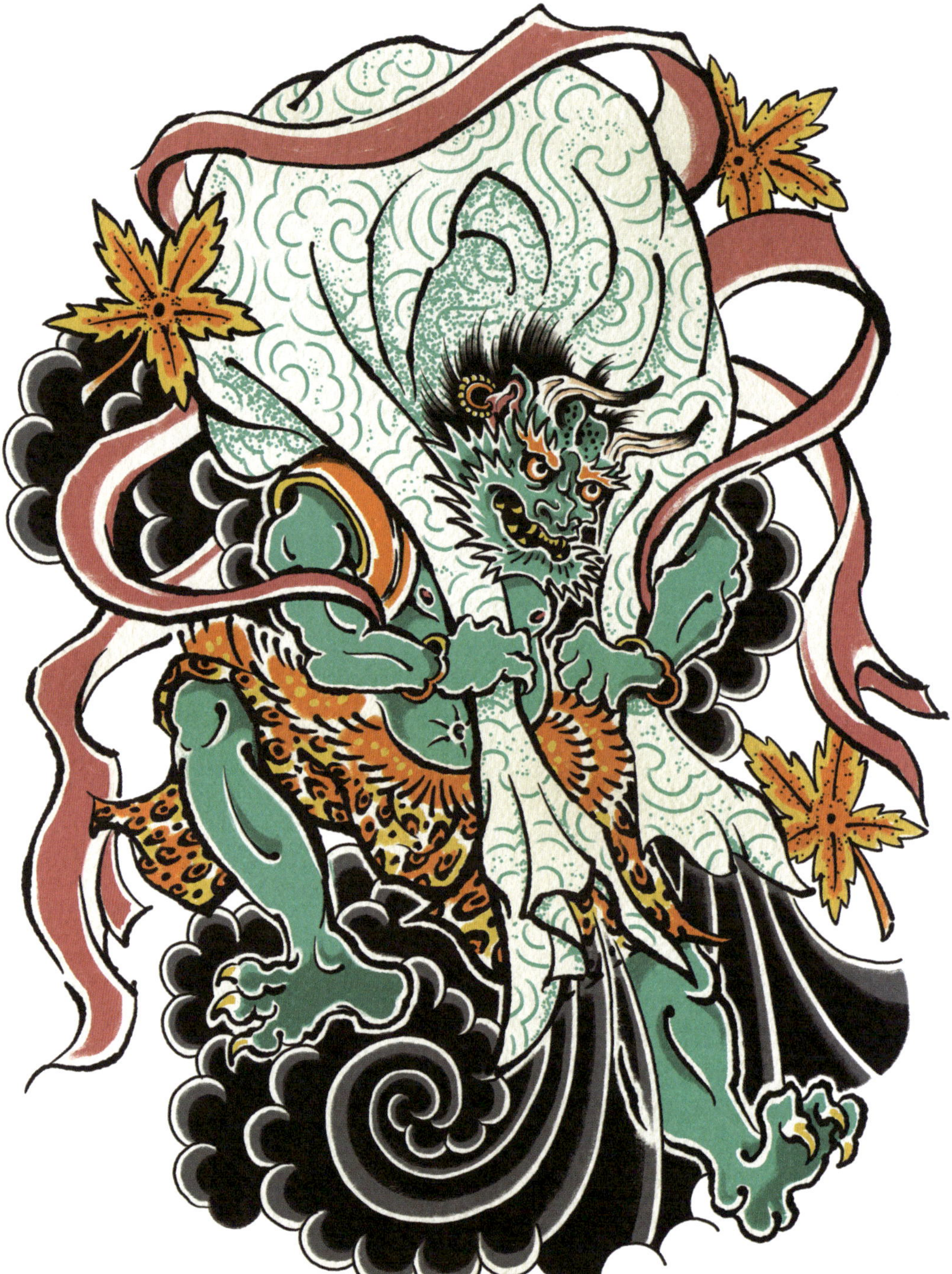

Fujin

Notable for horns on his head and clawed hands and feet, Fujin is the Shinto god of wind. He wears a leopard pelt and, in his bag, carries the winds, which according to his story were let out to create the space between heaven and earth. This in turn, allowed the sun to shine. Despite some positives, association with Fujin is largely cautionary as his winds are mostly known to cause harm.

Broken Chain

Tattoos of a broken chain convey a simple, but powerful message: an unshackling from a negative force. It serves as a very clear visual representation of strength of inner will and a triumph over a dark period of life.

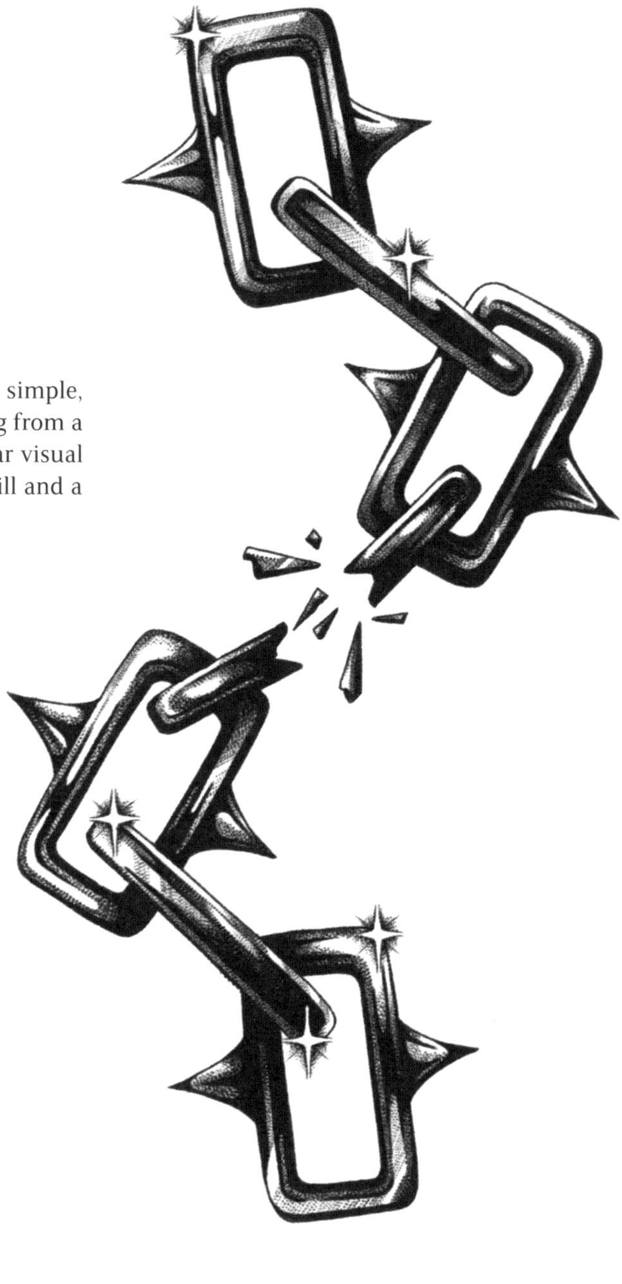

Stag

In several traditions, including Buddhism and Celtic lore, the stag is celebrated for spiritual regeneration and authority. The animal is viewed as a messenger and problem solver, guiding people away from traps. For Christians, the behaviour of stags (for example, helping one another to cross a river), represents the idea that members of a community should support each other.

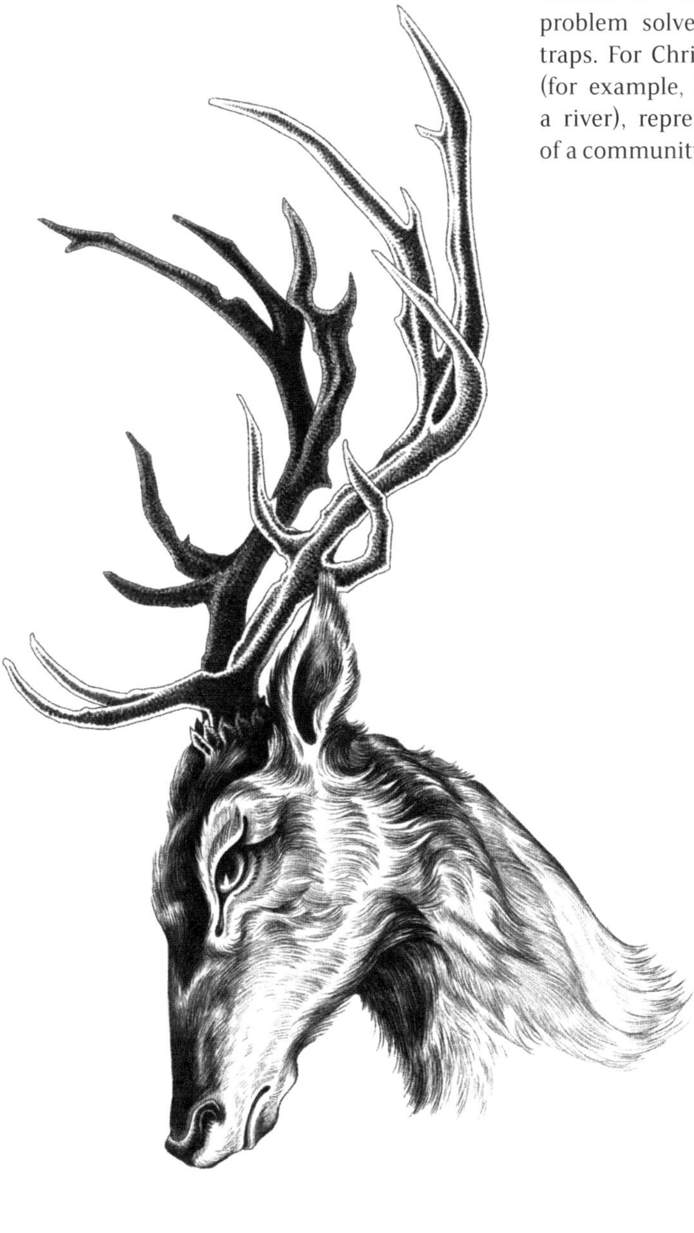

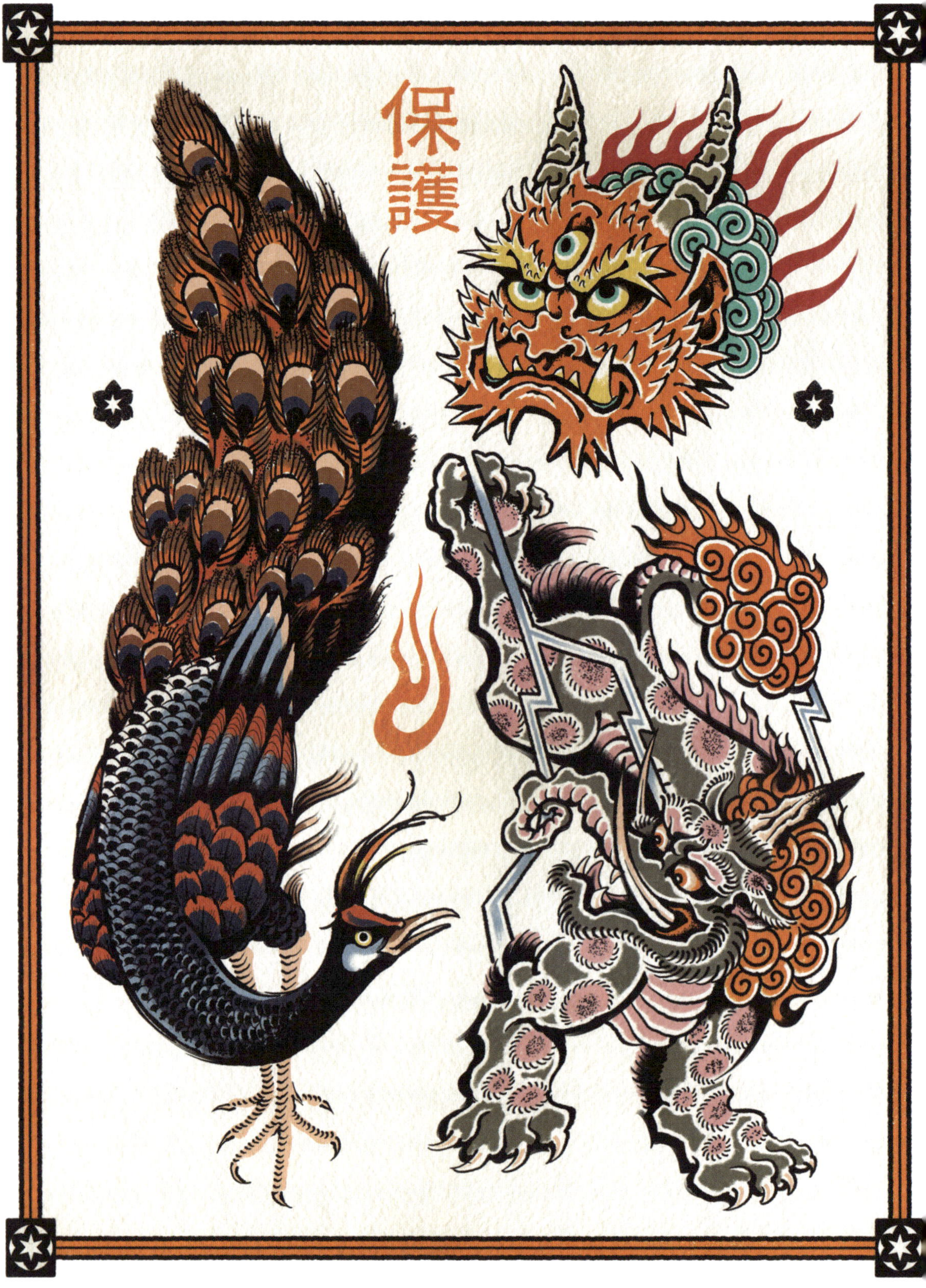
保護

3

PROTECTION AND GUIDANCE

Closely connected to themes of faith and spirituality, protection and guidance symbols often have direct religious origins. Of those, the Rock of Ages, in all its dramatic glory, stands as one of the clearest examples of how an image has been appropriated through tattooing, becoming iconic in the process.

Several seafaring symbols feature in this category, such as the nautical star, the shark and the compass. Underscoring the interconnection between mariners and tattoos, their application today honours the transference of that history to the contemporary landlocked bodies who need their own safeguarding. A third lineage in the theme flows from Japanese mythology, and a fourth from the appropriation of professional symbols (such as the caduceus). Reference is also made to hieroglyphs from the ancient world.

Most of the symbols presented here counter or ward off evil, shifting attention from a negative circumstance to a positive outlook. Other symbols, such as the peacock, allow for a more subtle articulation of these themes, with an emphasis on historic association.

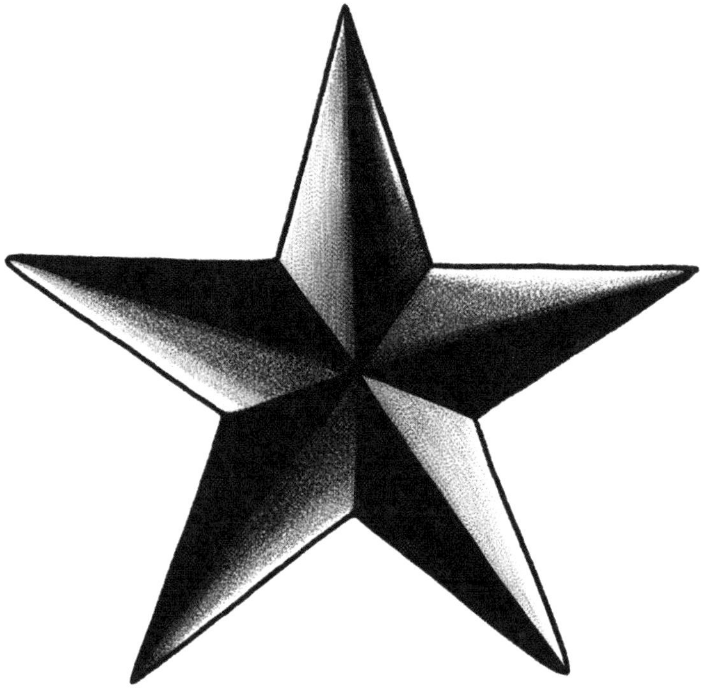

Nautical Star

Nautical star tattoos relate to the North Star as a navigational guide at sea. A symbol of protection and guidance, the nautical star became rooted in tattoo culture through the seafaring community – particularly those enlisted in the coast guard, marines or navy – and has blossomed as a western traditional icon since the mid-19th century.

Various forms of the nautical star have been employed by tattooers (both on skin and in flash books). Honolulu-based, Sailor Jerry (born Norman Collins), regarded as the master of 20th-century American tattooing, famously produced the nautical star in red and black, five or six pointed, or in the shape of the compass rose. The design reflects a desire to stay on course and, predominantly, free of danger, while wider interpretations suggest self-determination. Through veneration of Jerry in the 2000s, the star gained renewed popularity, further diversifying its integration within the contemporary tattoo vocabulary, but always remaining tightly connected to the spirit of its original usage.

Shark

A shark tattoo was said to protect a sailor from danger. The association connects to Polynesian and Hawaiian reverence for the shark as family's *aumakua* (guardian and protector).

Western traditional tattoos give the shark a one-dimensional, almost cartoonish, character. Examples include the famous Sailor Jerry version, which depicts the shark in a 'sailor's grave' design – playfully toying with all the inherent fears presented in a life at sea. Contemporary designs are more varied. While some elaborate on the Jerry-style composition, the alpha predator of the ocean is also beautifully rendered in black and grey. Of course, Polynesian tatau designs are also among the most visually arresting.

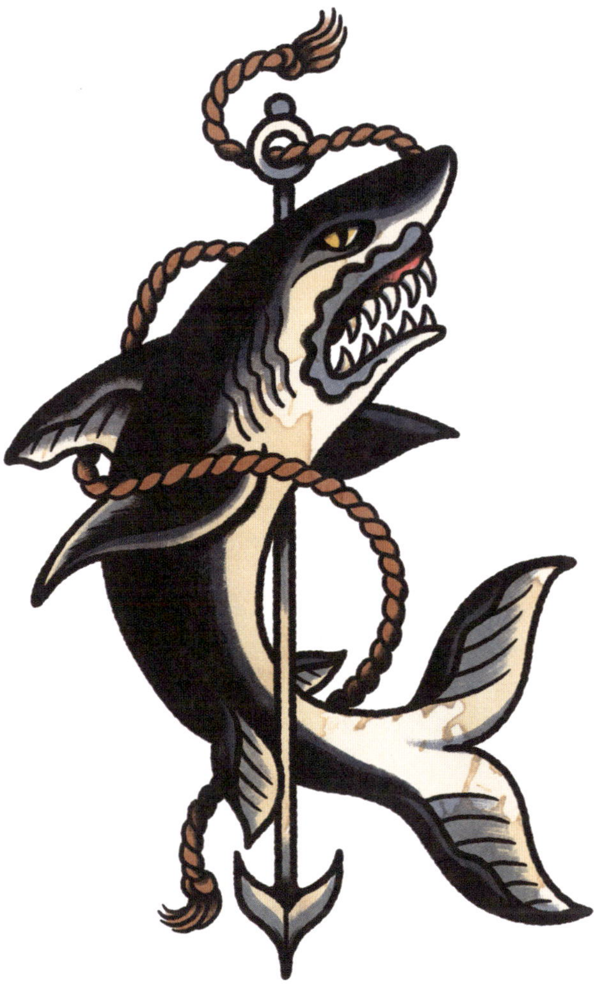

Compass

Like the nautical star (see page 54), compass tattoos emerge from the maritime tradition to reflect a sense of wanderlust. Symbolic of guidance and good fortune, the compass serves travellers of all types, as well as dreamers.

Though the compass was invented in Han dynasty China, the common compass in tattoo culture derives from the maps of early modern Europe, which begat the compass rose – a multipoint star used to display the cardinal directions of the wind. The dynamism of the compass rose, with its star-shaped centre, allows for depth and deviation of composition. Meanwhile, the positioning of the arrows against north, east, south and west allows for individualized meaning.

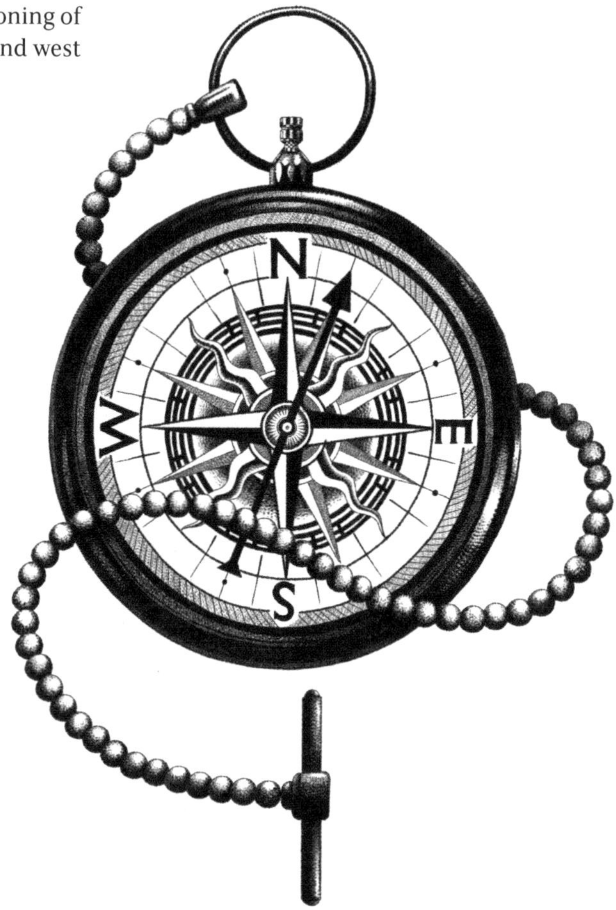

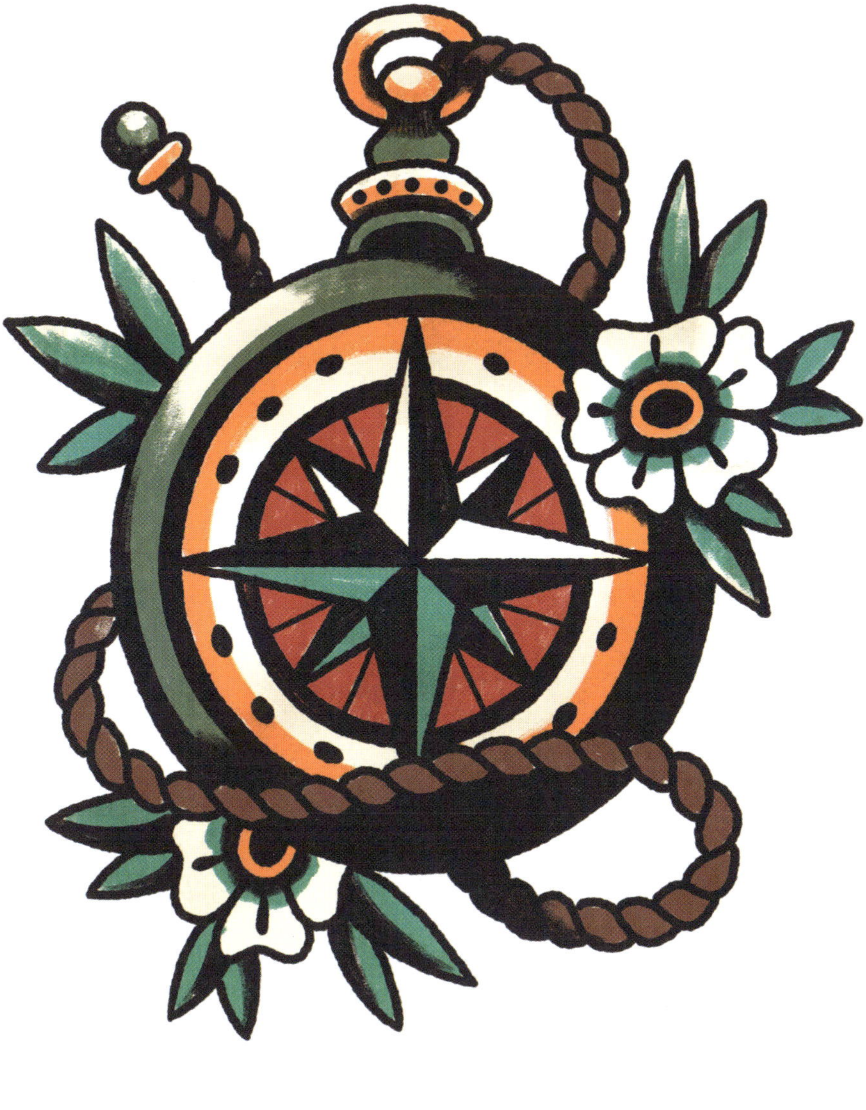

Rose of No-Man's Land

Arising from the atrocities of World War I, the rose of no-man's land embodies courage and compassion. The design embodies an image of the type of Red Cross nurse who would have supported wounded soldiers in no-man's land – the unoccupied area between opposing trenches. It is one of the finest examples of an otherwise ephemeral image gaining immortality in tattooing.

Though coined by soldiers, the rose of no-man's land moniker was cemented in popular culture through song. Leo Feist recorded a version of the song 'la rose sous les boulets' in 1918 and an English version by Boston-based songwriters Jack Caddigan and James Alexander Brennan followed. Sheet music for the latter, published in 1918 by Jack Mendelsohn Music, features an image of a nurse's head settled within a rose – a vision that certainly inspired the composition of the now famous tattoo.

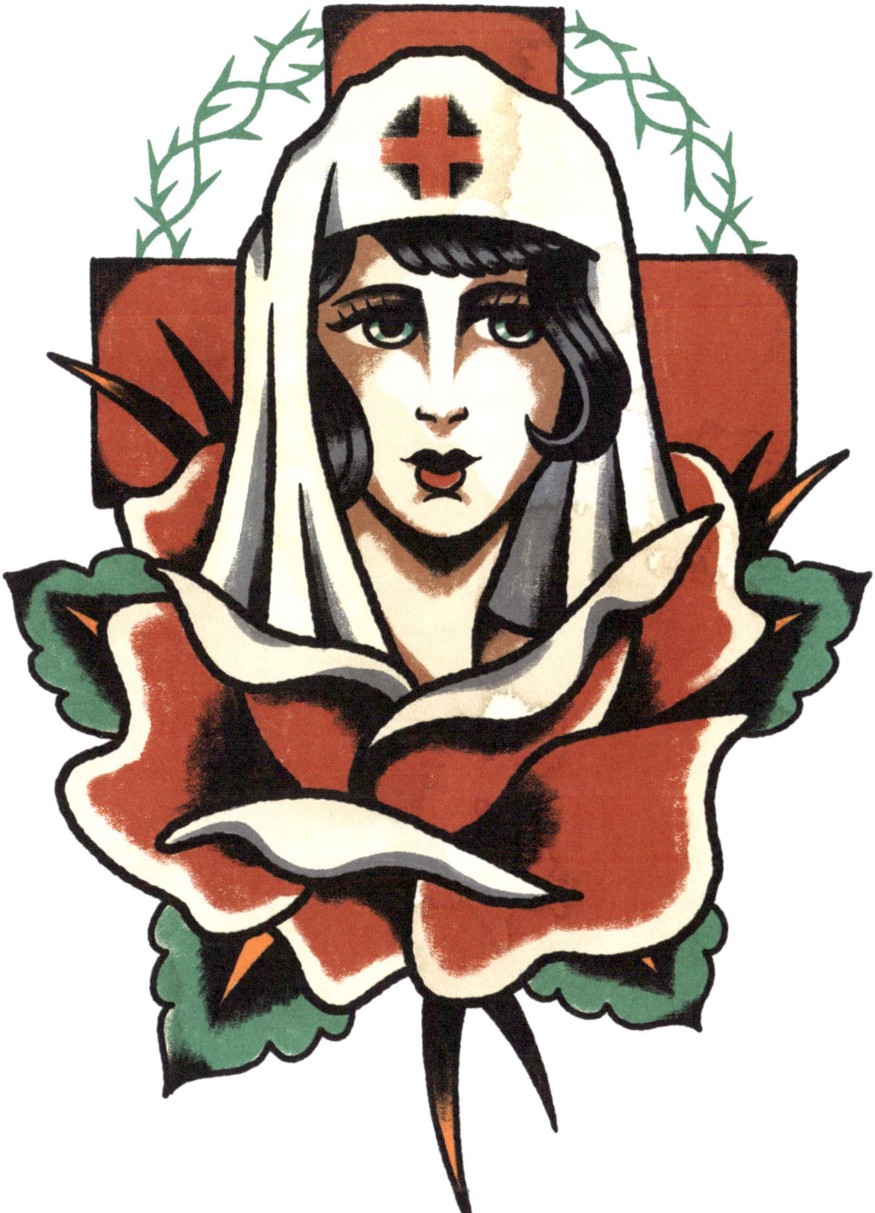

Rock of Ages

Written in 1763 by Reformed Anglican minister Augustus Toplady, the hymn 'Rock of Ages' was inspired by the author having taken refuge from a storm in Burrington Combe limestone gorge, in Somerset, England. The lyrics reflect a religious shift – from Calvinism to Methodist – and celebrate salvation.

More than 100 years after the hymn was written, the 'rock of ages' found visual form through a painting by Johannes Oertel, *Saved, Or an Emblematic Representation of the Christian Faith*. Oertel's dramatic depiction, complete with crashing waves surrounding a single female figure gripping to a stone cross, was reproduced as the *Rock of Ages*, and proliferated quickly in a variety of print forms (including versions distributed by the successful New York printmakers, Currier and Ives) through the 1870s and beyond.

The image, like others featured in popular Victorian-era religious prints, almost immediately gained popularity within tattooing, particularly in the works of 19th-century New York pioneer Samuel O'Reilly. Since that time the 'rock of ages' design has continued to intrigue artists and clients alike, continually evolving, while communicating the protective aura of the original painting.

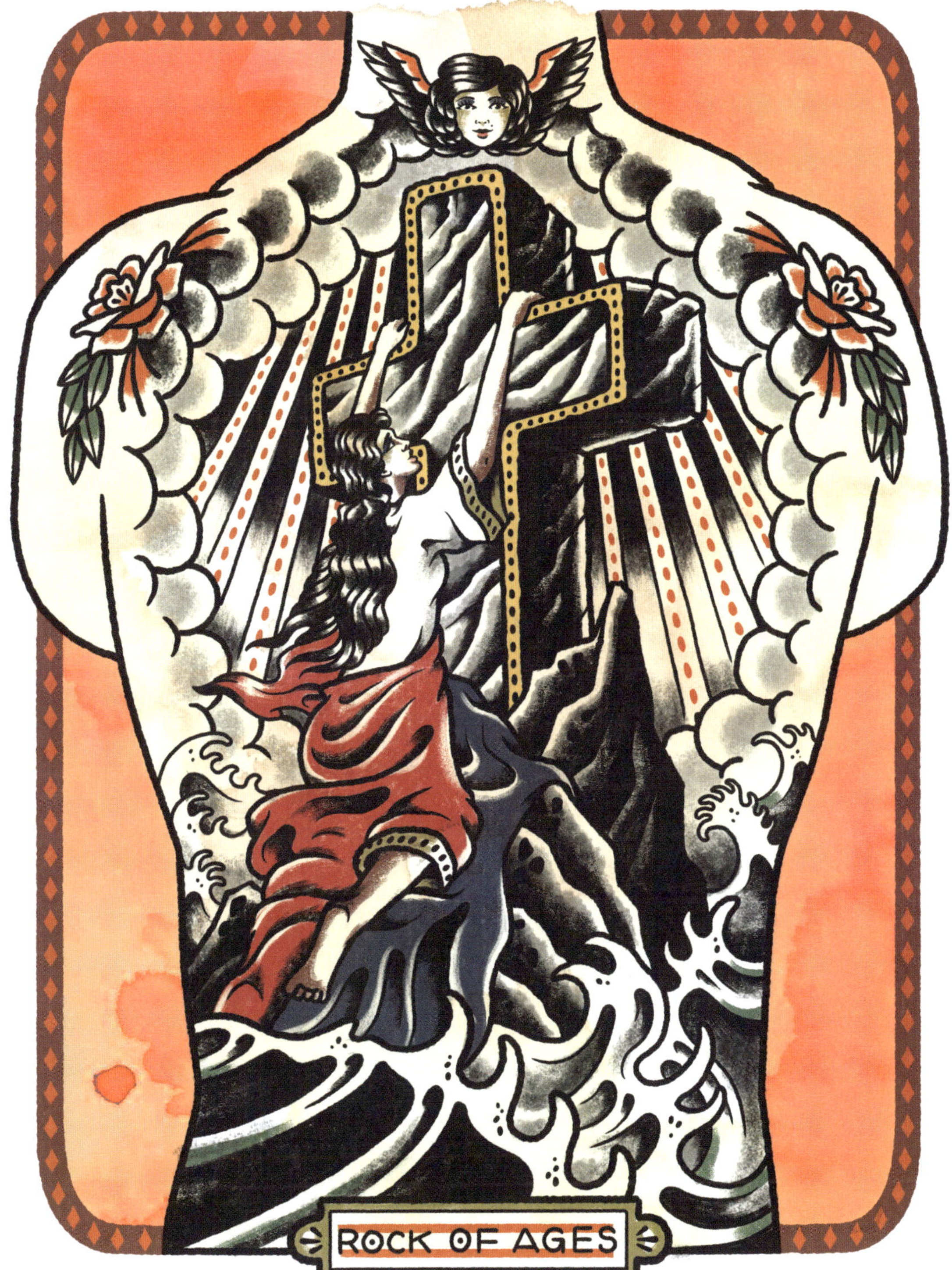
ROCK OF AGES

Ship's Wheel

Meanings attributed to ship's wheel tattoos derive from functional interpretation – the wheel itself defining direction. Nautical association grants the wheel a practical and nostalgic connotation; the wheel worn both by those commemorating a particular position at sea and those relishing the graphic sensibility of the western traditional style.

For the latter, a wheel represents clarity of purpose. It becomes a metaphor for life, relaying a sense of control or certainty of path despite inevitable rough patches. As with other nautically inspired symbols, the wheel can be paired with other icons in composition, such as an anchor, to strengthen the message. Additionally, one might add a banner or surrounding text to underscore intent.

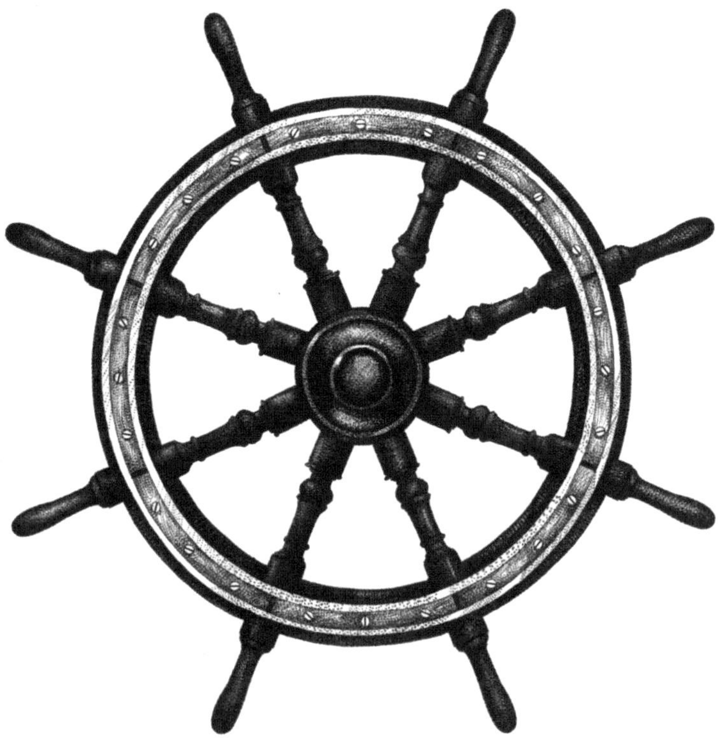

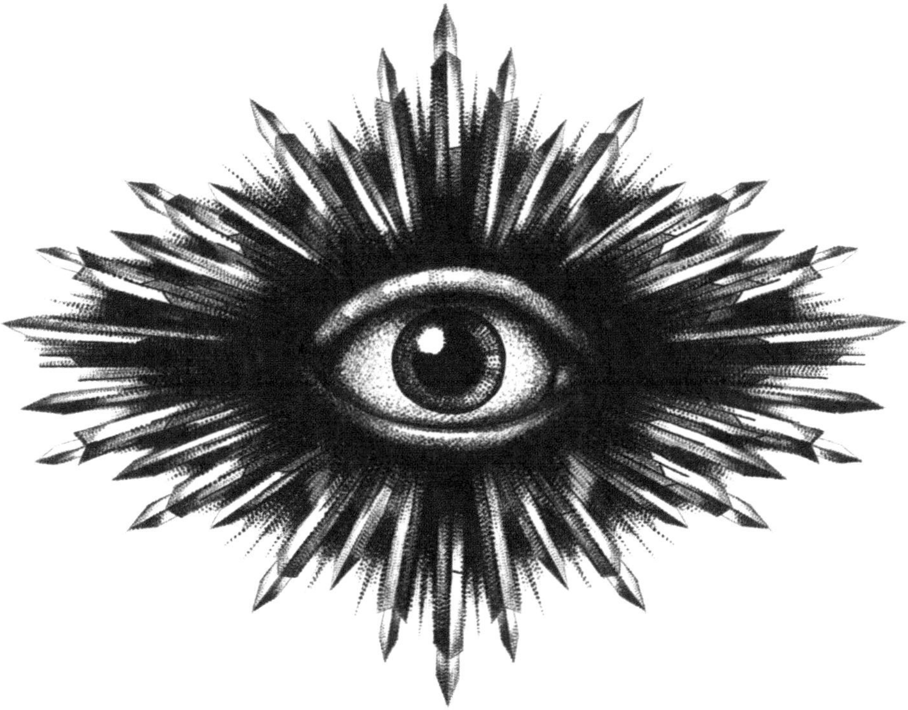

All-seeing Eye

Commonly read as God's omnipresent eye, the all-seeing eye design often follows from the Eye of Providence. Here, the eye is enclosed in a triangle, with light rays emanating from behind. The image itself is omnipresent, too, having been adopted as an American symbol in the early republic. Earlier renditions of the image – and, in fact its origin – come from ancient Egypt, the Eye of Horus, and depictions steadily spread around the world from the 16th through to the 18th centuries.

Of course, the idea of omniscience features in many belief systems and religions, making the all-seeing eye an incredibly adaptable symbol (and one of flexible interpretation). As a tattoo, one may choose the Eye of Providence or the Eye of Horus. But through choice of style – neo-traditional, black and grey, dotwork and more – an allowance for unique articulations also emerges. Thus, whether you lean to historic accuracy or surrealist aesthetics, there's likely an all-seeing eye design for you.

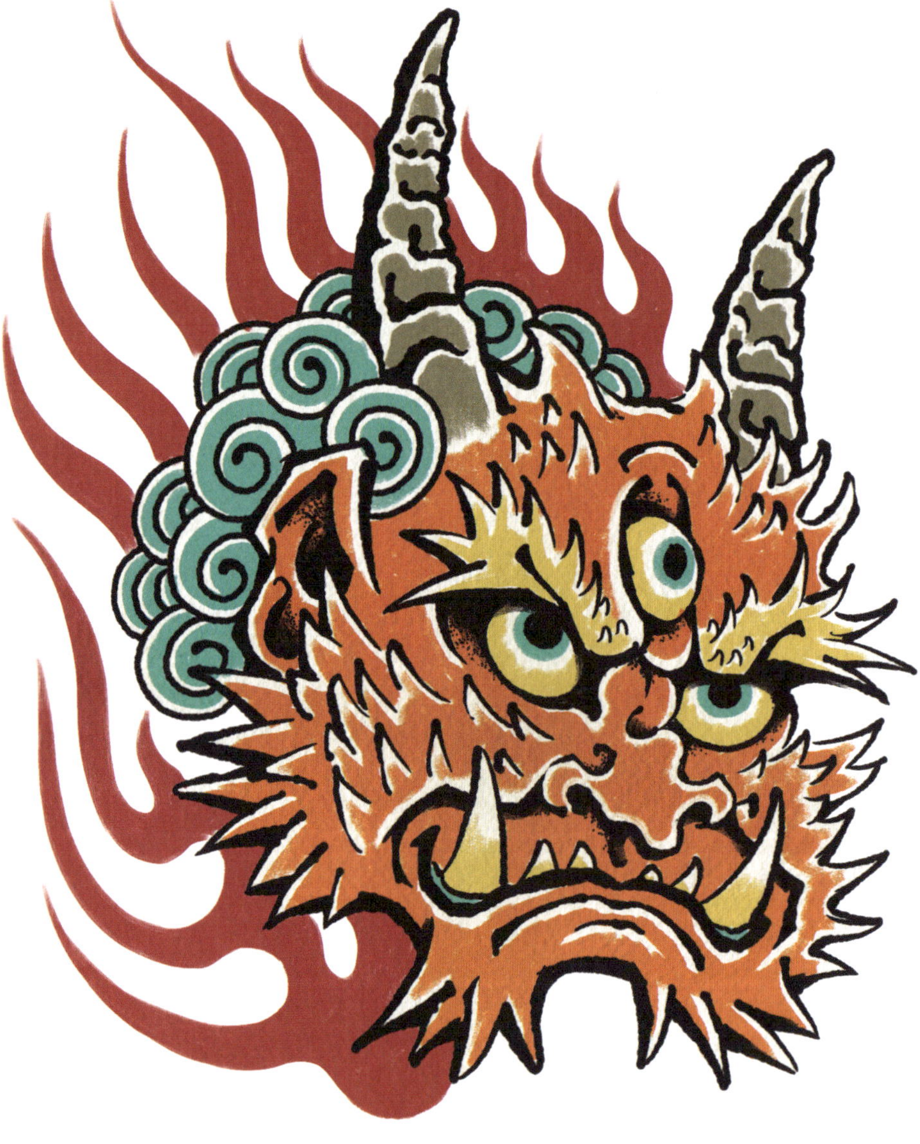

Oni

An *oni* is a Japanese folkloric demon, initially viewed as symbolizing a tormented soul. These evil elements were to be driven out of the home as part of the Setsubun festival, marking the change from winter to spring. During the festival, roasted soybeans are thrown out the front door or at a family member wearing an oni mask.

Oni are also symbols that themselves can ward off bad luck and evil spirits. The oni mask typically exaggerates features – bulging eyes, horns, toothy mouth. Naturally, the look is moderately to very intimidating, underscoring its associations with torment and evil.

Scorpion

Scorpion tattoos communicate protection and control. Like the black widow, another poisonous insect, the scorpion also suggests a sexual charge.

The Egyptian goddess Serket, a woman with a scorpion crown, was closely associated with predynastic rulers – as protector and healer – Scorpion I and Scorpion II. It was believed she could ward off the effects of venomous bites... and deploy scorpions to punish those who fell foul of her wards. Her role as guardian extends to tales of Isis, Horus and Ra, as well as of the canopic jars that were used during mummification.

As a tattoo, the arachnid lends itself to a variety of styles, including black and grey and western traditional.

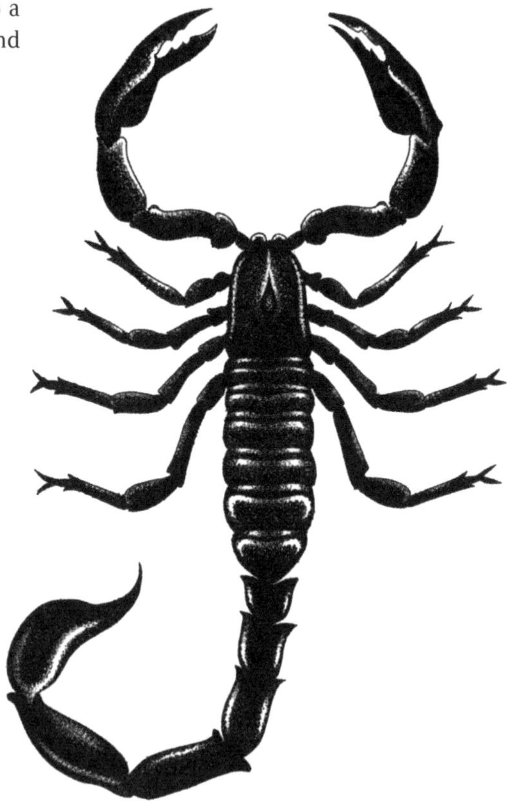

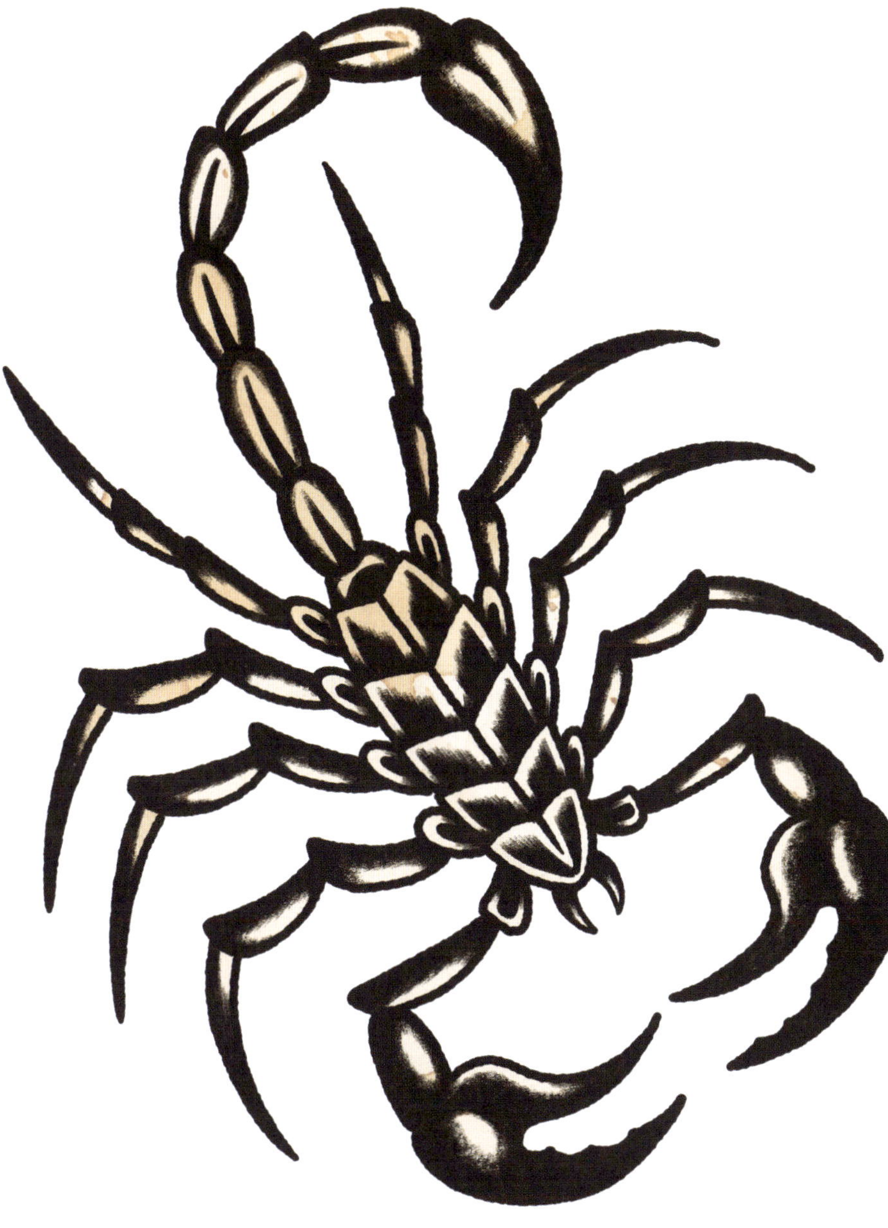

Lighthouse

Symbols of strength abound in maritime culture. One of the motifs most readily rendered as a tattoo, a lighthouse illuminates spiritual associations with hope and safety. Of course, the lighthouse structure is built to withstand storms and to protect ships from disaster.

In design, the lighthouse takes the focal point – as a beacon it attracts attention and reminds the viewer of the vitality of the building's function. While there are centuries of artistic depictions of the lighthouse (as a building type it was birthed in the 5th century BCE), lighthouse tattoos take their own inspiration. In the western traditional style, the composition is sometimes augmented with banners and other nautical symbols. Black-and-grey, blackwork and dotwork styles also lend themselves to lighthouse tattoos.

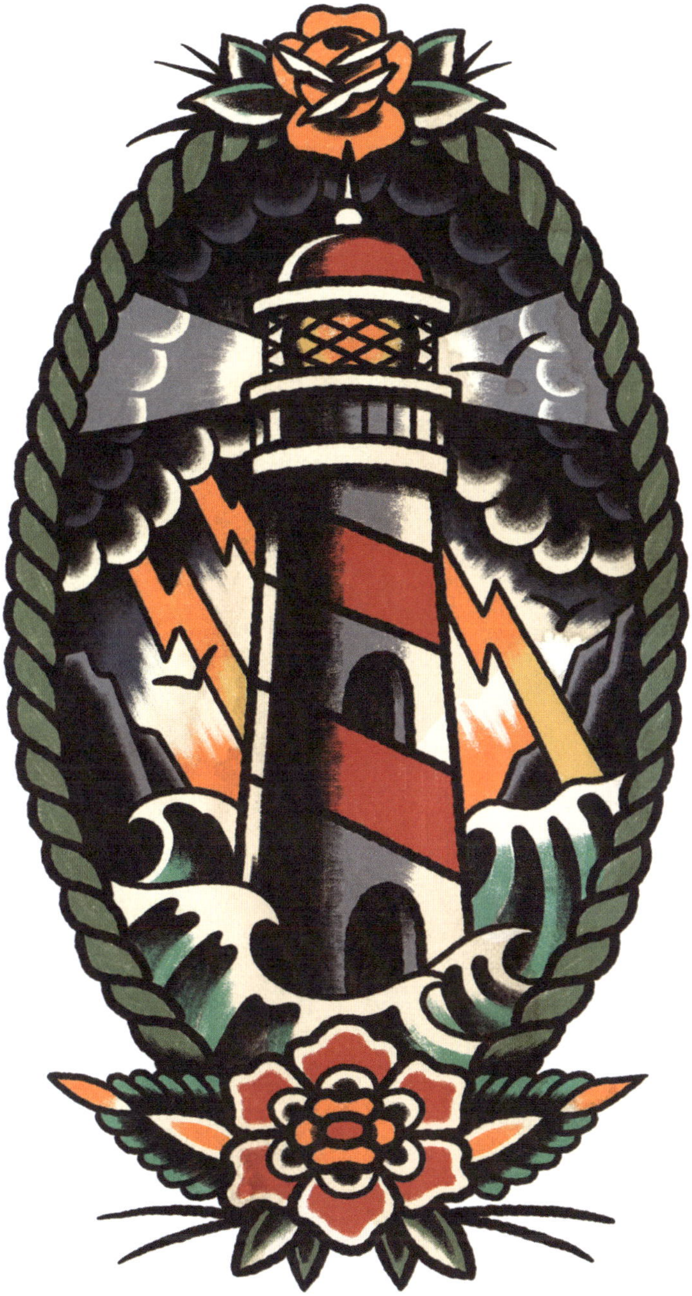

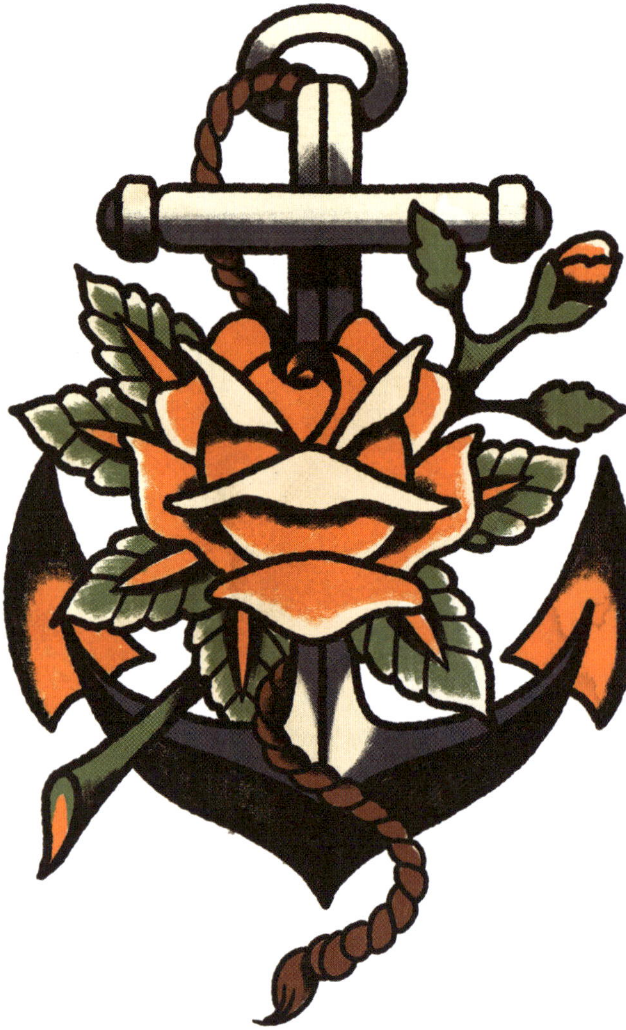

Anchor

Anchor tattoos have adorned bodies for well over 150 years. Symbolic of hope, safety and security, the image's meaning doesn't deviate much from the object's function. However, there are subtleties to the design that imbue individual nuances, including the addition of lettered banners or specific national flags.

For mariners, an anchor tattoo marks the crossing of the Atlantic. A fouled anchor, which is entwined with rope or chain, has held naval associations since first appearing in 1402 within the Scottish navy and was quickly adopted throughout the British services and later the American navy, too.

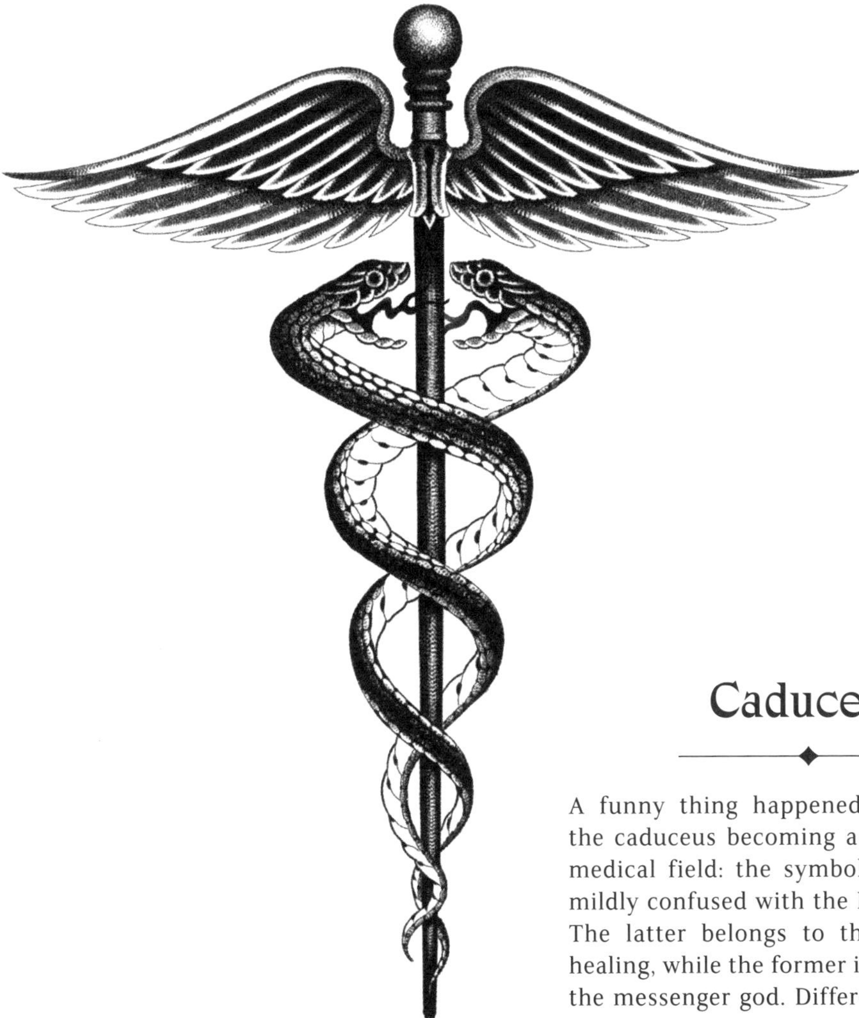

Caduceus

A funny thing happened on the way to the caduceus becoming a stand-in for the medical field: the symbol of Hermes was mildly confused with the Rod of Asclepius. The latter belongs to the Greek god of healing, while the former is associated with the messenger god. Differences are stark – a single snake versus a double snake – but today, due to adoption in the 20th century by the US Army Medical Corps, both articulations convey a spirit of protection.

Building around the staff, the caduceus design is naturally balanced. However, the image need not be staid. Individual articulations (ranging from angels to daggers) allow for a shift in the central element, and can help convey more personal protections and other professional peculiarities.

Baku

The supernatural *baku* are famed for eating nightmares. They are protectors of sleep, arriving in Japanese mythology from Chinese origins in the 14th century. In Irezumi, baku stand alongside dragon, kirin and foo dog among the most popular mythological monsters.

The creature itself, a chimera, draws characteristics from elephants (trunk and tusks are evident in pre-Meiji woodblock prints) and other animals, including the tiger and the ox. In articulation, baku often resemble a tapir. However, there is space for quite a lot of individual choice in the depiction, including coloration, horn shape and location and associative elements (such as maple leaves or lightning).

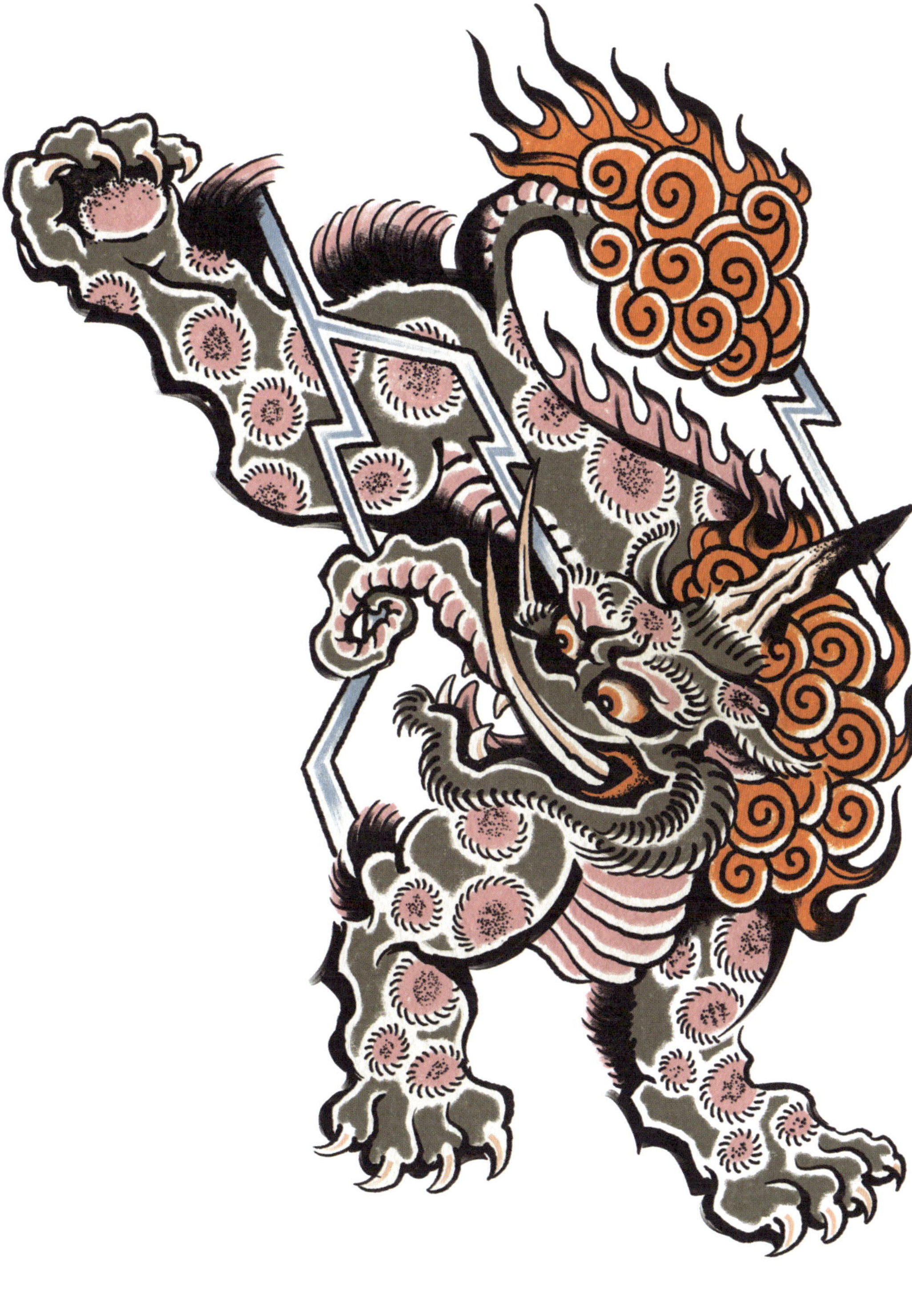

Peacock

Go back to ancient Egypt or Rome, and images of peacocks are easily found in relation to wealth and funeral tradition. Through the Middle Ages, the bird decorated Roman catacombs, symbolizing resurrection and renewal. The birds are associated with watchfulness and protection – particularly in connection to royalty.

And while the peacock has been depicted in art for millennia, it was through the Aesthetic Movement of the 19th century that it became a defining symbol of beauty – particularly in view of the male's stunning feathers. This consideration was affirmed in the Art Nouveau era, with the peacock again emphasized for its exquisite grace.

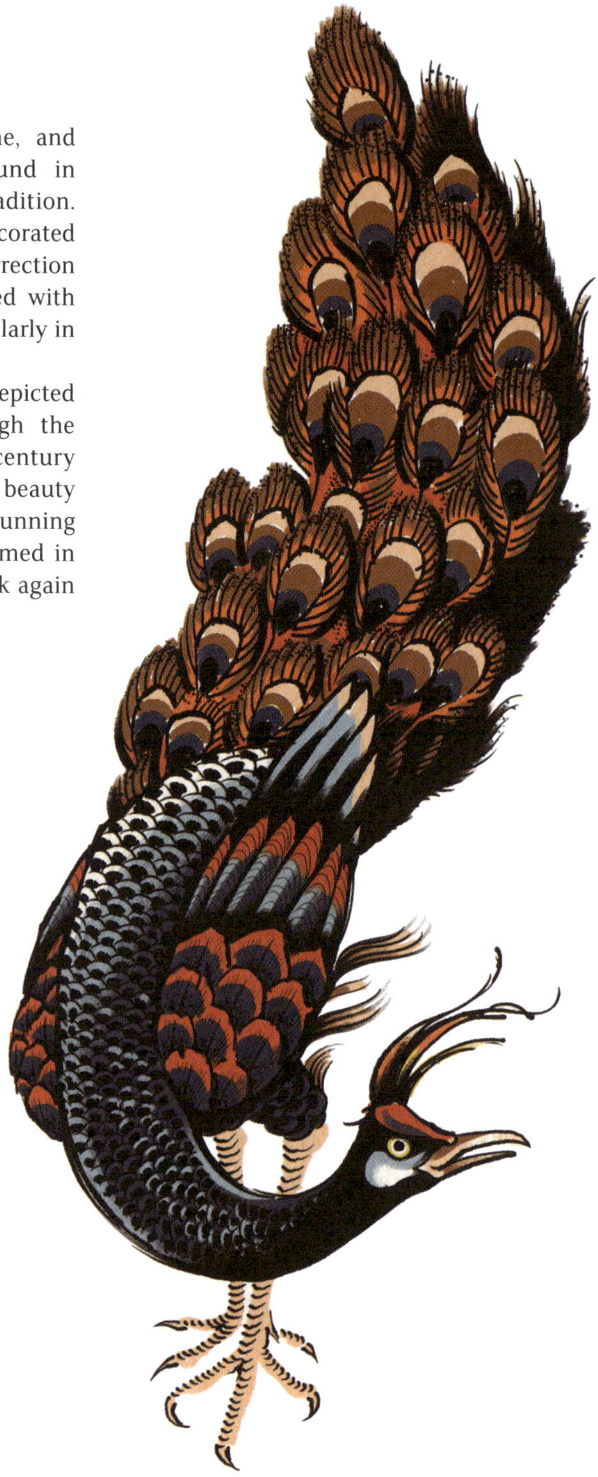

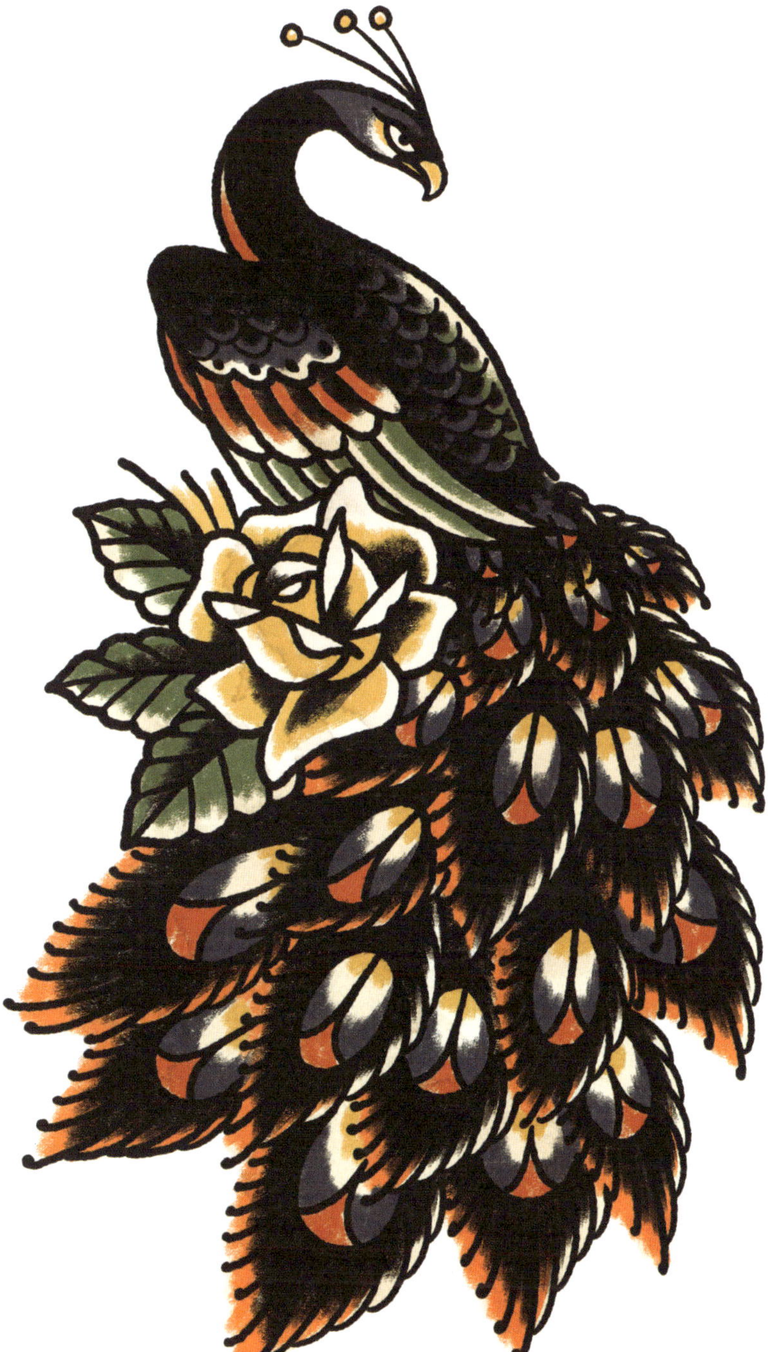

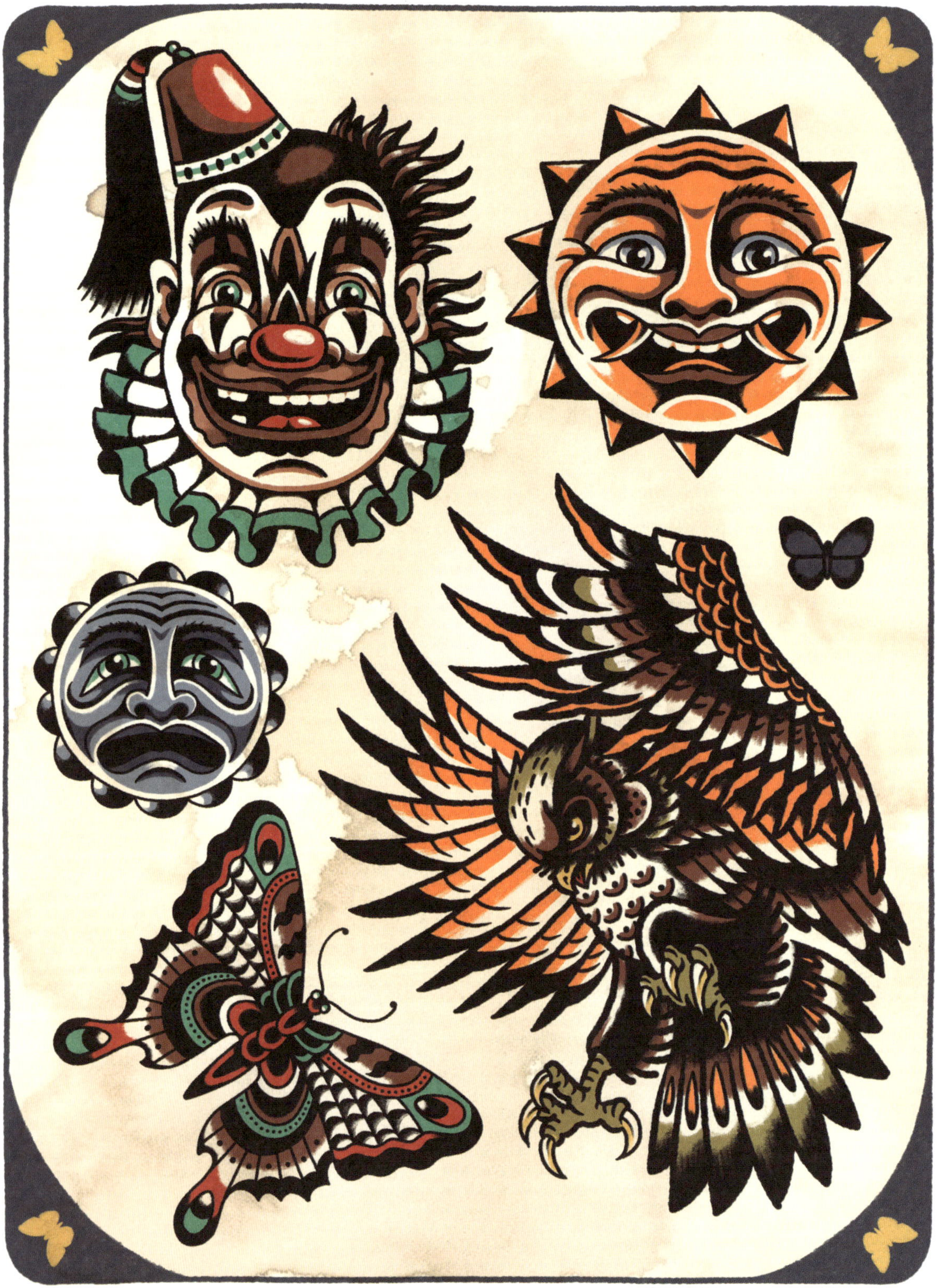

4

TRANSFORMATION

Tattoos offer beautiful ways in which to mark personal shifts. Fittingly, many symbols that convey a moment of transformation derive from ideas connected to rebirth. They present life as a cycle, privileging optimism and allowing a smooth passing to the future.

The theme shares a variety of influences that include Buddhist thought, Celtic tradition and Haida mythology, among others. It also highlights the graphic ingenuity of tattooists as, within the theme, we share the sun and moon designs pioneered by the legendary Bert Grimm. These two symbols remind us that, while designs are often appropriated or adopted by tattoo culture, some are truly unique to their originators.

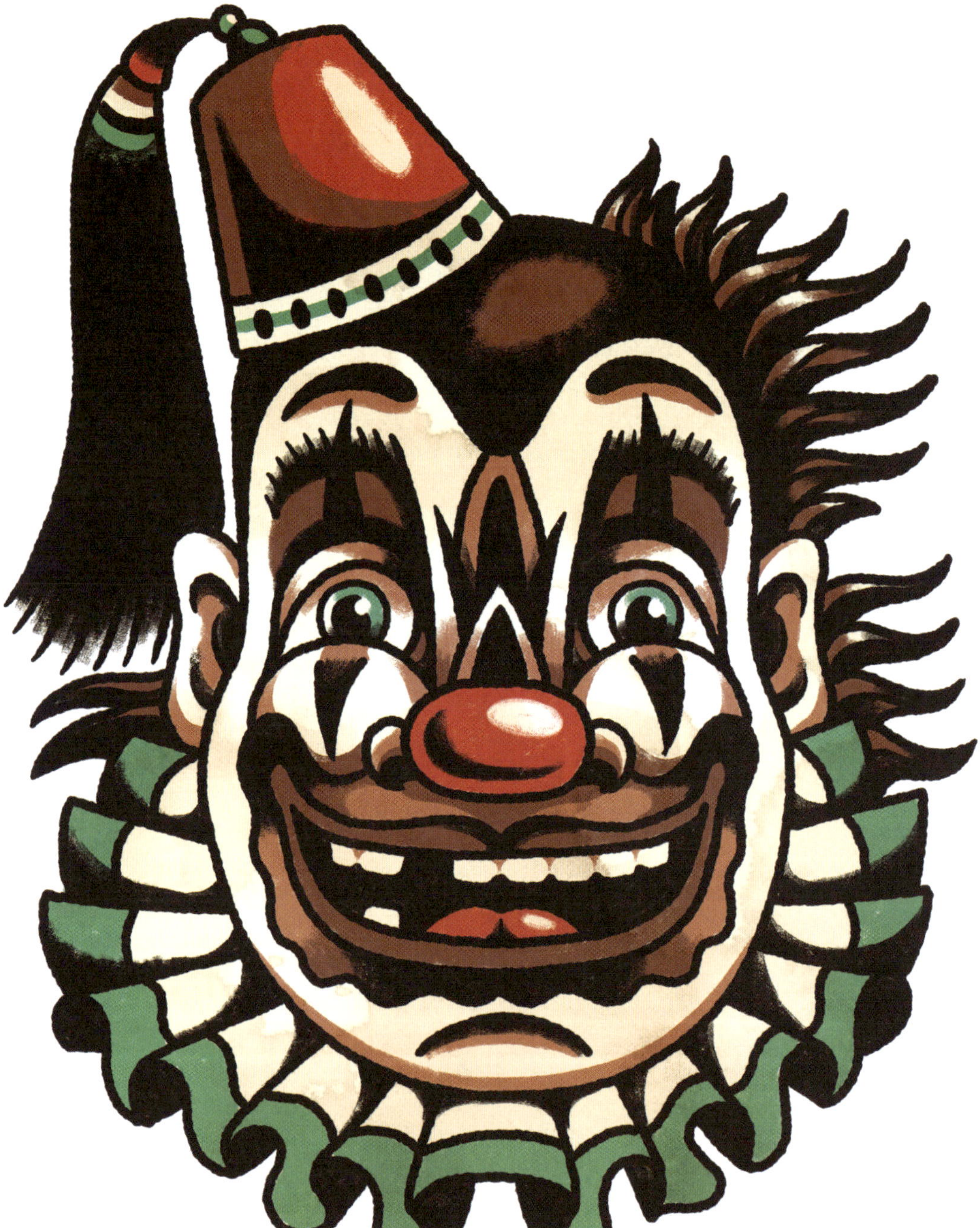

Clown

While there exists a wide variety of clown tattoo designs, within the western traditional style meaning derives from a tragicomic portrayal defined by 19th-century circus performers. Often with oversized features and exaggerating emotions such as happiness and sadness, worn on the body, these clowns convey a certain happy-go-luckiness and a tongue-in-cheek approach to life's challenges.

Butterfly

Butterfly tattoos have been popular for well over a century. Cap Coleman, the famed early-20th-century tattooist from Norfolk, Virginia, decorated the left shoulder of an advertising figurine with a butterfly sometime between 1910 and 1920, and by mid-century, butterflies were near ubiquitous on flash sheets throughout the United States.

As a symbol, the butterfly most commonly represents change, hope and metamorphosis. In sailor's lore, the butterfly carries a negative connotation – to see one before setting off is considered an omen for death – but it is the transformative associations that are most pervasive. While history within the western traditional style has led to myriad bold butterfly designs, the symbol rings just as true rendered in sharp, black linework.

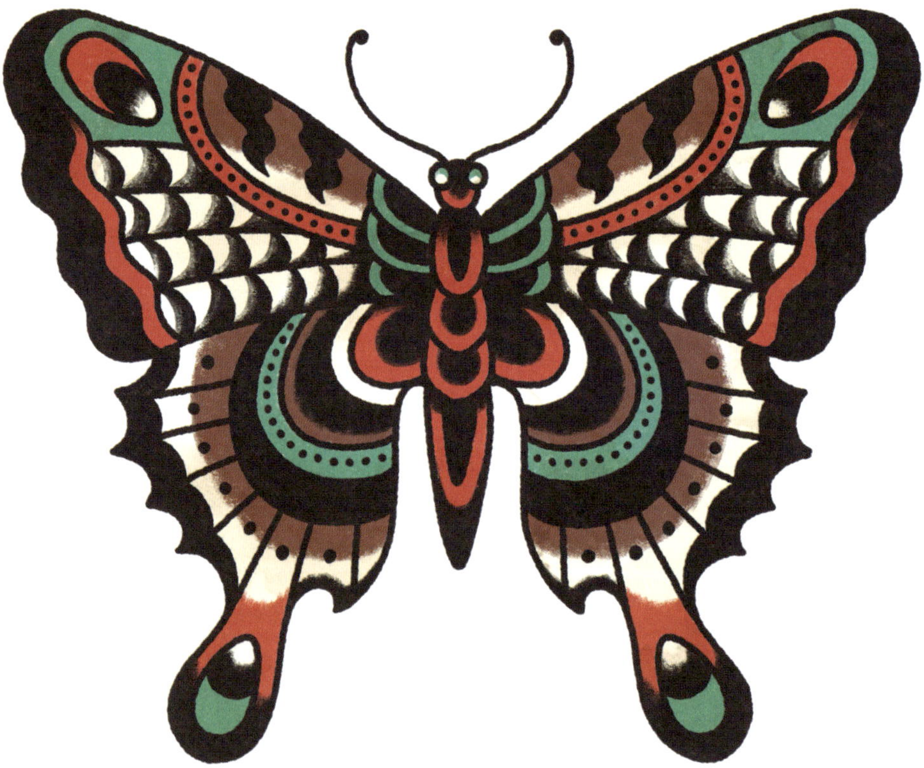

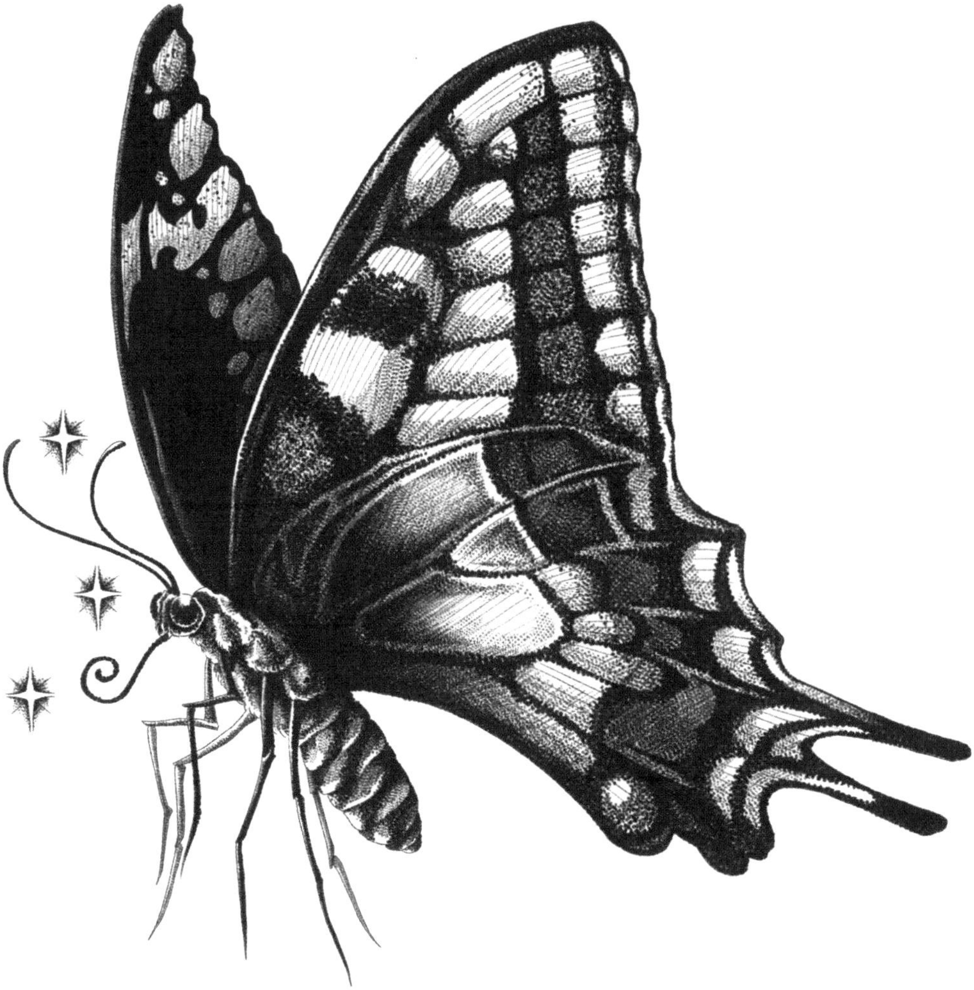

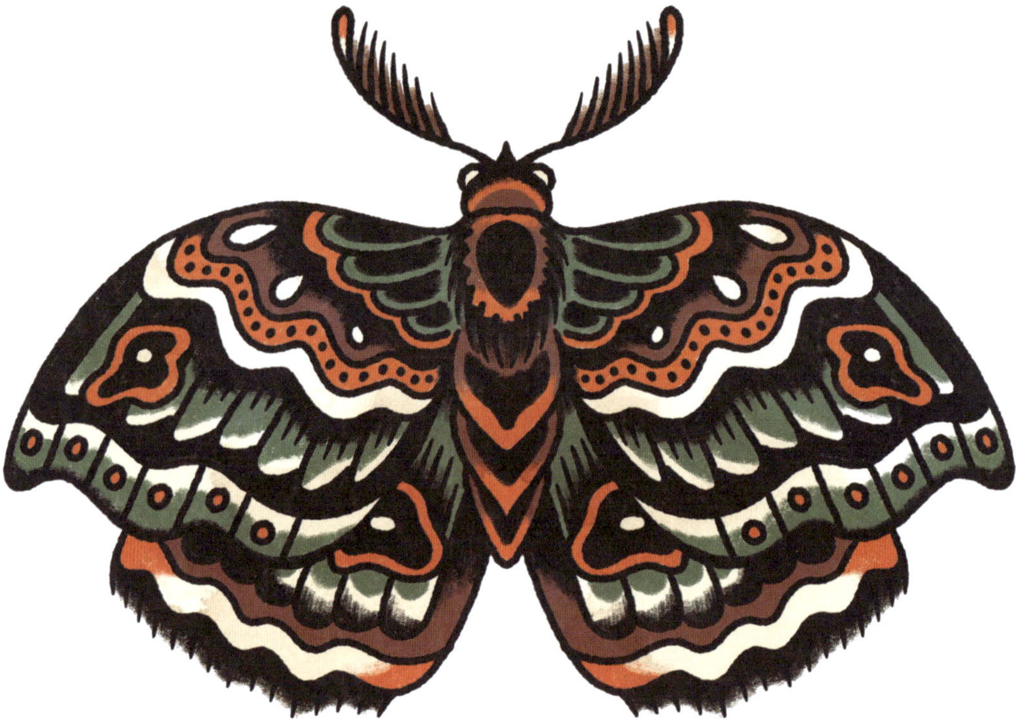

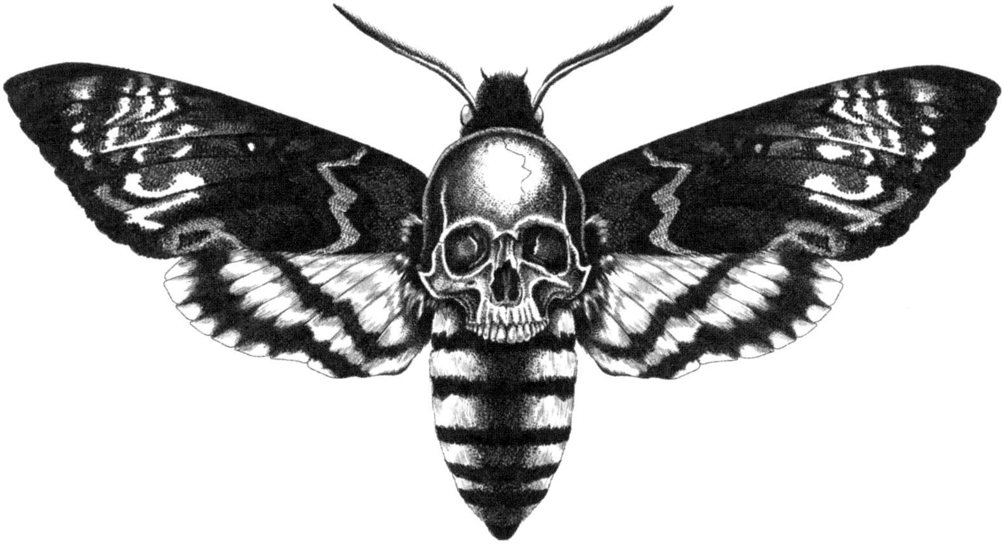

Moth

As with the butterfly, the moth represents metamorphosis. In subtle contrast, the nocturnal life of the moth links the insect to the dreamscape and even death. Meaning is derived from these contrasts, the moth symbolizing freedom to recognize danger and avoid corrupting forces. In a quest for change, the moth becomes a perfect icon.

Additionally, the centrality of the moth in a variety of cultures, including Christian tradition, Native American mythology and European folklore, allows for a range of design considerations.

Snake

While there are snake tattoos that stand for strength and power (the cobra) or protection (the Japanese *hebi*), there are also snake tattoos (and figures such as the ouroboros) that symbolize rebirth and continual renewal.

It is important to consider how a design represents the snake. Take, for example, an image of a snake removing dead skin by sloughing. Through the shedding, the snake readies itself for the future. For this reason, particular snake tattoos are popular among people wishing to commemorate a moment of rejuvenation.

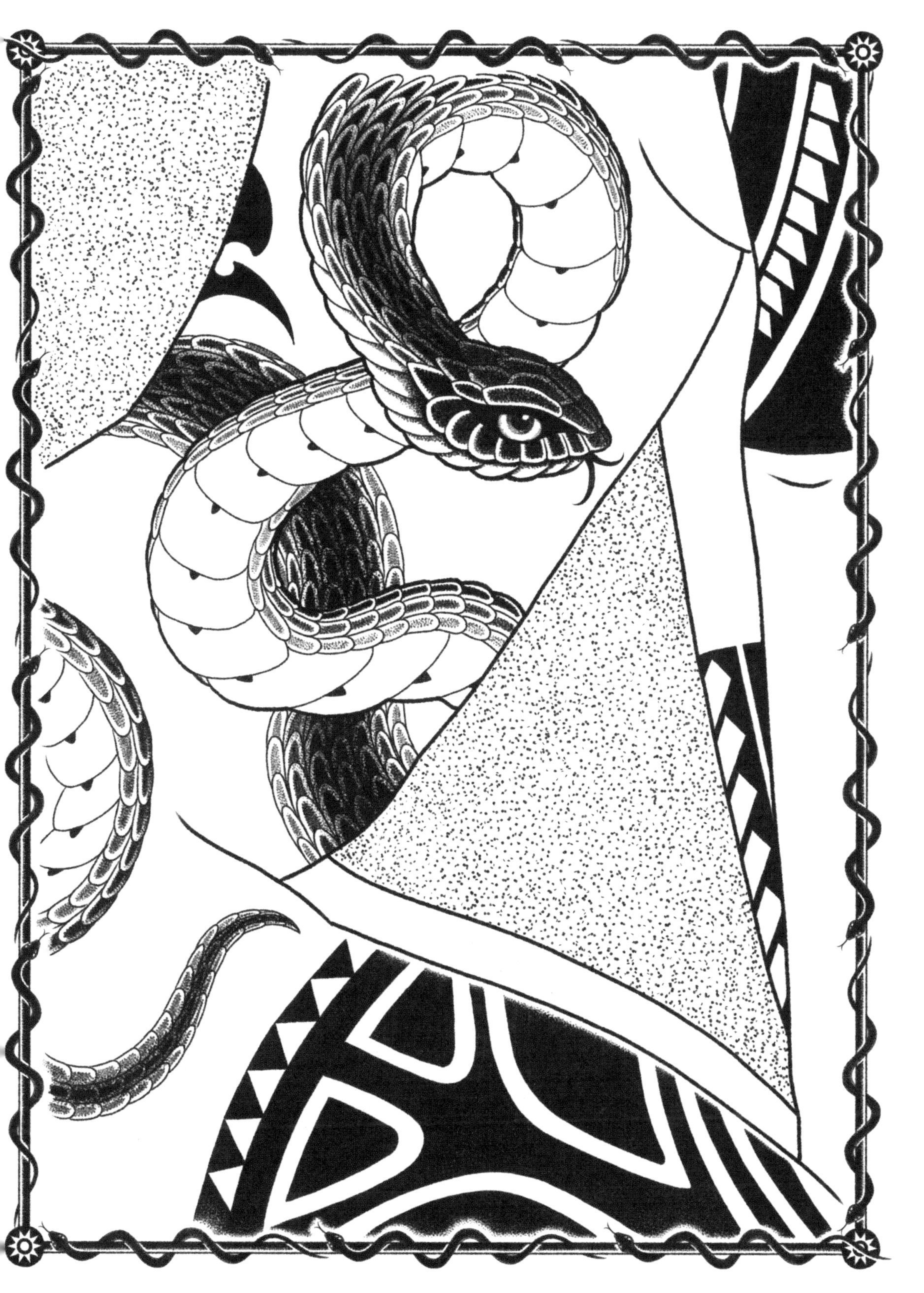

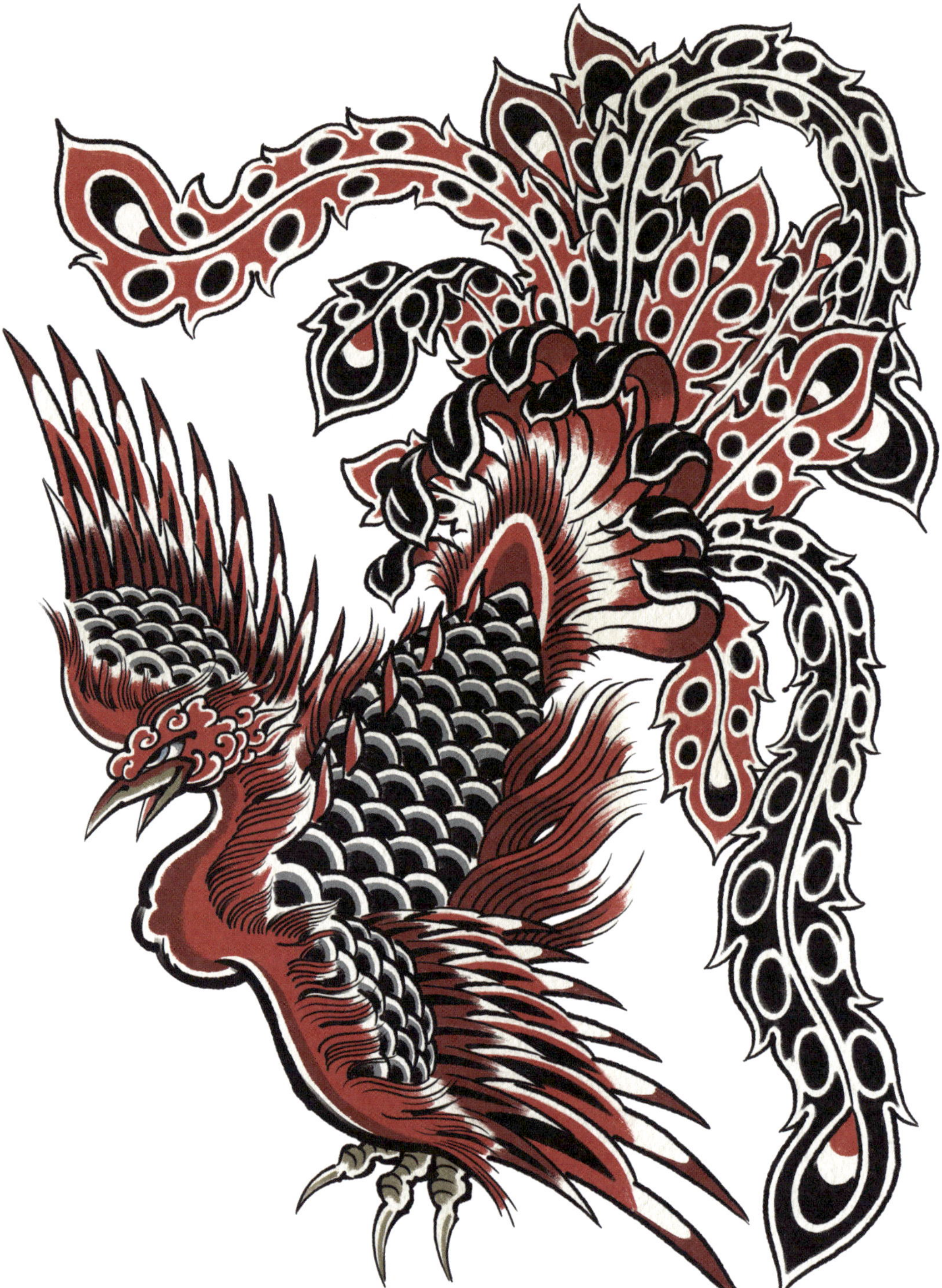

Phoenix

Phoenix tattoos represent transformation through several associations. The first connects to the mythology of renewal and the cycle of life. This is the bird rising from the ashes, a story spread from ancient Egypt to early modern Europe, and beyond. It is a motif that serves cities, institutions and sports teams wishing to represent rejuvenation following a tragedy (inclusive, of course, of fire).

A second reading of the phoenix, or *hou-ou*, originates from the Japanese Irezumi tradition. The design stems from ancient Chinese depictions and, as with other popular Japanese tattoos entered the genre during the Edo period. This form of phoenix symbolizes a balance of positive and negative change.

A further rendition, of a phoenix descending from heaven to earth, signals peace; the opposite is conveyed in return. Balancing two phoenixes allows for a yang-yang interpretation, reflecting the concept of a perpetual cycle.

Sun

Bert Grimm's anthropomorphic sun stands as one of the great 20th-century designs in the western traditional style. Over his career, which began in the 1910s and stretched into the 1960s, Grimm diligently stripped down classic icons and helped create a unique new aesthetic. With the sun, Grimm incorporated a brilliant grin, offering sharp optimism for a new day, moment or period of life.

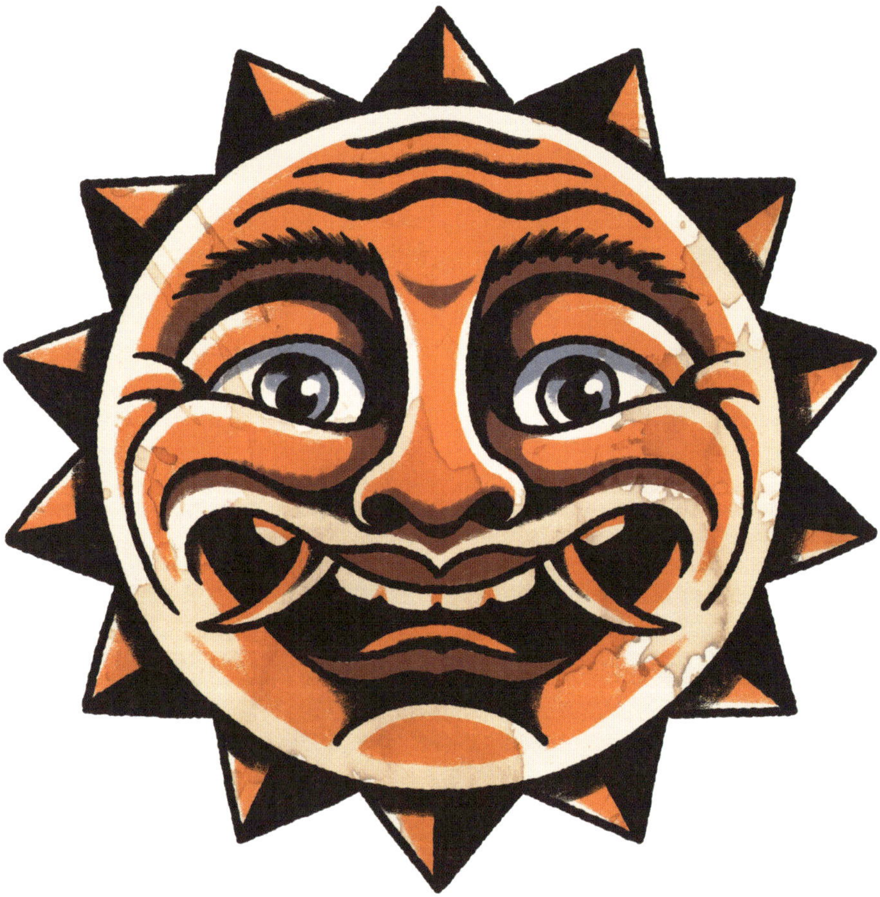

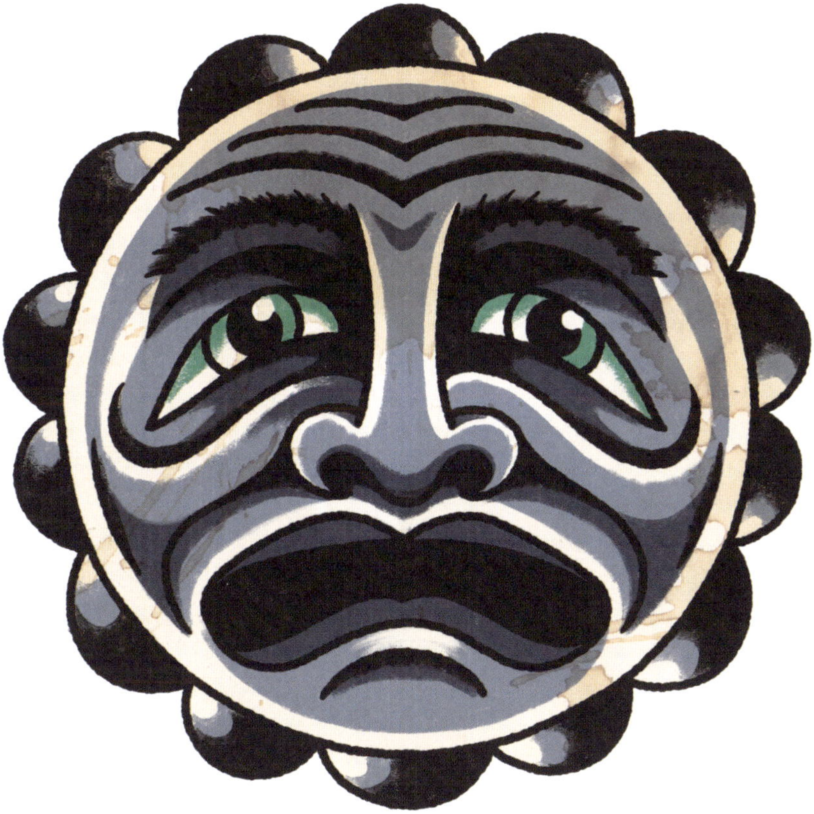

Moon

Like his sun design, Grimm's anthropomorphic moon, complete with sorrowful frown, gives a comic appeal to a transformative moment. Often tattooed in tandem with the sun (for example, on the backs of hands or tops of feet), the moon supports an honouring of the duality of life: good and bad; dark and light; masculine and feminine energy. Inherent to the juxtaposition, too, is the acknowledgement of a transformative cycle.

Lotus

As a Buddhist symbol, the lotus represents purity and enlightenment. The flower is celebrated as much for its stunning bloom as for the circumstance of its growth. It comes from mud, rooting underwater and bursting out in glorious, dramatic fashion. This makes the lotus a popular symbol for human transformation from a tough stage of life, often one mired in materiality, to one of greater freedom.

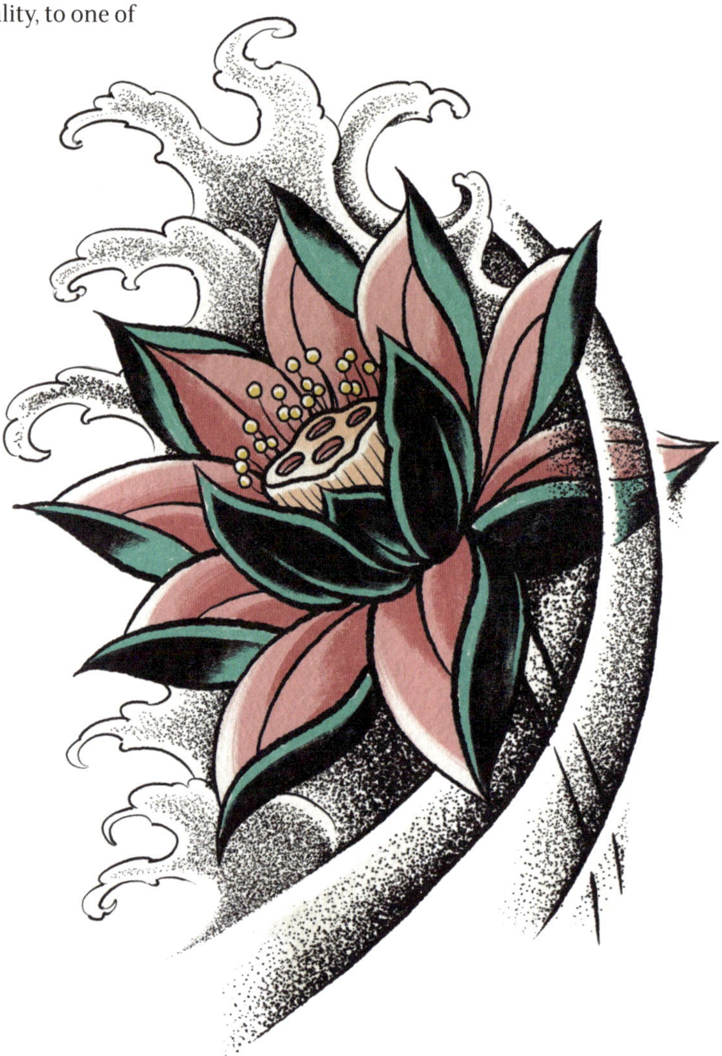

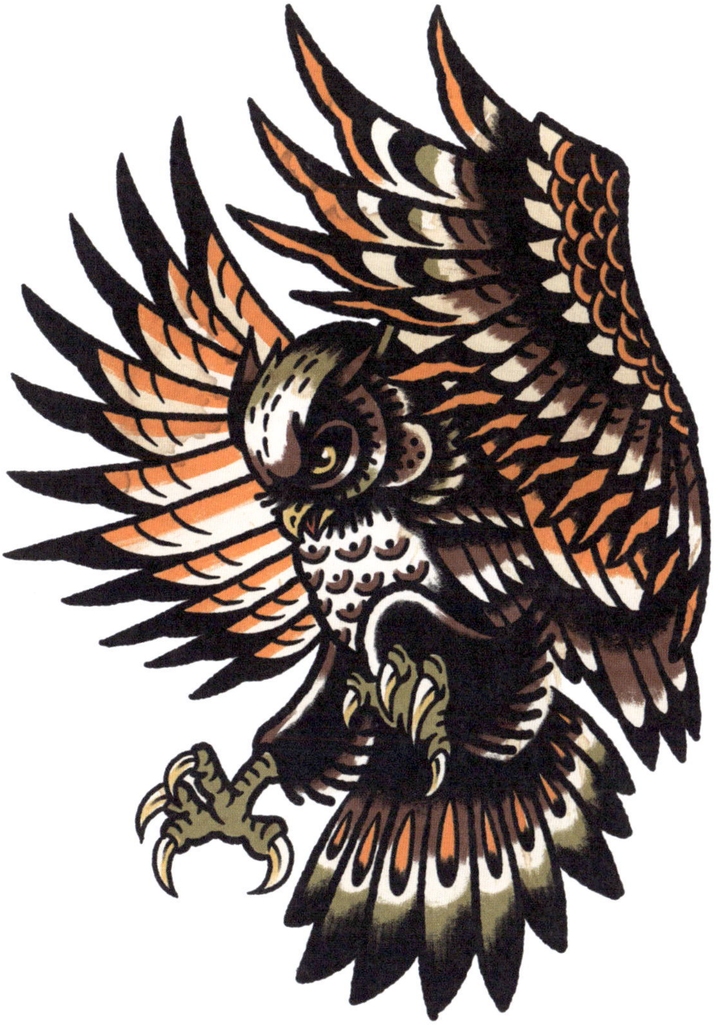

Owl

Though the owl has no fixed symbolism – it can represent everything from death to wisdom – contemporary associations often relate to signal change. These present the owl as guide, a subtle shift of position as psychopomp (in some traditions the owl escorts the soul to the afterlife), from one space to another.

As designs, owl tattoos tend to be very adaptable. They render well in fine line or western traditional styles, and allow for both faithful representation and fanciful colouring.

Frog

The frog has been used as a symbol of rejuvenation since ancient Egyptian times. The goddess of water, Heqet, was depicted with a frog-like head, and frogs had associations with rain and rain ritual. Within Christian tradition, the frog is associated with the life, death and rebirth of Christ. More abstract readings see the frog as a good omen for positive change and personal transition. Thus, frogs are often personified in tattoos (artist, boxer, and so on) and take playful shapes in a variety of compositions.

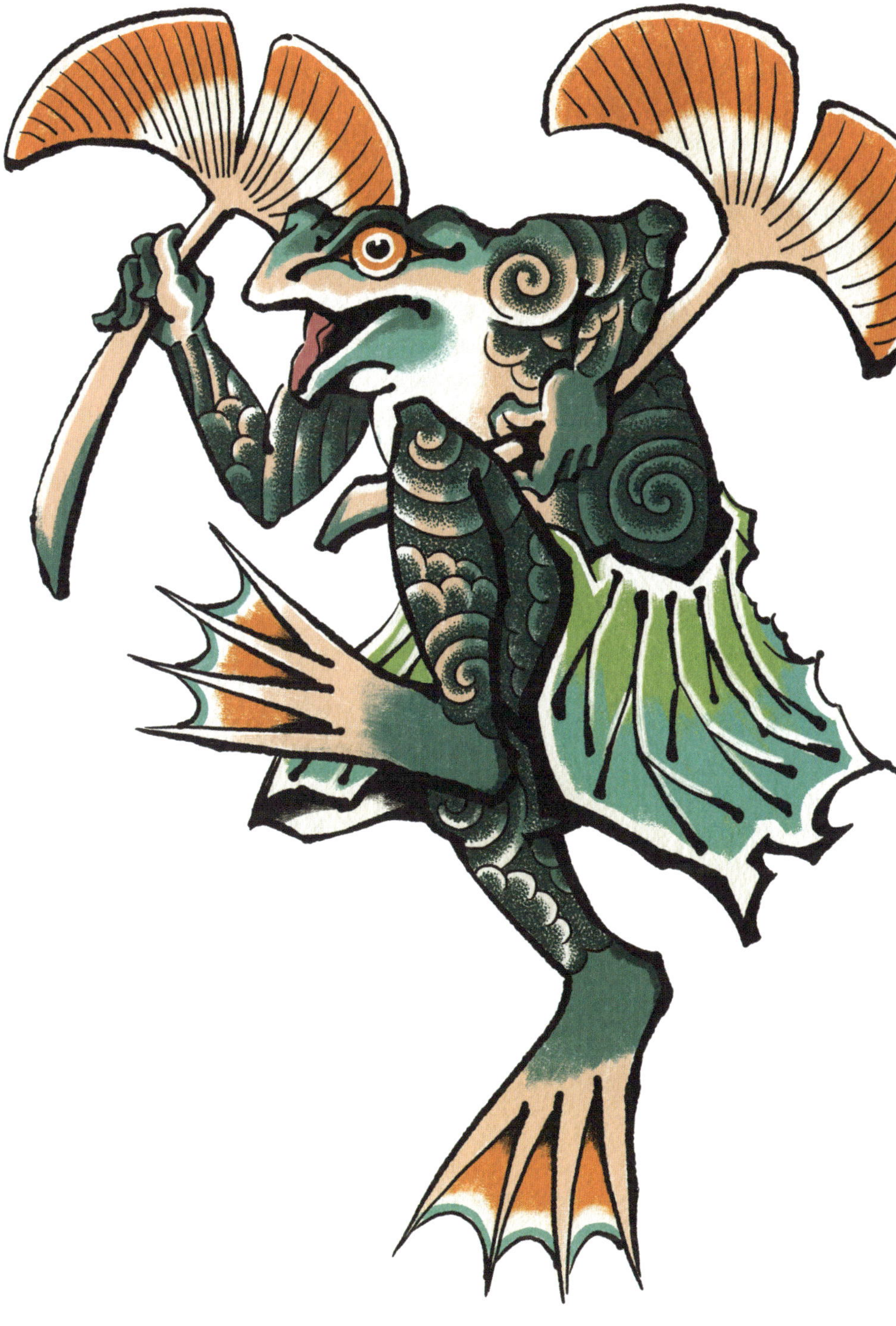

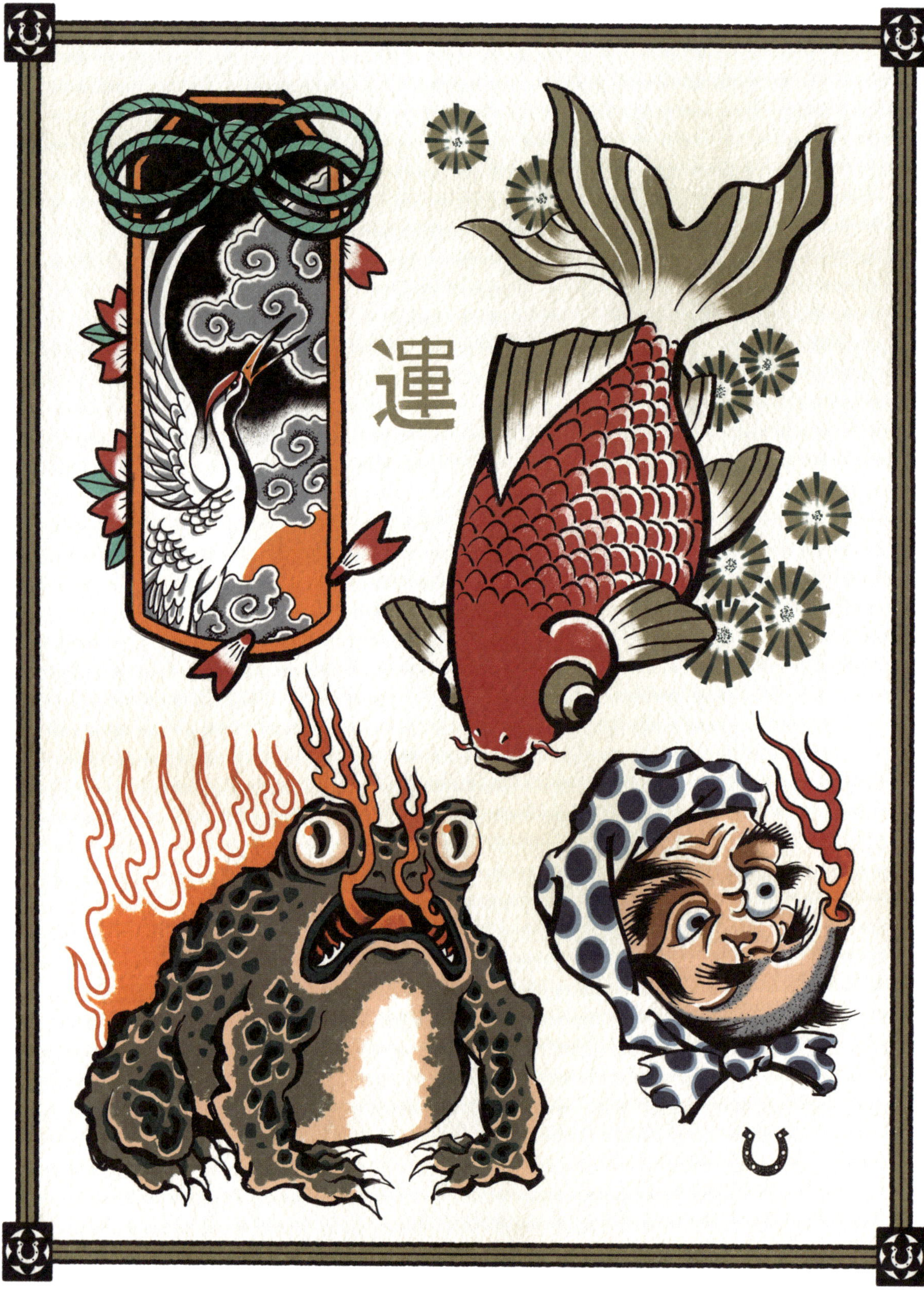
運

5

LUCK

Like acknowledgements of love, symbols reflecting an acceptance of luck are ever present in modern tattooing. In some designs, they follow a mid-20th-century, happy-go-lucky attitude countering the dark side of vice. In other designs, they are faith based. These include renderings of omamori, the amulets seen at Shinto shrines and Buddhist temples. Commonly, symbols of luck are served up as charms.

Each of the above options signifies, in a unique way, an individual's perspective on opportunity, and the best way to articulate these symbols is with conviction. Therefore, the language of luck matches best with the language of tattoos when presented using bright colors and bold lines. Thus, a healthy mix of ideas exist in both Japanese or western traditional styles. But there are also a few more nuanced symbols, such the hamsa, the fairy or the spider's web, that allow for delicacy in line. Above all, symbols of luck highlight a universal desire for good fortune – whatever shape that may take.

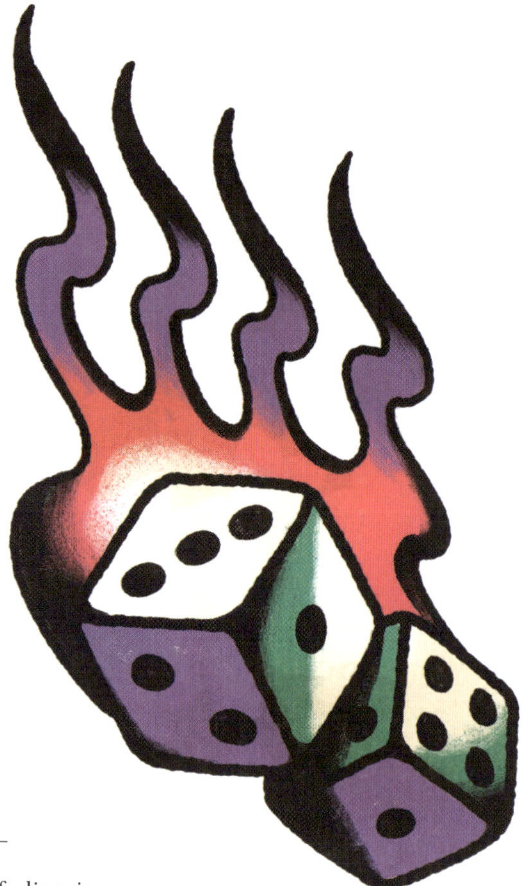

Dice

In traditional tattooing, a set of dice is a surrogate of luck – but with a twist, for dice can also represent risk and vice as a stand-in for the gambler. However, the dice tattoo allows these ideas great elasticity. The choice of rolled number, whether snake eyes or lucky seven, runs the gamut of fortune from loss to success. As such, dice are considered a metaphor for life.

Compositionally, dice can tie in nicely with other 'lucky' symbols, such as the horseshoe (see page 100). A surround of flames adds an eye-catching ornamental punch. Lady Luck, the black cat and other traditional favourites are also easily incorporated into dice-focused tattoos.

Uchide no kozuchi

Uchide no kozuchi, the Japanese lucky hammer, or magic wishing mallet, has origins in 12th-century folklore. While a variety of myths involve the hammer, including stories related to the deity Daikoku (the god of wealth) or the Issun Boshi (one-inch boy), each finds the mallet-wielding, wish-granting character a central element. The term, *uchide no kozuchi* derives from the idea that it shakes or strikes out whatever is desired.

As a tattoo, the *uchide no kozuchi* serves as a lucky charm and can be rendered simply or ornately. It works well both as a standalone image and incorporated into a more complex composition. The standard design for the tattoo draws from its ubiquity within Japanese art and craft, where it can be found as part of the popular iconography of Daikoku, singularly on textiles or as a discrete charm.

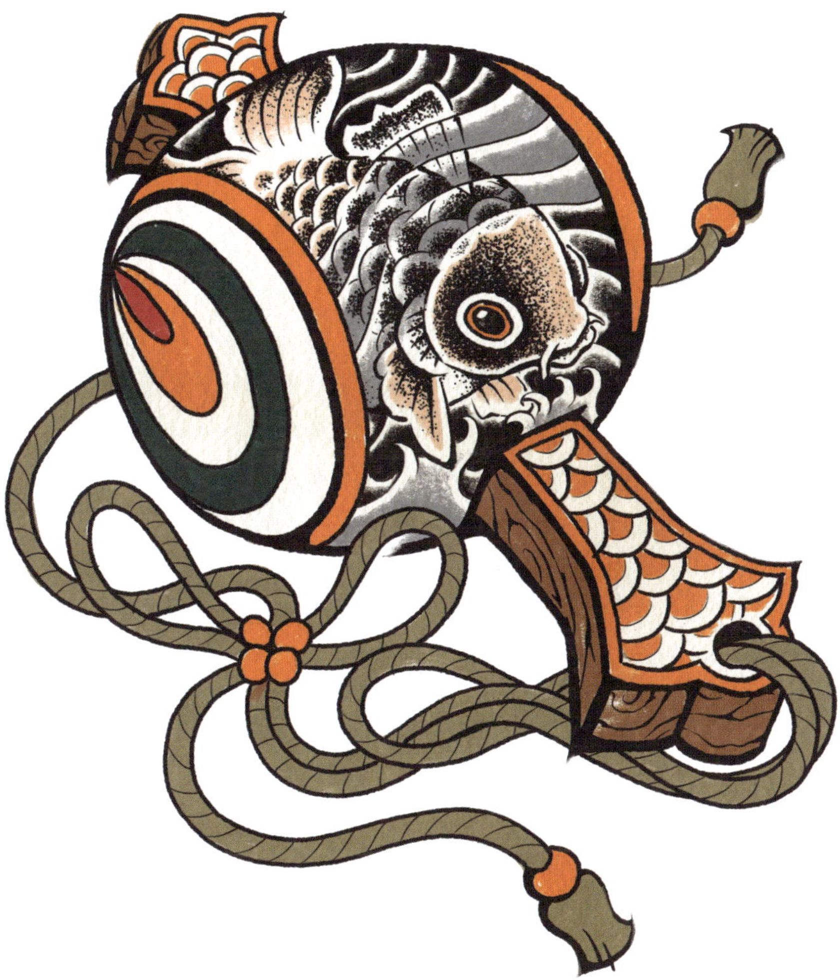

Lucky 13

Throughout the 20th century, tattoo iconography toyed with playful irony and the lucky 13 exemplifies the period's humour. Mocking superstition, the symbol represents a certain joie de vivre, and augments a catalogue of similar images that celebrate chance, fortune and possibility. Often the lucky 13 will feature on a spread deck of cards. Other times, it's intertwined with other lucky emblems, such as the horseshoe, or – for equally tongue-in-cheek interplay – a black cat.

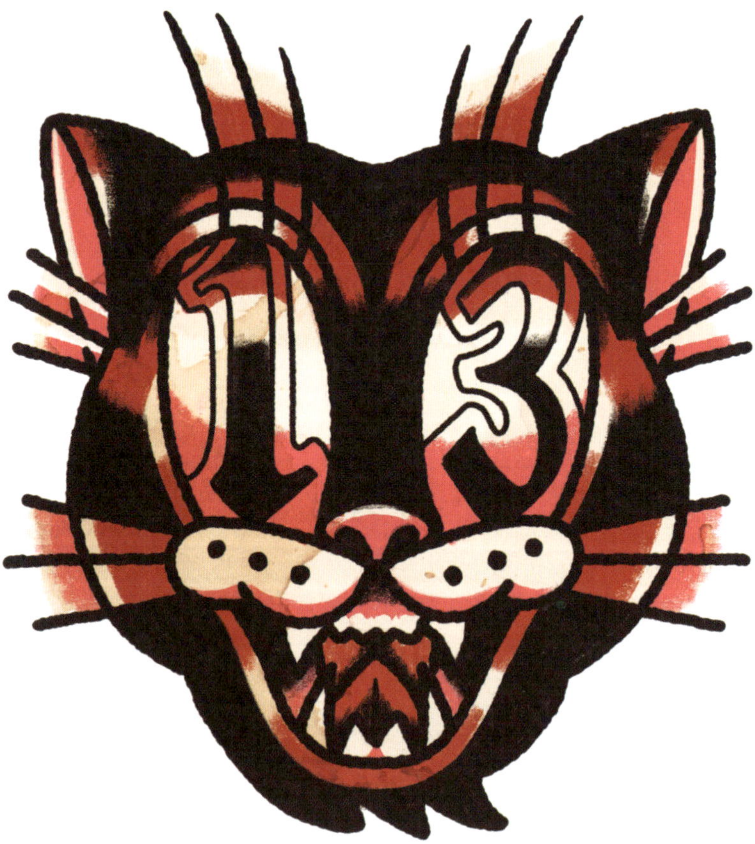

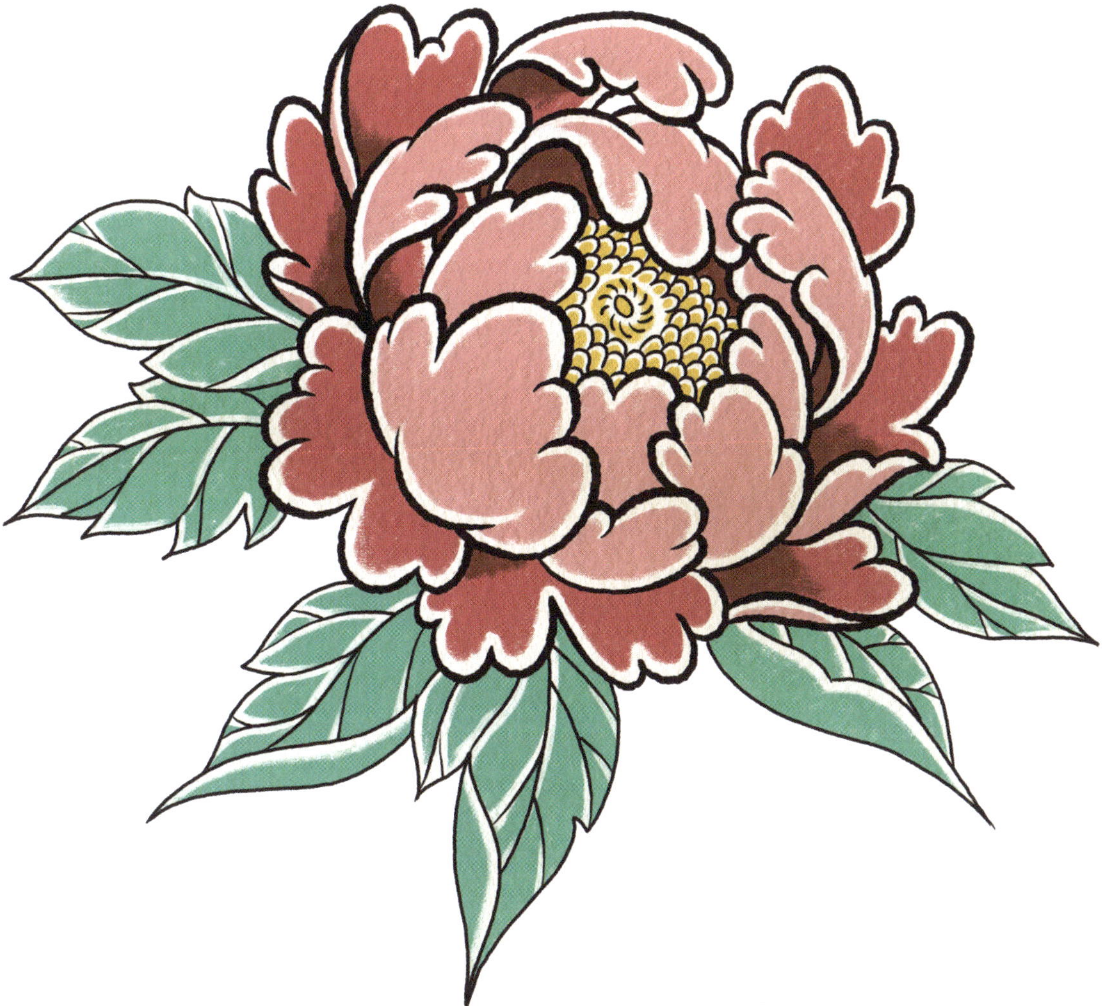

Peony

Coming to Japan from China during the Nara period (710–794), the blossoms of the peony tree emerge in spring, along with those of the *sakura*. But while cherry blossom symbolizes grace in transcience, the peony (*botan*) is a potent reminder of the power of the emperor. Of course, some of this association derives from the tree's health benefits, so lending good fortune and prosperity to the symbolism.

Horseshoe

Luck, health and prosperity are meanings ascribed to the horseshoe. As a symbol, the crescent shape has held power in popular imagination since ancient Greece, where it was linked to the moon goddess Artemis, through to the Celts, who believed it to be a talisman for keeping mischief-makers away – an association reinforced in ancient England through the tale of St Dunstan.

Born in Somerset, Dunstan was a prominent monastic figure and leader of the Anglican Communion during the 10th century. A famous interaction between Dunstan and the devil established the horseshoe as a ubiquitous symbol of luck. Working as a blacksmith, Dunstan nailed a horseshoe to the devil, agreeing only to alleviate the pain, and remove the horseshoe, if the devil agreed never to cross into a space in which a horseshoe hung at its entrance.

This tale cemented the horseshoe as ward against evil and, more widely, an object welcoming positive outcome. Hung facing up, the horseshoe catches good will; meanwhile, a fisherman hangs it upside down so that luck pours into his nets. This breadth of use is easily transferred to its application as a tattoo – it's adaptable to many styles, including fine line and western traditional. Elements such as banners and flowers can be added to augment it. Any choice speaks to belief in luck and an optimistic outlook.

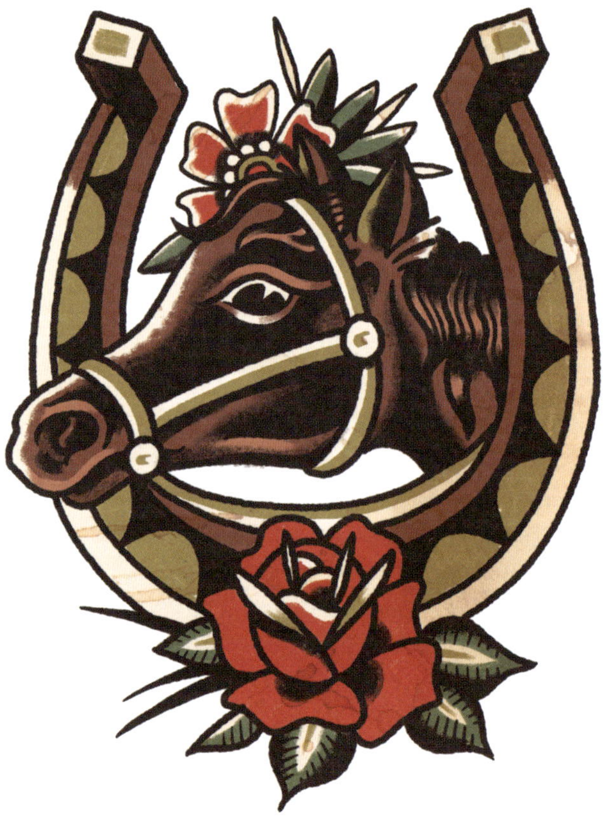

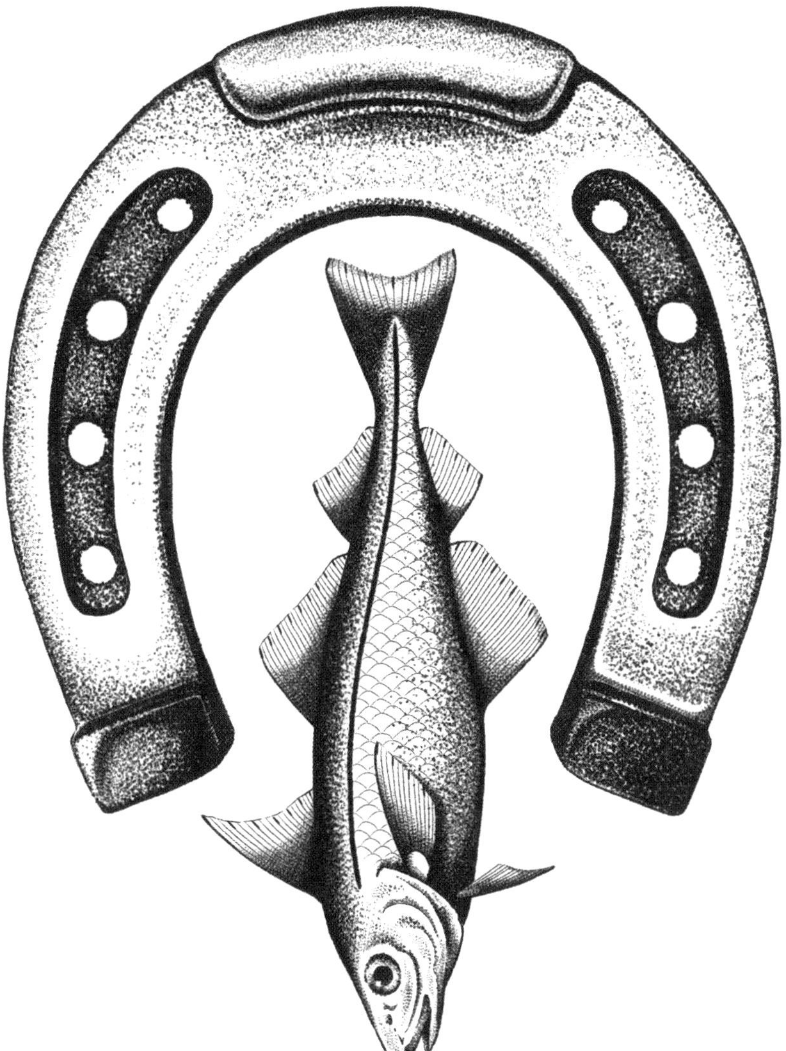

Omamori

Omamori are colourful amulets sold at Shinto shrines and Buddhist temples across Japan. Translating as 'protect' or 'protection', an omamori most commonly manifests as a brocade pouch. In general, omamori serve as good-luck charms. There are several types, each connecting to a clear, identifiable theme, such as success or happiness, good health or good fortune. More specific versions might convey safety in travel or a healthy pregnancy. As omamori are designed to be worn or carried, there is a natural transference to tattooing.

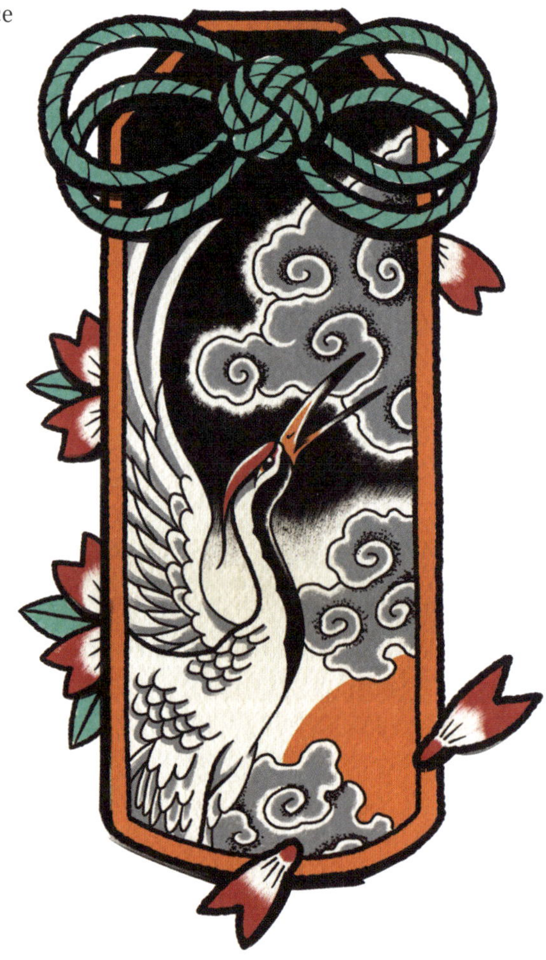

Maneki-Neko

The beckoning cat, a maneki-neko, symbolizes good luck. As a figure, the maneki-neko first appeared in the Edo period, in either Tokyo or Kyoto, and it traditionally used to bring fortune to businesses and places of study. Compositionally, several nuances of the maneki-neko pose are worthy of consideration. A raised right paw attracts good fortune, while a raised left paw attracts others to conduct business (one hand often holds a koban, or oval coin, too) Closed eyes reflect short-term opportunity, while open eyes reflect a deep optimism for future luck. Typically, the cats are coloured in calico, but other colours may be employed to convey specific fortune (for example, green for academic success or pink for romance). Tattoos of the cats also allow for rather playful composition, as the maneki-neko is adaptable to both a range of styles and the addition of additional symbols representing love or luck.

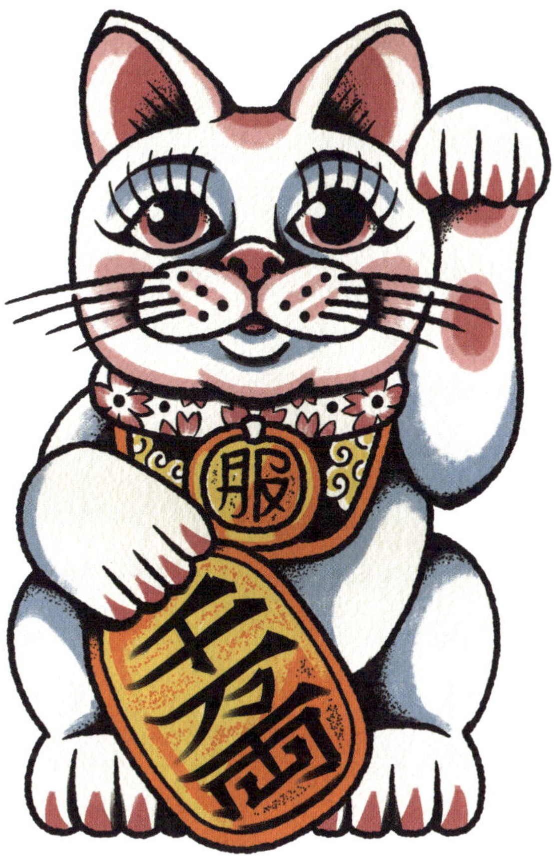

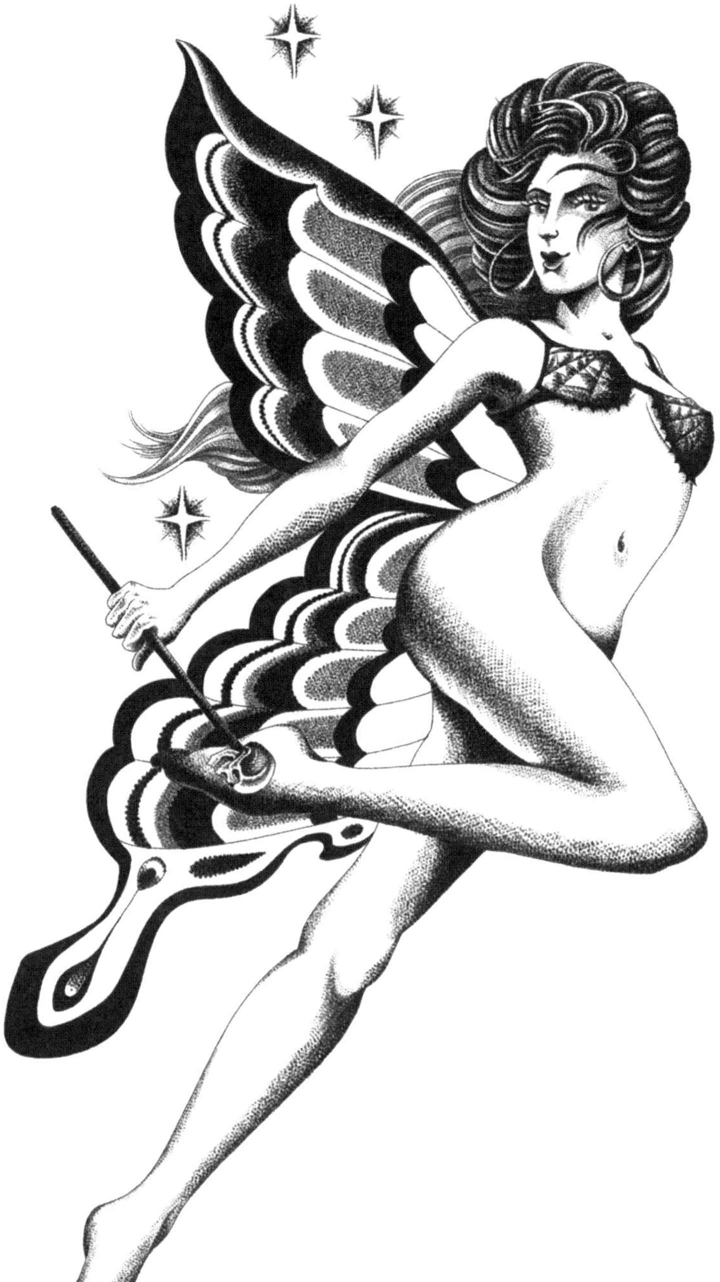

Fairy

There is a magical romance associated with the fairy. This being, often winged, delicate and beautiful, features in Arabic, Arctic, Greek and Samoan myth, but its name derives from European oral and written history. Less attractive incarnations also exist – hobgoblins and the like. However, the more sinister folkloric associations faded in the animated universe of the 20th century and the contemporary fairy remains dainty, spritely, slightly mischievous, but always, ultimately, in favour of a positive outcome. Tattoos depicting fairies thus invariably celebrate luck and wishful thinking.

Tennin

Tennin are heavenly persons, male or female, celebrated within Japanese Buddhism. In some respects, they are similar to angels or fairies. The figured form of the Tennin draws most commonly on its female version, the beautiful Tennyo, dressed in a flowing, ornate feathered kimono, called a *hagoromo*.

Common legends and folktales related to the Tennyo involve the theft of the *hagoromo* by a human suitor. Unable to fly without the garment, the Tennyo marry into the mortal world. Later, the indiscretion is revealed, the *hagoromo* returned and the courtesan returns to the heavens.

Characteristics of grace, refinement and beauty define the Tennyo, and these qualities are thus reflected in tattoo composition.

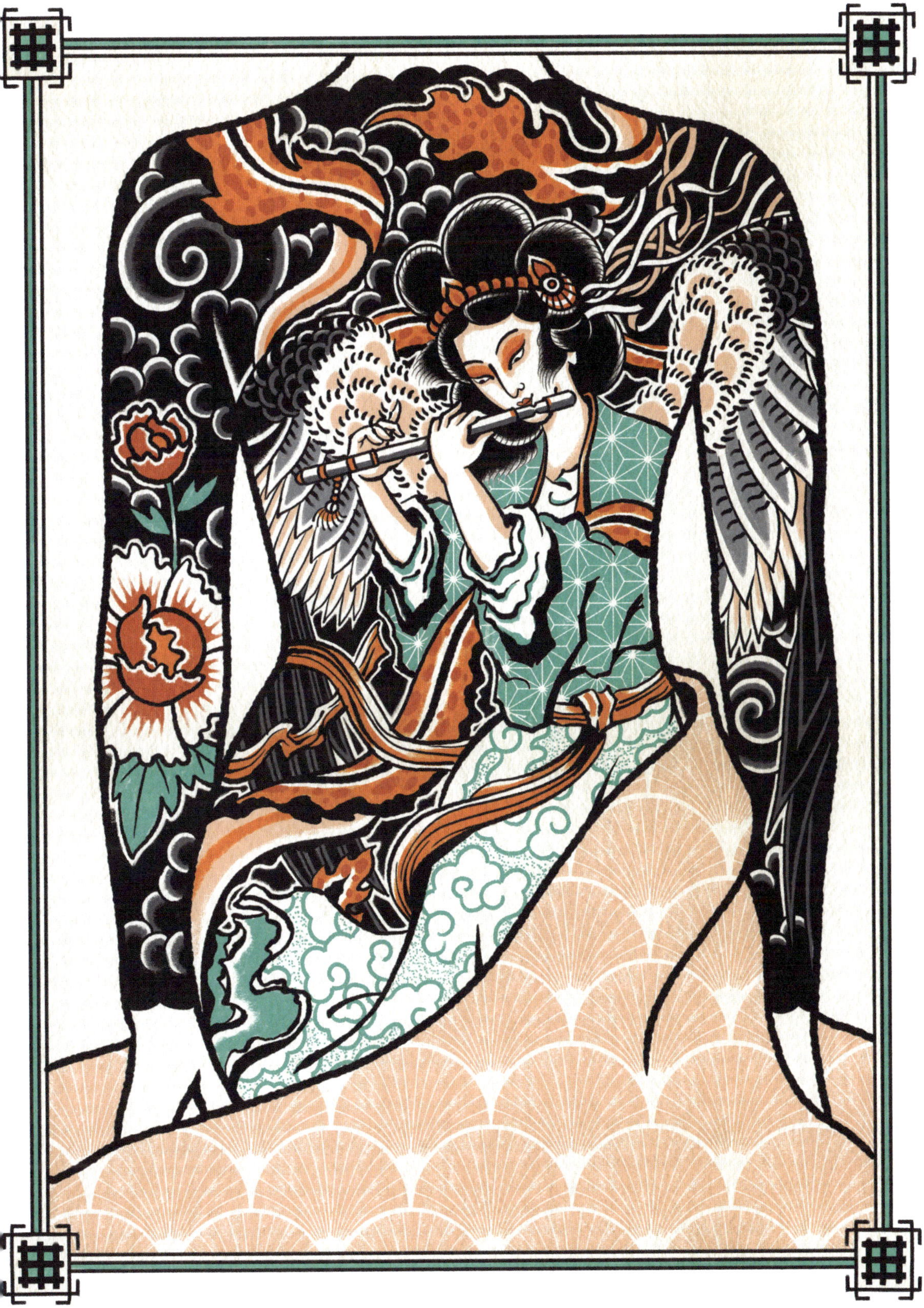

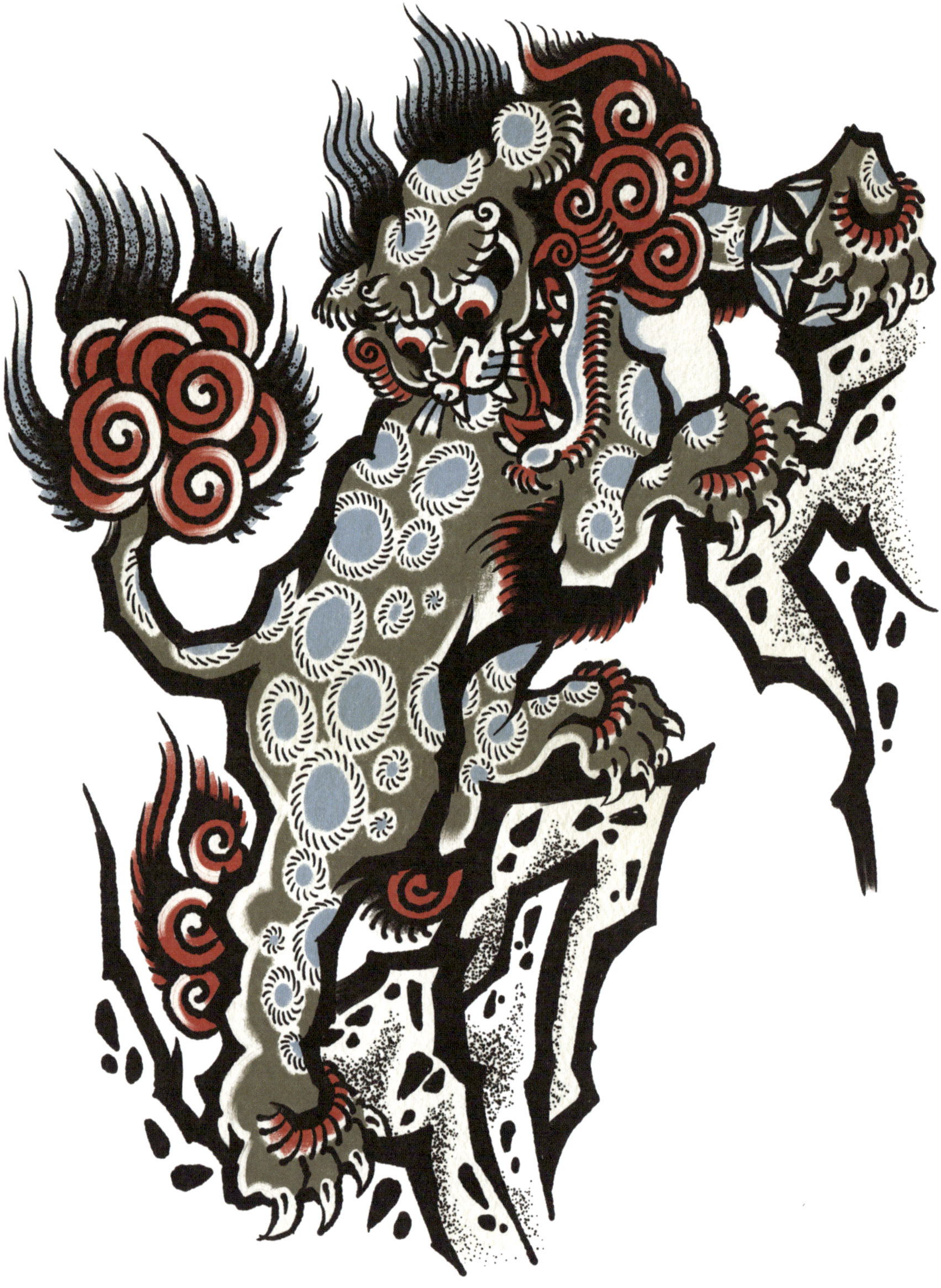

Foo Dog

The foo dog, or *shishi*, originated in Han dynasty China. Its image, decidedly neither feline nor canine, flourished via commissioned sculptures and talismen, and was created to ward off evil. Commonly, these were placed in pairs at the doors of palaces and temples. In Edo period Japan, they featured in woodblock prints, becoming cultural icons.

Male and female foo dogs carry different meanings. The female, depicted as a head alone, brings good luck to women in childbirth. This is based on the legend of the foo dog's own procreation: while it gave birth to 100 cubs, only the toughest is allowed to live. A male foo dog combined with a ball symbolizes power. Depicted together, a male and female symbolize the external and internal – the male defends the structure, while the female guards the dwelling – assuring that the tattoo itself serves as a protector of mind, body and spirit.

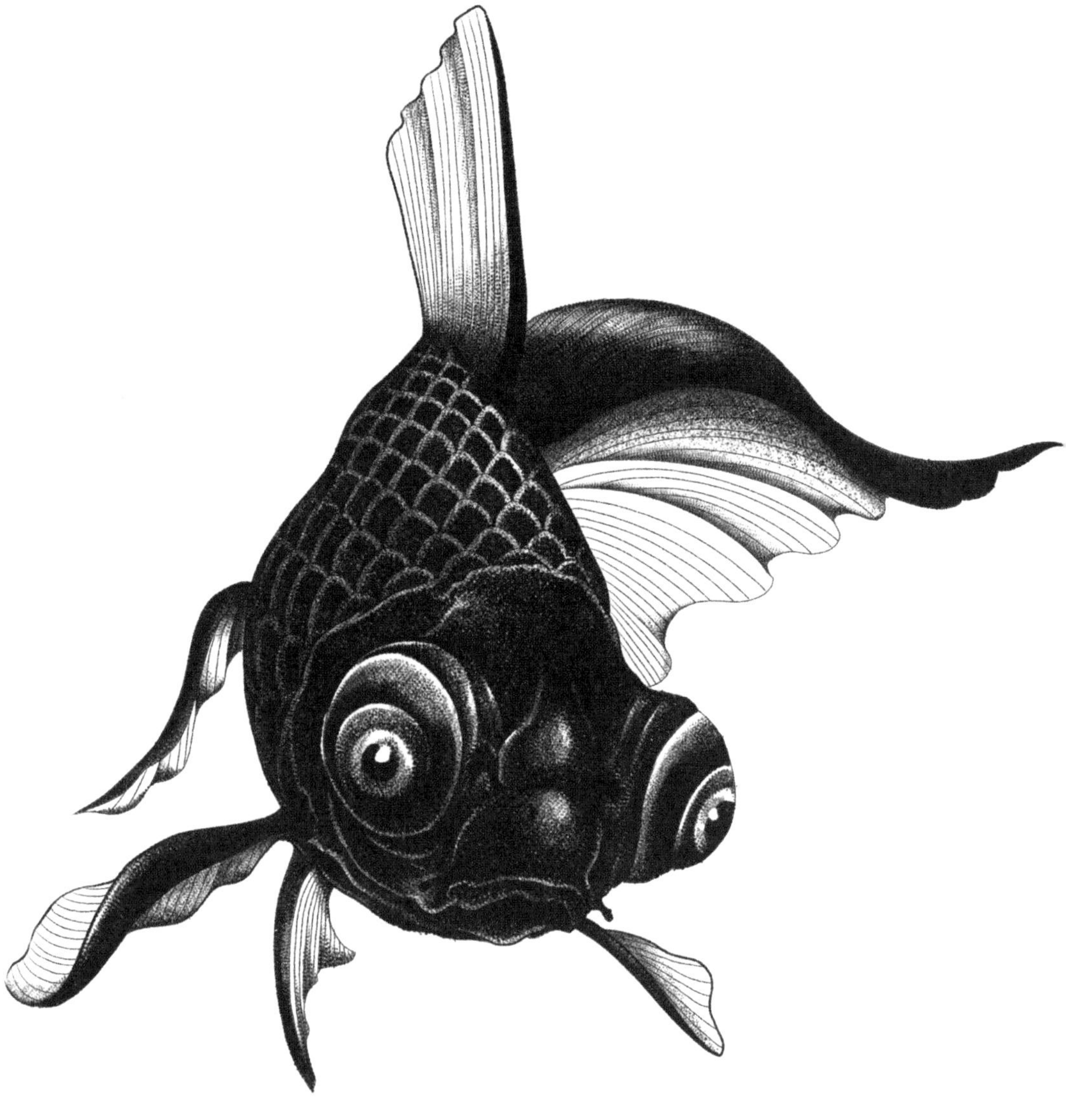

Kingyo

Consider the kingyo (gold fish) the proletariat version of the koi. It may be less regal, but it is no less potent in its association with abundance and happiness.

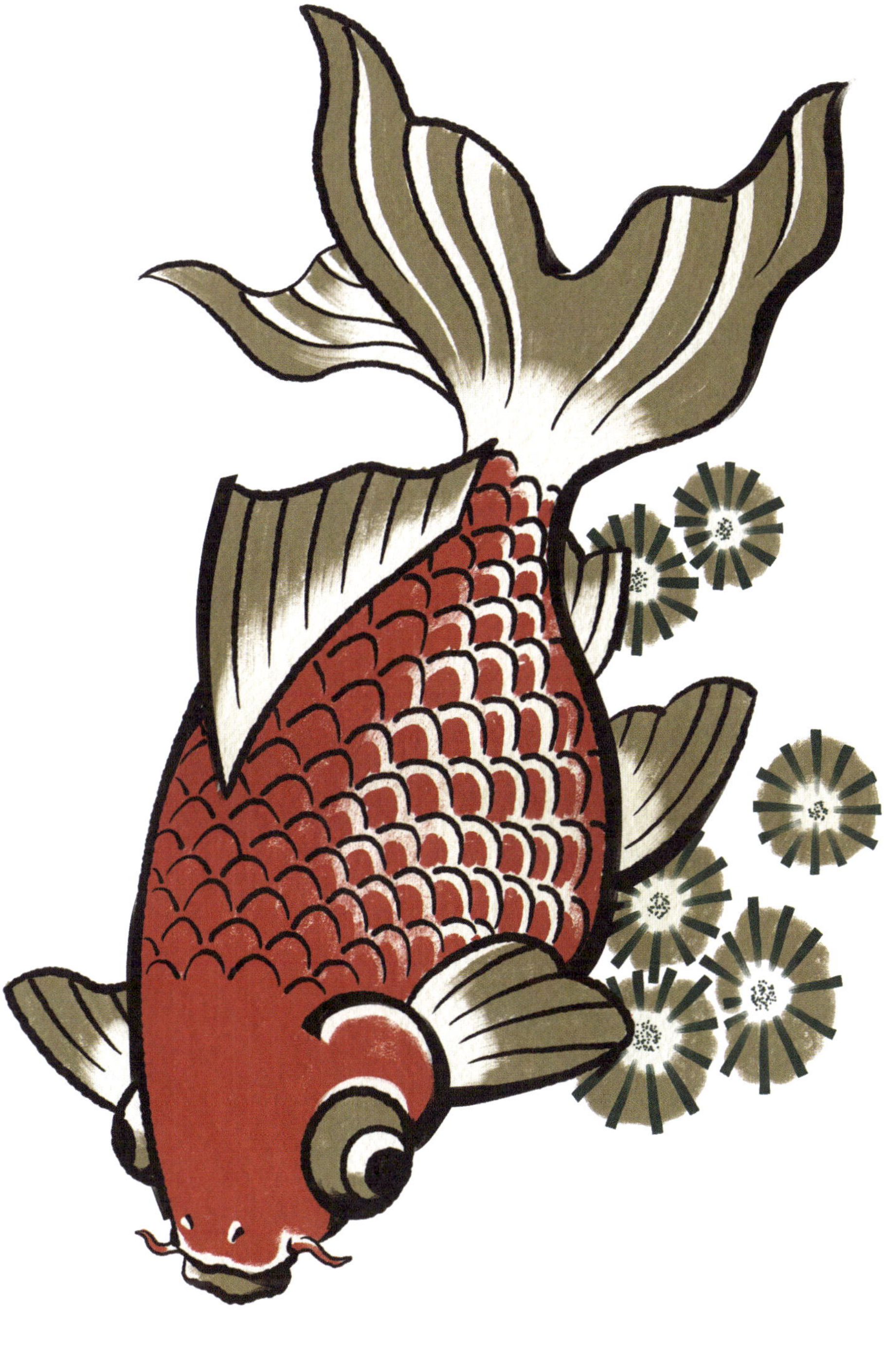

Toad

Toad tattoos are among those that symbolize wealth, success and good luck. One of the symbols that reinforces this association is the greedy three-legged Jin Chan, the feng shui money toad, known for its red eyes and flared nostrils. Jin Chan sits atop a pile of coins and is known to invite prosperity. Further, the toad represents long life and continued good fortune.

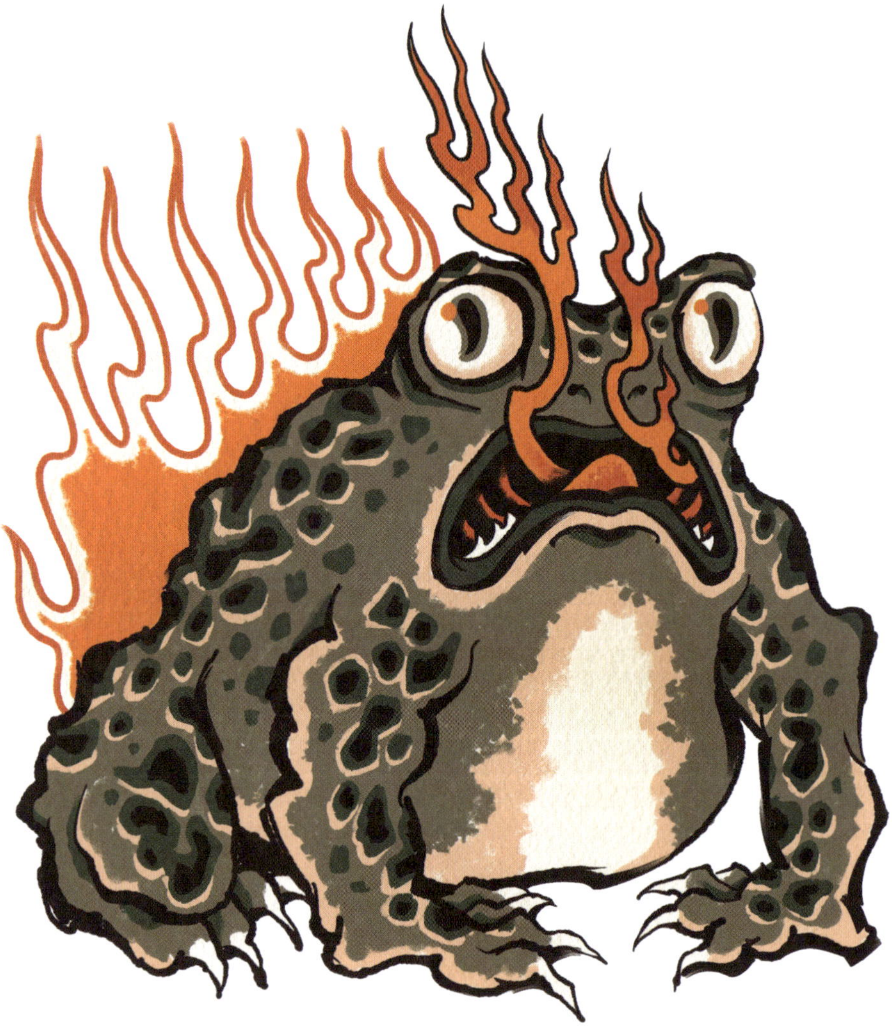

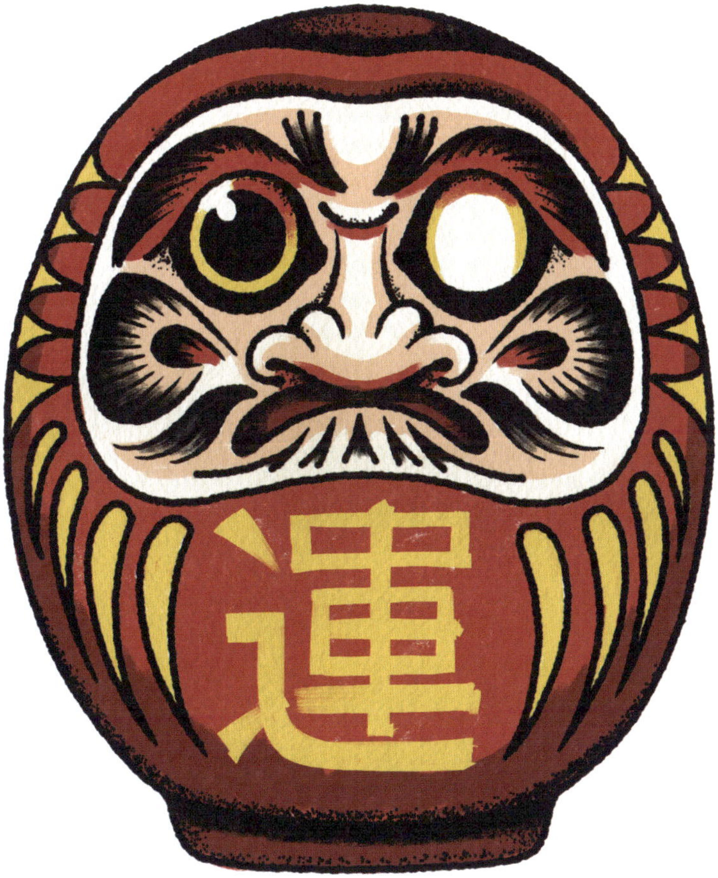

Daruma

Common in Japanese culture since the 18th century, the daruma is a good-luck charm modelled after Bodhidharma, the monk credited with founding Zen Buddhism and Shaolin kung fu. Bodhidharma was famed for extreme practices. For example, he gazed at a wall in meditative state for close to a decade. During this time, he took no breaks and closed his eyes only once – during the seventh year. He was so furious at this perceived lack of self-discipline, that he sliced off his eyelids. This mutilation, combined with loss of limb use from sustained sitting, inform the design of the daruma, complete with big, doll eyes and distinct beard (shaped like a turtle) and eyebrows (which reference cranes). Together, the elements of the daruma read as tribute to longevity, and its lack of body speaks to the power of perseverance, regardless of struggle.

Okame

The Shinto goddess of mirth, happiness and good fortune, jovial Okame is easily identified by her large cheeks. She is also a popular female character in Noh theatre, where she embodies long life and joy, particularly to whomever she marries. In both art and theatre, Okame is commonly partnered with the comedic Hyottoko.

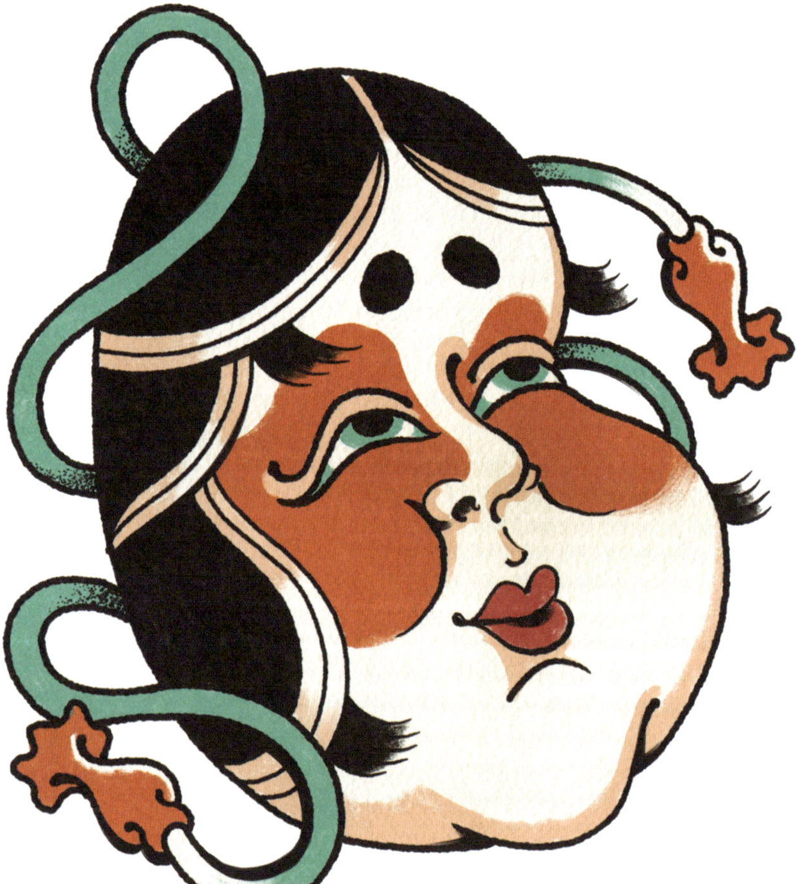

Hyottoko

Regular partner to Okame, Hyottoko derives from the Iwate prefecture myth of a boy with a strange face who could conjure gold from his belly button. In death ritual, the Hyottoko mask may be placed on a mantelpiece to bring good fortune. In Noh theatre, the character serves as comic relief. With puckered mouth, pushed to one side of the face, bushy eyebrows and asymmetrical eyes (one squinted, one wide open), Hyottoko is easily identified – especially when partnered with Okame.

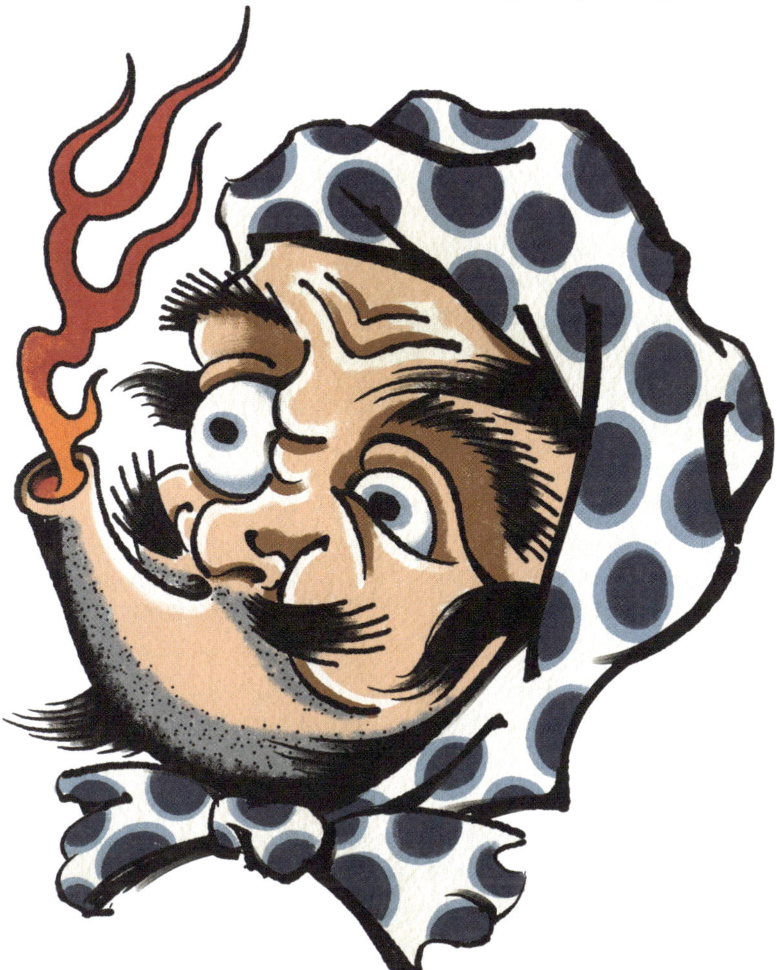

Spider's Web

It is worth noting negative connotations with the spider's web first: associations with criminality, incarceration and even hate groups are well rooted in the public imagination. However, the spider's web is also considered an omen of good luck.

Historically, there are numerous folktales featuring the spider web as a symbol of abundance and protection. David, King of Israel, is said to have been protected from King Saul by a spider's web; a similar circumstance is said to have saved the prophet Mohammed from his enemies.

The duality of the spider's web – representative of both entanglement and liberation – makes it a tough visual read. Yet, the beauty is in the context, and opportunities abound to utilize the symbol as both a single design and a connective tissue in a more complex piece.

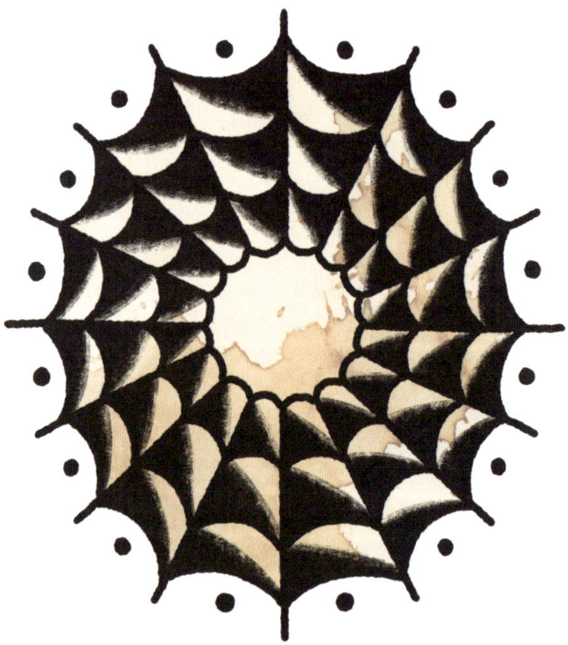

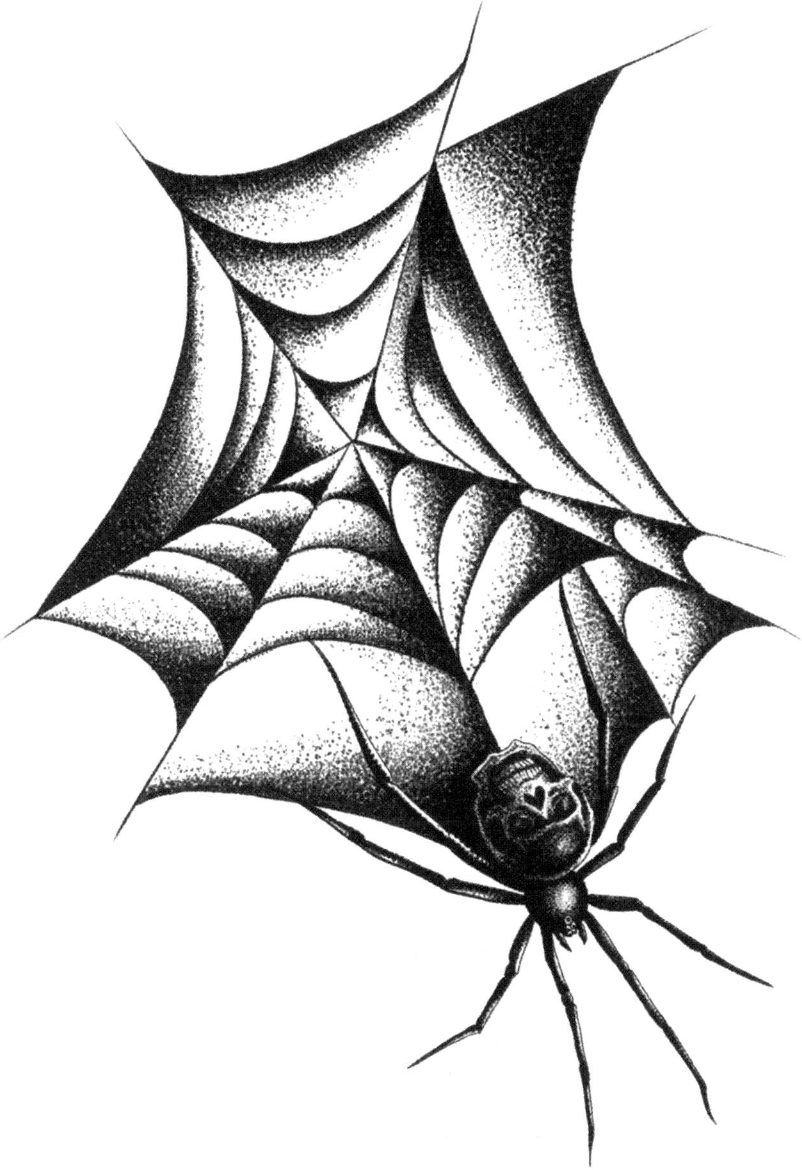

Hamsa

One of many ancient symbols appropriated in tattooing, the 'hand of the goddess' or 'hand of Fatma' welcomes positive energy and rejects negative energy. As such, the hamsa predominately carries associations of luck. Articulating the hamsa requires a simple choice: pointing up or down? Chose up, and the symbol wards off evil. Opt for down, and the hand welcomes goodness, including fertility.

Hamsa tattoos most commonly serve as protection against evil. Compositionally, the image is recognizable for its symmetrical thumbs (going downwards or outwards) and the 'evil eye' at the centre of the palm, which deflects the evil energy of others. The earliest use of the hamsa dates to artefacts associated with the Mesopotamian goddess Ishtar or Inanna. Over the centuries, the symbol has been periodically employed within Islamic, Jewish and Christian practice.

Given the sweeping adaptation of the symbol culturally, there is widespread use in the tattoo world. Many pay respect to the symbol's ancient roots, but there are also deviations that incorporate modern iconography as well.

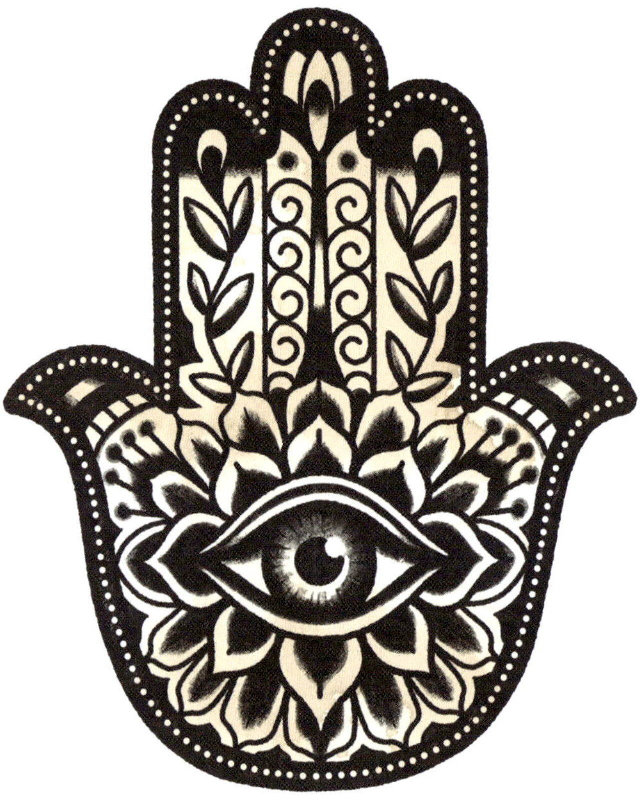

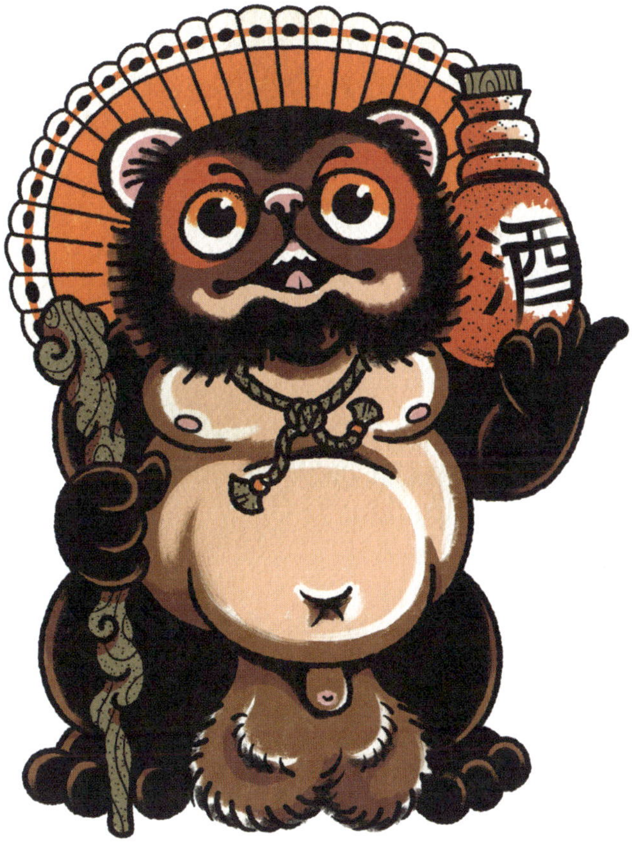

Tanuki

In Japanese lore, the tanuki, or raccoon dog, is considered as mischief-maker. Since the 720s, depictions of the animal have shared tales of a particular magic: shapeshifting, to animal, human or material form, and a love of pranks.

Commonly, the trickery derives from a comic manipulation of the tanuki's testicles. Illustrations from the 19th century highlight this portion of tanuki lore – testicles shaped as bowls, cloaks, drums, raincoats, weapons and more abound. Contemporary articulations of the tanuki are derived from Shigaraki, Japan, where ceramic figurines portraying the trickster god became common in the mid-20th century.

Tanuki tattoos follow this popular portrayal in form and offer a jovial way in which to symbolize wealth and prosperity. As such, the character and belongings of an individual tanuki are important. If one holds a bottle of saki, it is trustworthy. Exaggerated body parts hold different meanings, too. For example, a tanuki with large scrotum conveys wealth; small eyes relay amiability; and a big belly reflects boldness in decision-making.

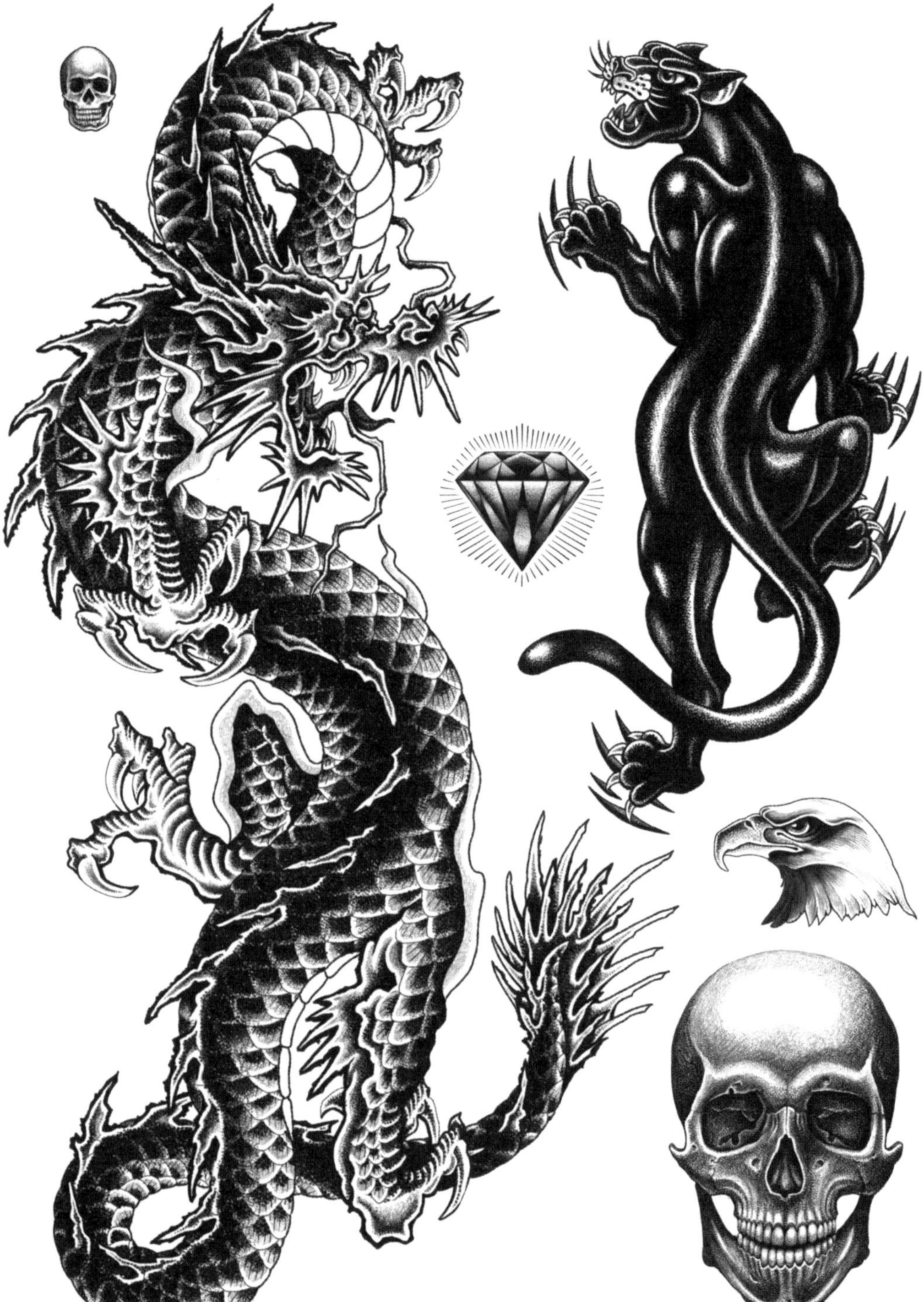

6

STRENGTH

Several tattoo symbols relate to narratives of overcoming obstacles. In strength, a symbol has the capacity to confront an issue through physical force. These are the images that convey dominance, masculinity, stamina and virility. Also among them are symbols that suggest feminine power and notions of longevity.

Another interesting throughline within the theme of strength, is durability of will and devotion. Symbols such as the 'golden boy' Kintaro, embody a mind-over-matter strength – the kind where the spirit fuels the physical and devotion to a cause compels a person to hold their ground. Of course, this characteristic has a correlation to resilience, while maintaining a direct connection to force.

Panther

Stamina, strength and virility are characteristics conveyed by a powerful and striking panther tattoo. Compositionally, panther designs privilege a masculine stance, either in full body or as a strong, open-jawed head.

The crawling panther tattoo, originated in the 1940s by William Grimshaw and made famous in drawings by famed Milwaukee tattooist Amund Dietzel, is an icon of mid-20th-century tattooing – best with stylized claws articulated as if ripping into the flesh. In connection to art history, it also has close ties to the Art Deco movement, which had a profound influence on Dietzel, and while perhaps not commonly associated with tattooing, surely influenced pronounced stylistic shifts in the practice.

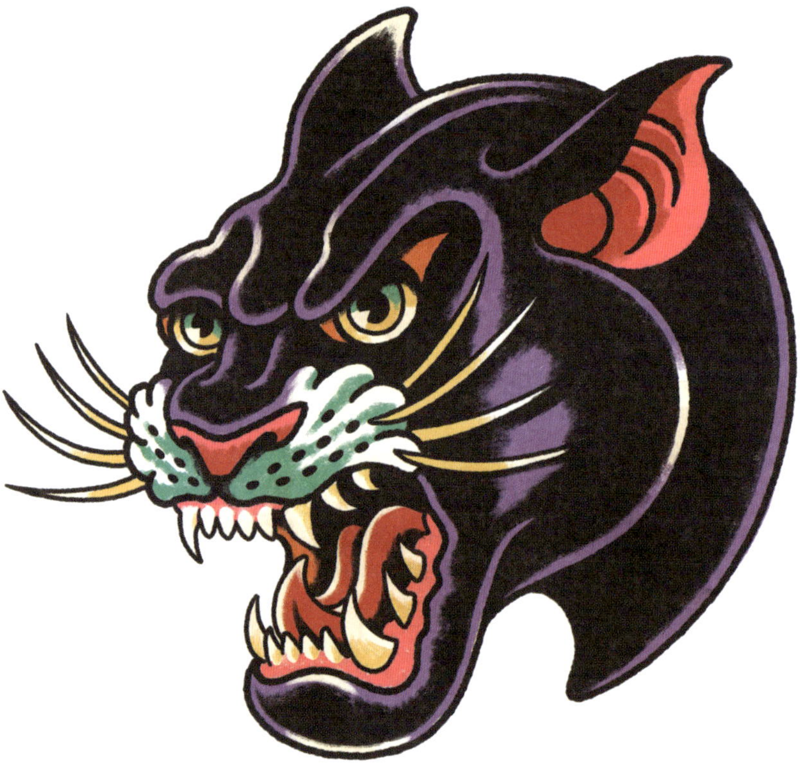

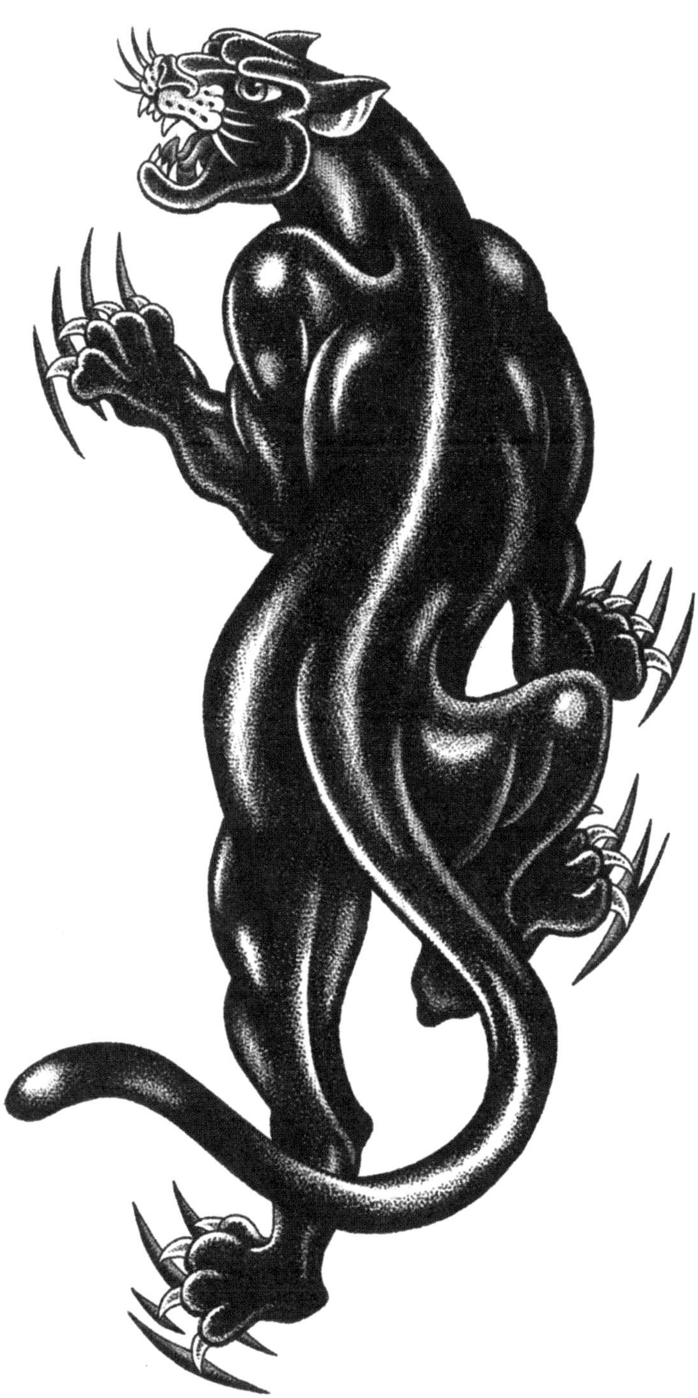

Dragon

Ryu, the popular form Japanese dragon, is a remnant of Edo period woodblock printing. The creature soars through the heavens, twists back to Earth, all the while granting wishes. Notable, is that these creatures are not singular, instead they form from a diverse body of myths that tie local Japanese folklore to legends from across Asia. Stylistically, Ryu finds commonality with the Chinese dragon, as a serpentine water diety without wings.

As a tattoo, Ryu takes on different meanings depending on which variety is depicted and the colours used. Importantly, the particular strength, physical and mental, of each dragon grants distinct (and positive) benefit to people encountered. Colourwise, red dragons are associated with power, blue with forgiveness and gold with virtue.

Western dragons, more commonly winged, also symbolize strength, but primarily in association with unstoppable forces (such as fire).

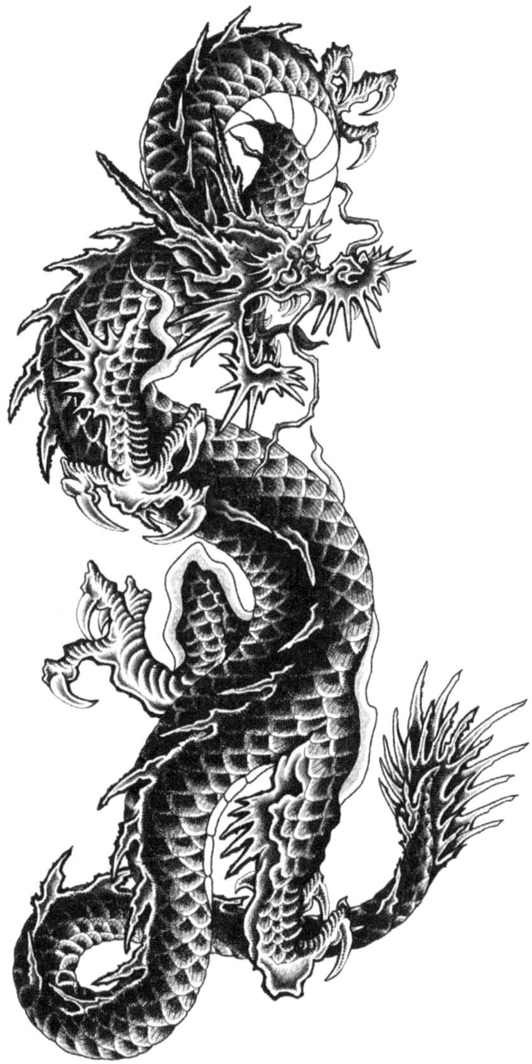

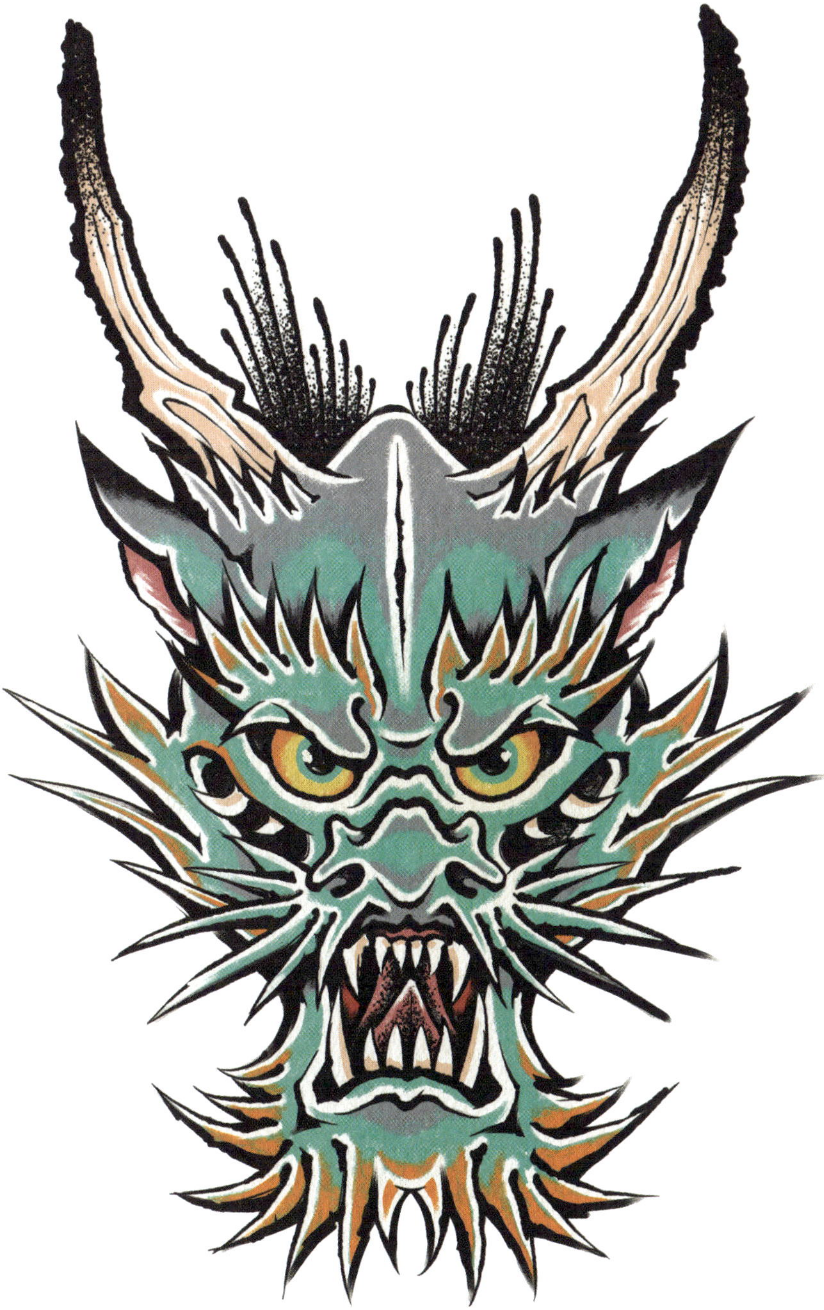

Diamond

Invincibility is the defining characteristic of a diamond, in direct correlation to the gemstone's physical properties, and is augmented by associations with love, faith, power and strength. Diamonds have been prized for their supernatural characteristics since discovery and have come to represent fortitude in many traditions over the centuries – from Greek mythology to the Buddhist sutra.

Associations with unbreakable love, and the adoption of diamond rings in courtship, dates to the 15th century and the union of Maximilian I and Mary of Burgundy in 1477.

The modern diamond trade began some 400 years later, reinforcing the stone's association with love, and rooting the practice of engagement rings. Though De Beers began marketing the idea heavily in 1938, diamond rings appeared upon clasped hands, celebrating betrothal, on some early 1900s tattoo flash sheets.

Typical contemporary tattoos articulated a faceted stone in clear, strong line work. While it is not uncommon to link diamonds with love, the majority of the tattoos are an expression of strength – be it of conviction, peace or will.

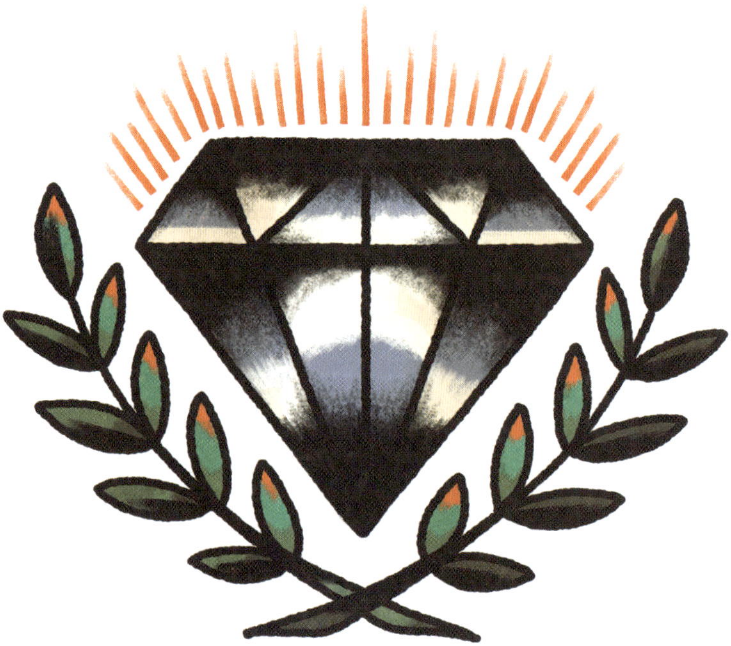

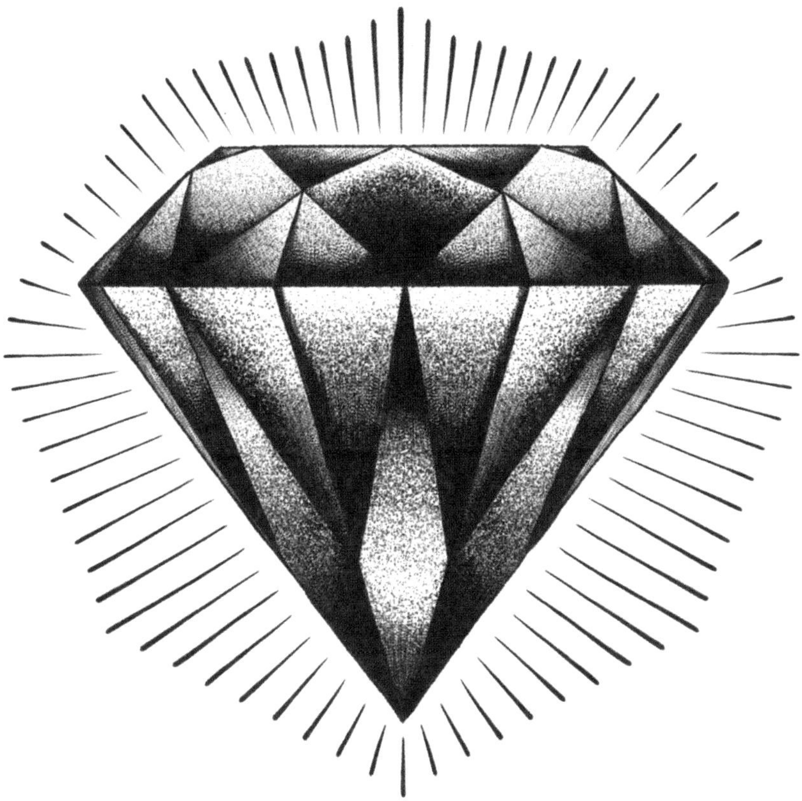

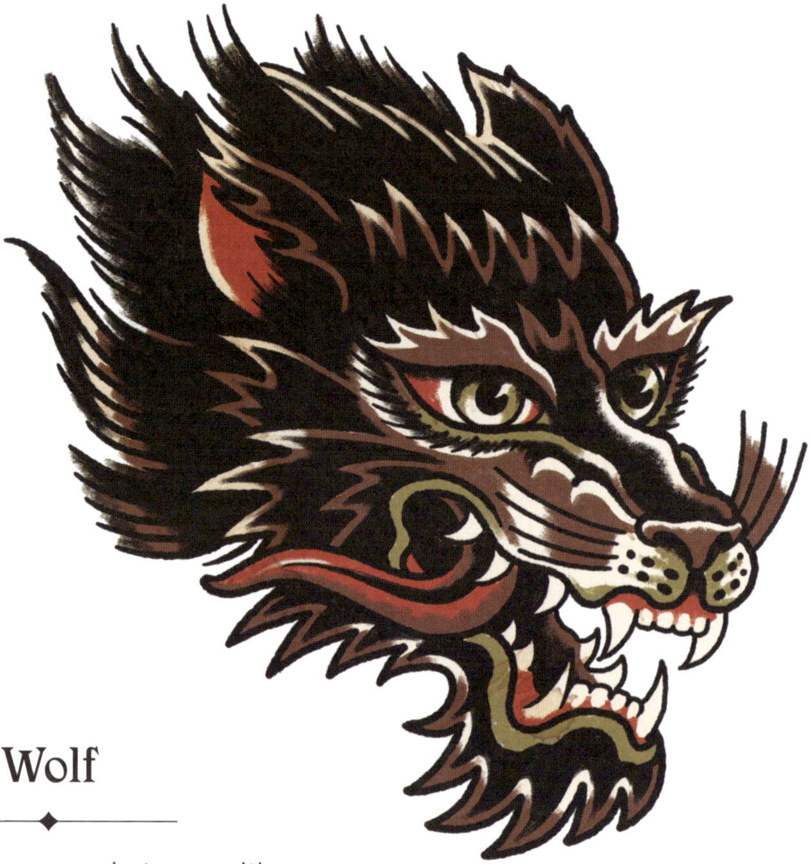

Wolf

Wolf tattoos communicate positive associations with the animal at the heart of much Native American mythology. There, it offers totemic guidance in intelligence, endurance, self-reliance and loyalty. Revered as a skilled hunter, the wolf finds its own path, suggesting qualities of courage and strength. The formation of a pack, which can be sparked by an individual quest to find a mate, correlates to contemporary ideas of family and further supports the universal popularity of the image.

Traditional style wolf tattoos, carrying bold black lines and bright red contrasts, are undeniably powerful. There is an inherent sense of strength, drawn from both the animal itself and the style of articulation.

Black Widow

The black widow represents strength and power. Most commonly, associations with the black widow are ascribed to femininity and sexuality. There is, of course, a pop cultural connection to the Marvel hero – a figure who overcomes stereotypes to become an unbreakably positive force – a reminder of the misunderstood nature of the arachnid. Tattoos depicting black widow spiders thus communicate traits that might be considered negative, but ultimately retain positive significance.

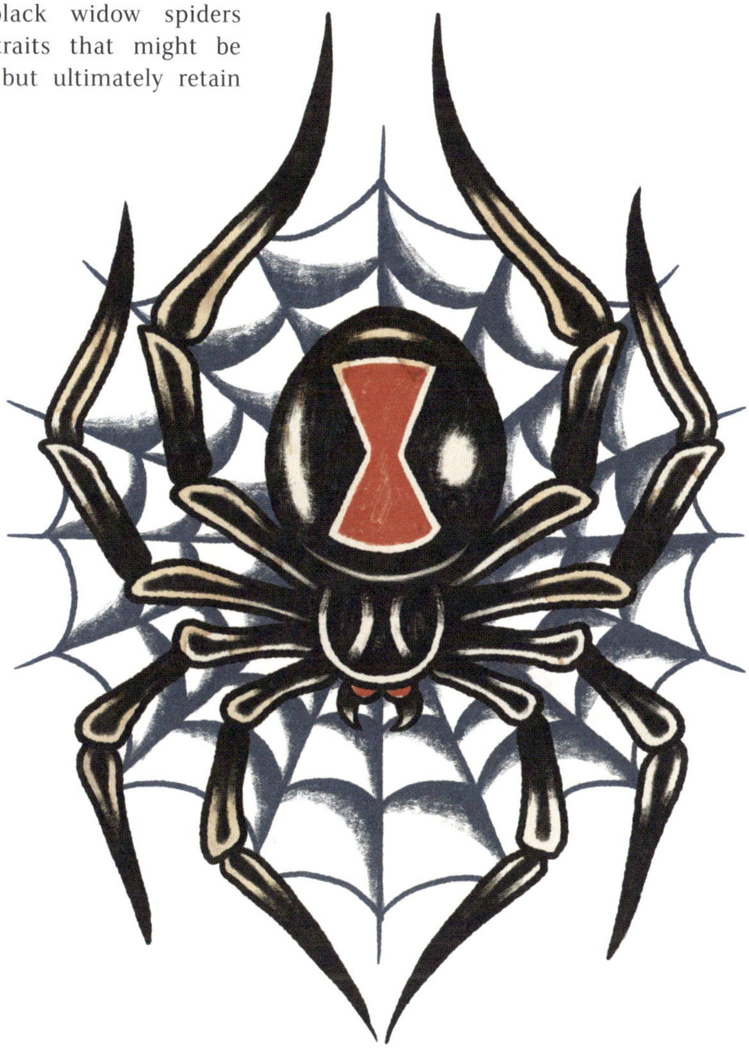

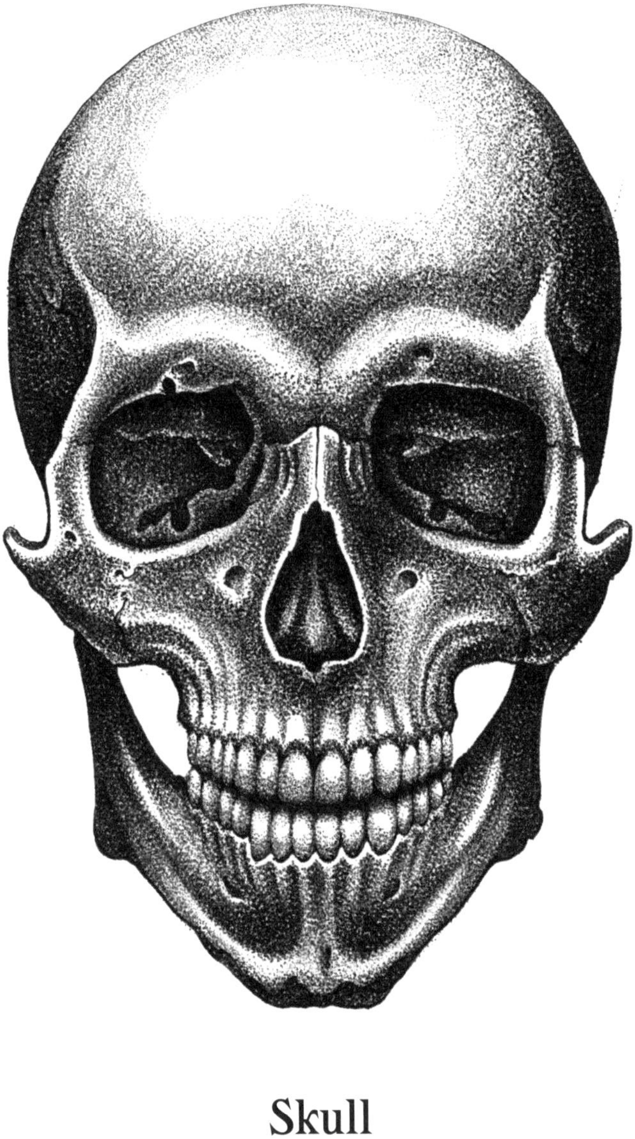

Skull

While there is a darkness associated with skulls, inclusive of mortality, as tattoos a skull communicates strength and protection. Wearers suggest overcoming challenge, even death, and the opportunity for rebirth.

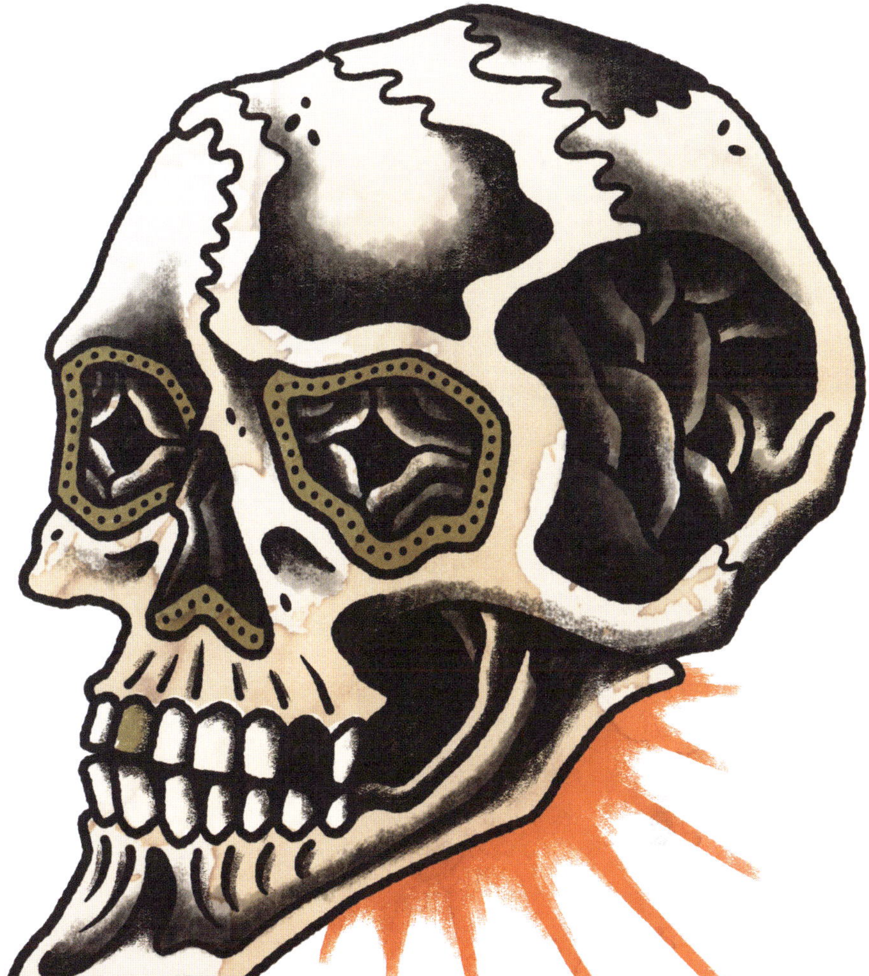

Pharaoh's Horses

A stunning example of 19th-century visual culture finding expression in tattooing, the pharaoh's horses design conveys resolution and strength of spirit.

The image, anchored by three Arabian horse heads, derives from a popular print of an 1848 painting by English artist J.F. Herring. While there is some debate as to the true origin of the composition (there is evidence that Herring himself may have been inspired by an earlier painting), the spread of the pharaoh's horses from the mid-1800s into the early 20th century assured its ubiquity in American popular culture. Familiarity with the image made it perfect for large-scale back, chest and stomach coverage on the era's famous tattooed attractions, among them Gus Wagner. By the 1920s, the design flowed freely within tattoo supply company catalogues (including those of Percy Waters and Milton Zeis).

Details of the pharaoh's horses design differ depending on articulation. The image draws influences from illustrations of Moses drowning the Egyptian army after parting the red sea. Commonly, the horses are pictured with a floral garland. As in the 19th-century etchings, the equine heads may also appear without further embellishment.

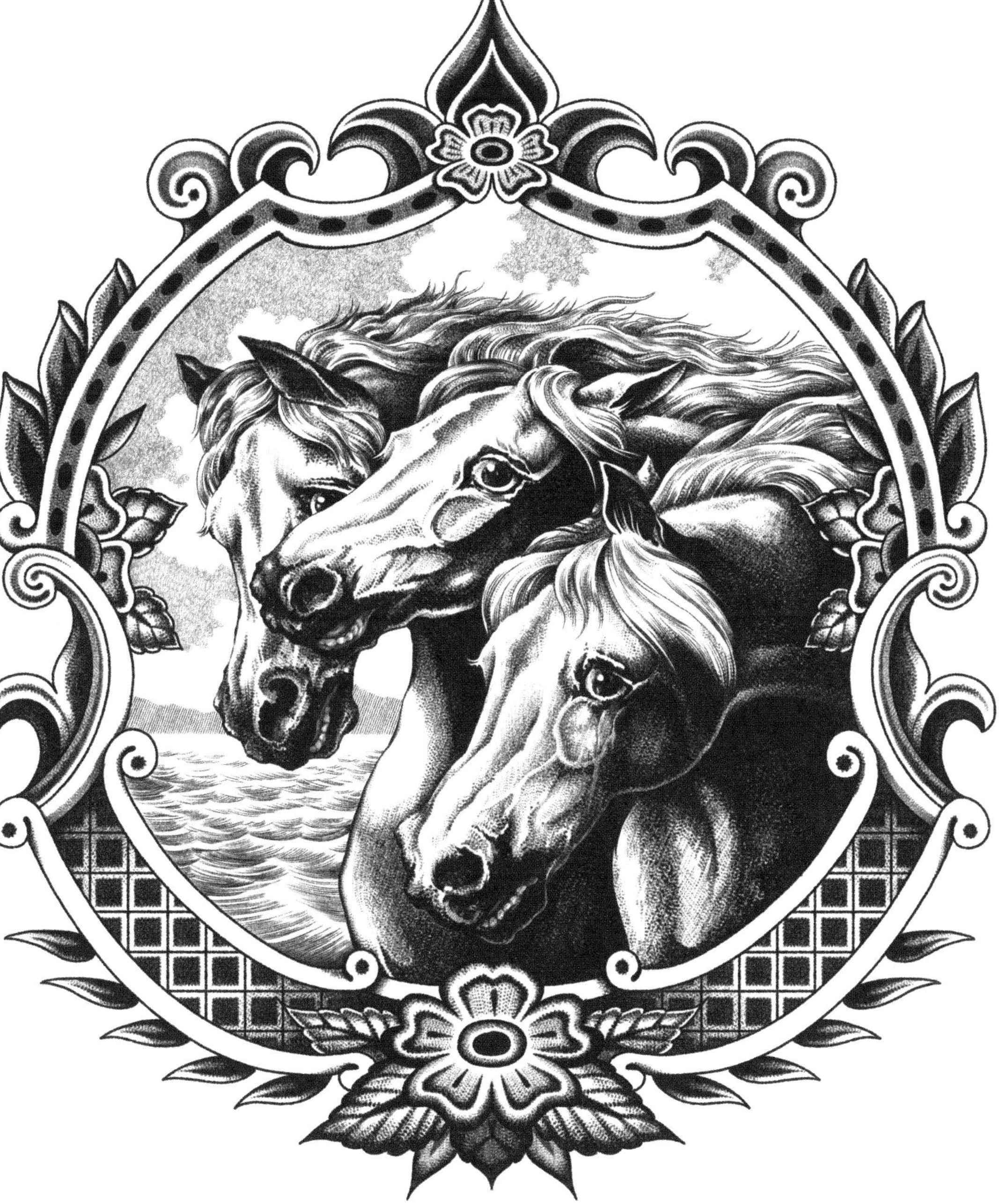

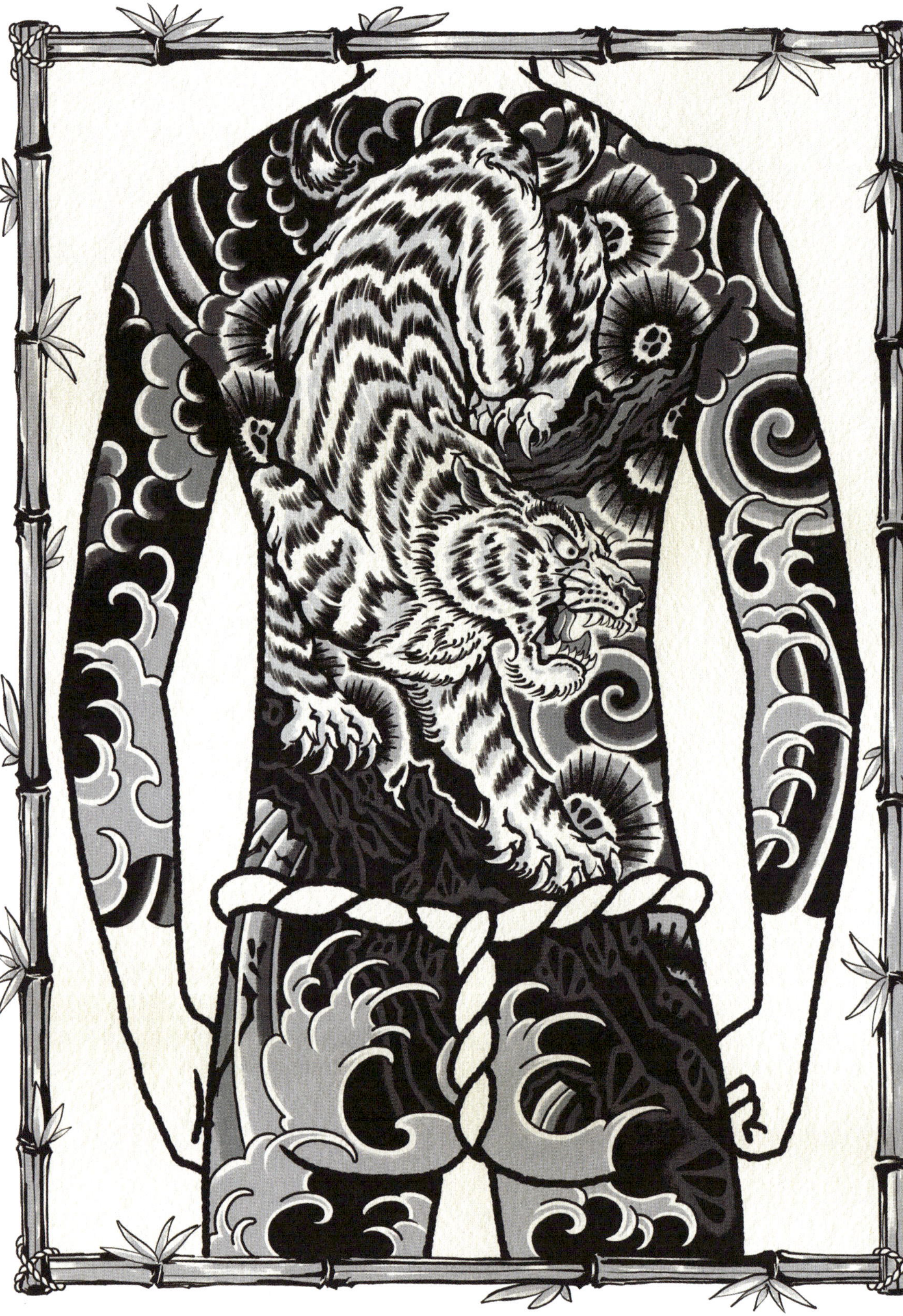

Tiger

Inclusion of the tiger in Irezumi compositions delivers a few distinct narratives. On the one hand, it may be placed in opposition to the dragon, a representation of misfortune against that of good luck. Other designs position the tiger among red peonies to represent full military power.

Another association connects the tiger to Buddhism. The animal is not native to Japan. Instead, its introduction to the country came with the arrival of religion from China. Within those views, the tiger represents an internal wild side to be tamed in order to find focus and fulfilment.

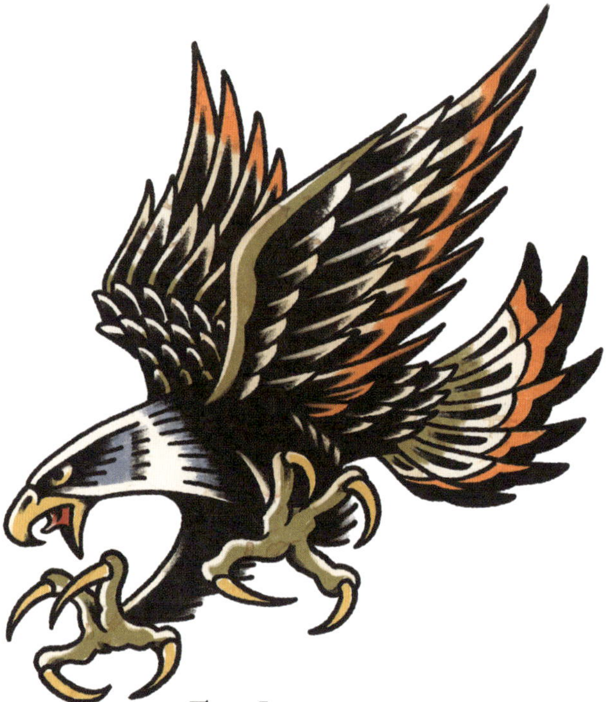

Eagle

On 20 June 1792, the United States welcomed the bald eagle to its Great Seal. Though naturalistic in interpretation, the use of the bird referenced the Roman Republic and gave a new vision to the strength and power of an imperial symbol. The current form of the eagle in American iconography has been in place since 1885, owing both to its ubiquity and the nationalistic association it rooted to American traditional tattooing.

In compositions such as the 'battle royale', which merge Japanese and western traditional styles, the struggle between occident and orient were displayed through use of the eagle. Its power conveyed a regional strength.

Of course, some rationale for this usage stems from spiritual and mythological associations between the eagle and the heavens, and with dominance and freedom. Hierarchically, it is at the top of the animal chain. In North American indigenous tradition, the eagle holds a special connection to the Creator. Depictions of struggle between eagle and snake in Aztec tradition represent a triumph of light over dark. And, within Greek mythology, the eagle is a patron of Zeus. These associations all intersect with the Roman, and thus modern, appropriation of eagle iconography as expression of dominance, whether through heraldry or more contemporary seals.

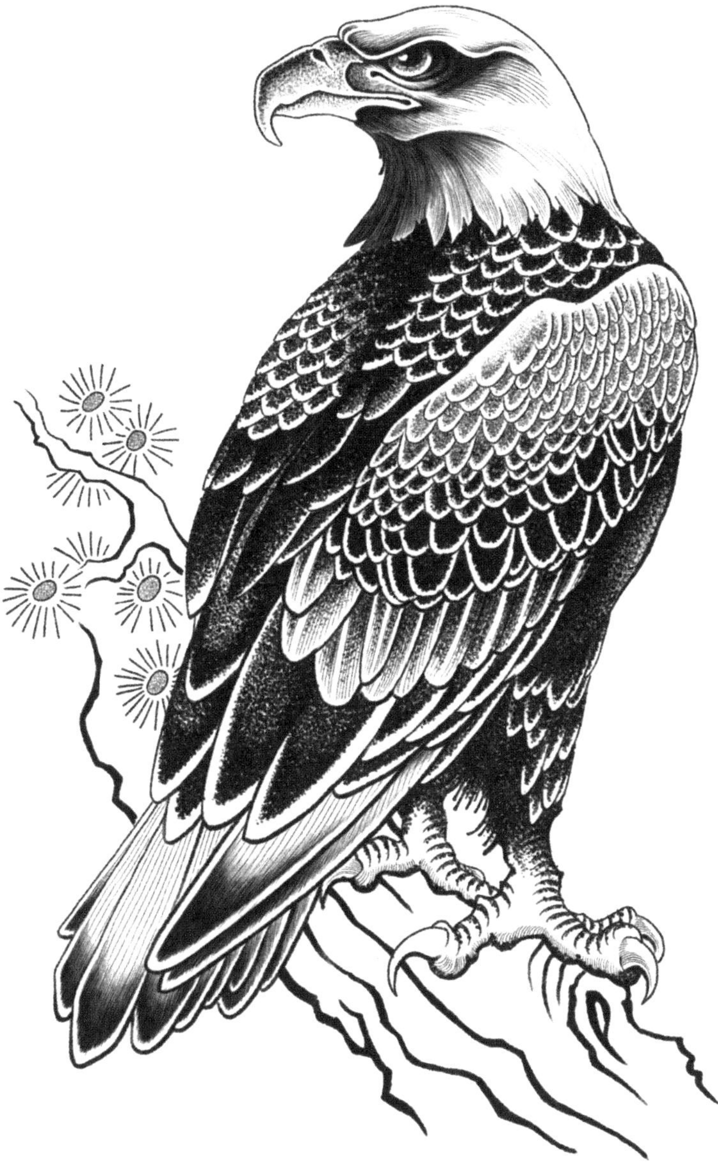

Kraken

The kraken is considered a terrifying sea monster. Squid-like in form, the creature has origins in Norse mythology as a forceful disruptor to seafarers – legend tells of the kraken's powerful tentacles, capable of pulling ships to the ocean floor.

Naturally, tattoos featuring the kraken play on the lore. The creature's strength is emphasized, along with its power. It is also a subject that, while uncommon in traditional sailor flash, gives contemporary voice to the associations of danger in the ocean, and taming them through absorption of the image.

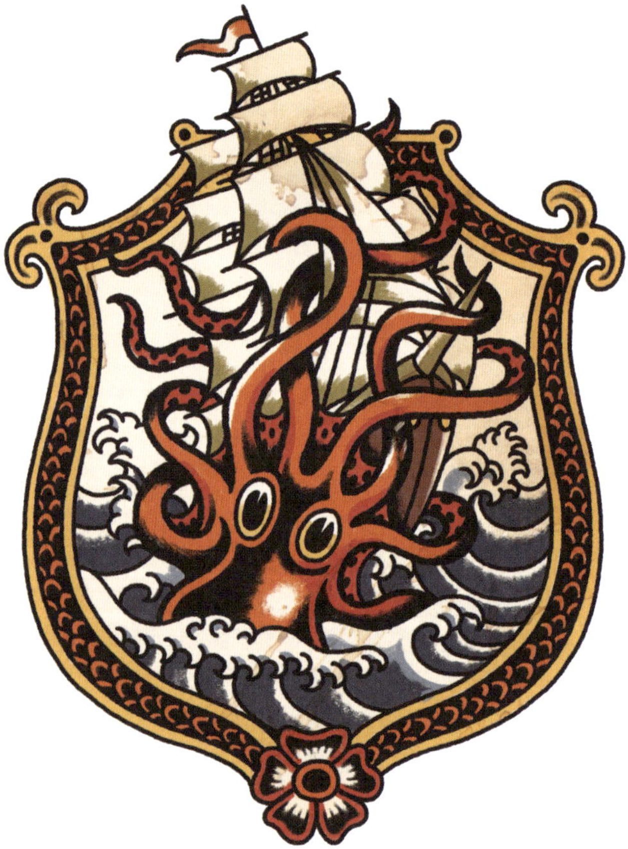

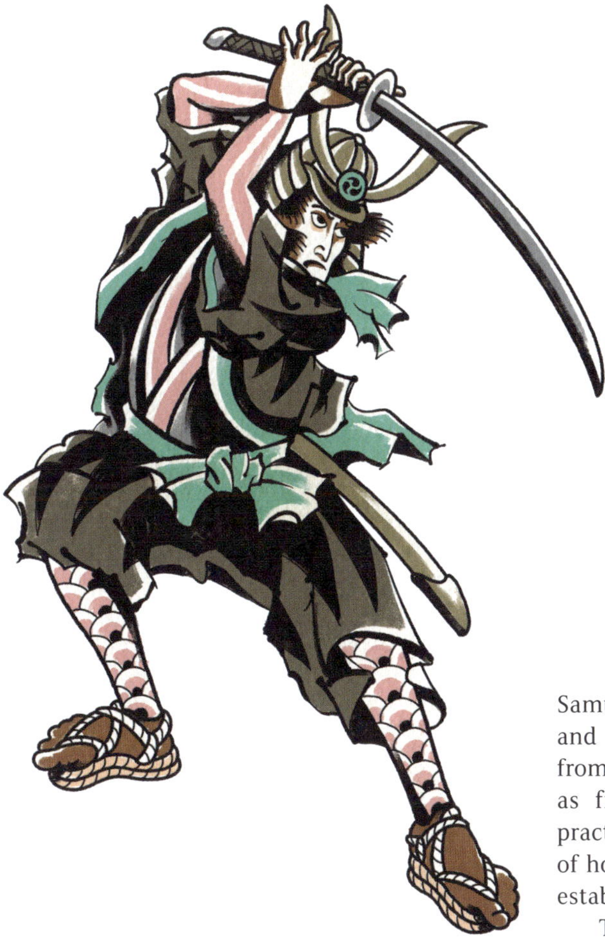

Samurai

Samurai tattoos convey courage, discipline and honour. Their meaning derives as much from true history of the Japanese officer class as from modern mythology around their practice; particularly in relation to the code of honour (*bushido*) among them, which was established in the late 17th century.

The rise of the samurai in the 10th century coincided with a period of feudal rule in Japan's Heian period. During this time, private armies were raised to protect the landed nobility (*daimyo*). In the following era, the Kakamura period, samurai followed emerging military dictators (*shogun*). They were abolished at the end of the Edo period, in 1867.

Easily identifiable by their highly specialized armour (including metal and lacquered elements), samurai within tattoo compositions may appear in a variety of ways. Paired with a dragon, the tattoo suggests protection of family. A samurai in an oni mask might suggest the wearer is facing an inner demon.

Kintaro

Tattoos featuring the 'golden boy' revel in the dynamism of his legend. Thought to be based on Heian period samurai Sakata Kintoki, who served feudal lord Minamoto no Yorimitsu, Kintaro's most famed exploit revolves around diving into a river and wrestling a giant koi. It is this exploit that forms the majority of tattoo compositions.

Often rendered as a sleeve or a backpiece, Kintaro-based designs find the boy either steering the koi or holding on for dear life. In either instance, the tattoo conveys the strength of his conviction and willpower.

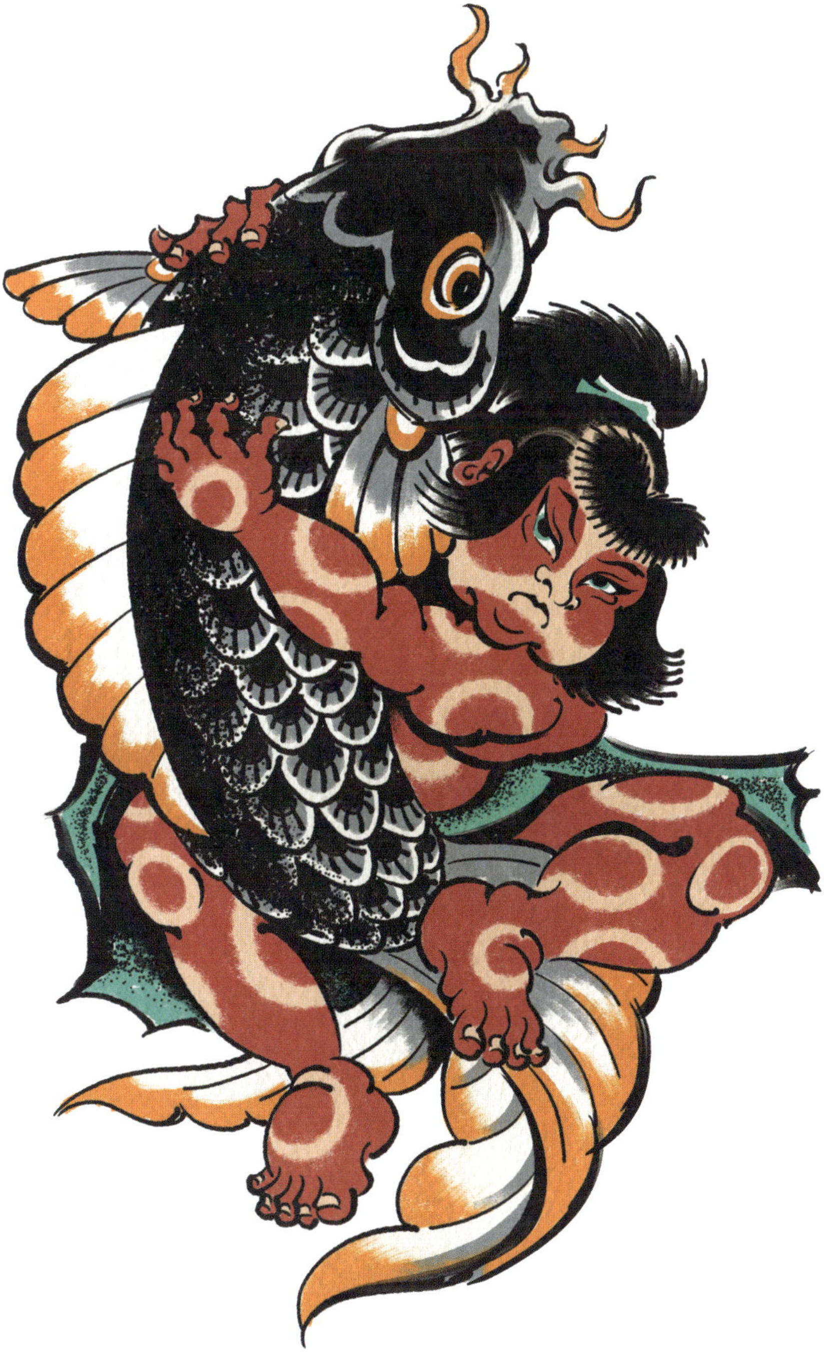

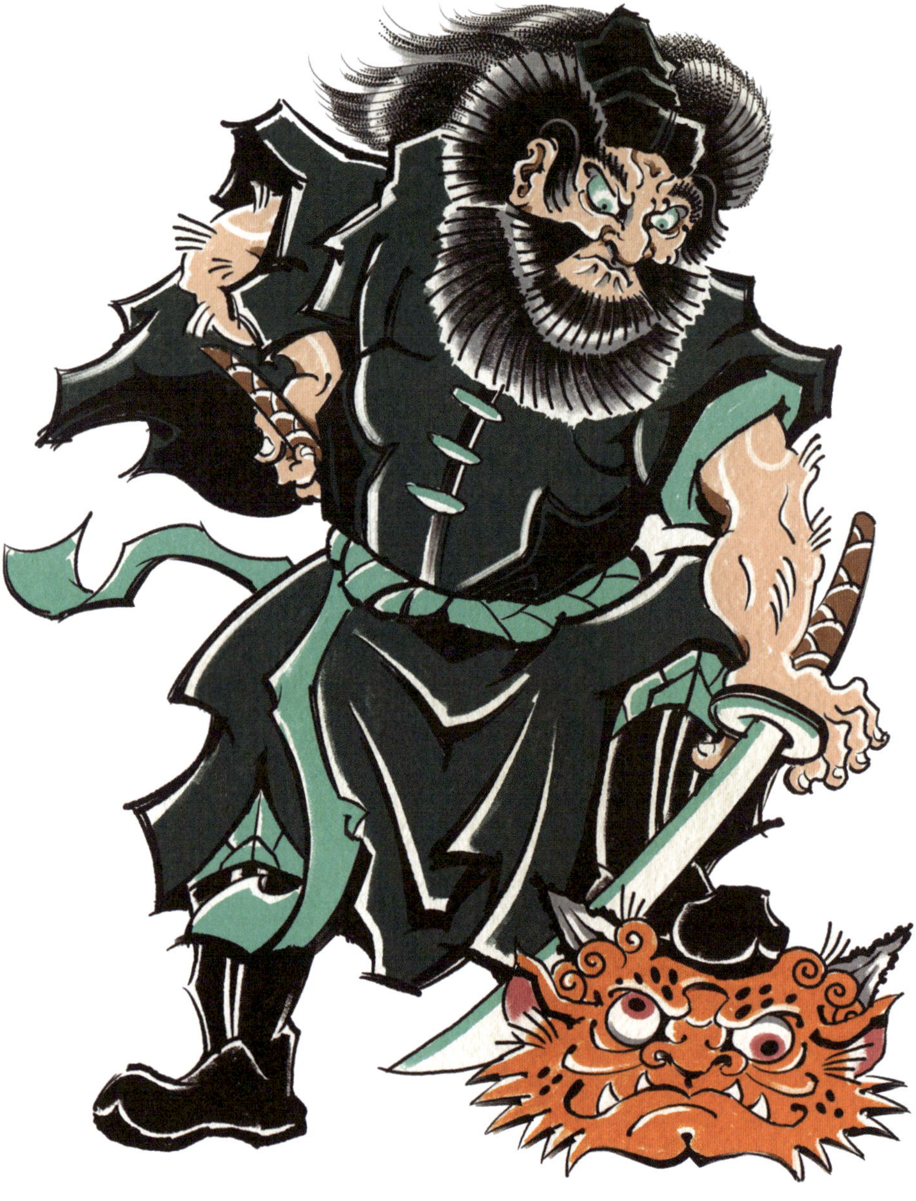

Shoki

A vanquisher of evil, Shoki is best known as a protector against illness. The mythology around him is rooted in 8th-century Tang dynasty China, with the story of a medical student Zhong Kui, who dreamed of becoming doctor to the emperor. Though he passed his exams with flying colours, Zhong Kui's appearance frightened the emperor, compelling him to deny the man of his lifelong goal. Distraught, Zhong Kui took his own life. Soon after, the emperor became ill and was troubled with nightmares. Within these, a spirit emerged to defeat the emperor's symptoms, and revealed himself as Shoki.

The fearsome appearance that put off the emperor is celebrated in depictions of Shoki. He is large, wears a beard and scholarly robes, and often a pair of black boots. His faithfulness to the emperor, despite initial denial of Zhong Kui, makes him a symbol of devotion. In Japan, the legend was revived during the smallpox outbreak of 1865, and Shoki remains in contemporary culture, featuring in Children's Day celebrations.

Cobra

The cobra is defined by two things: it is highly venomous and its upper neck ribs expand to form a distinctive hood. In a tattoo, these two aspects give a clear 'don't mess with me' message. Posed coiled and ready to strike, a cobra tattoo symbolizes a warding off of danger, whether it be the prospect of misfortune or of potential conflict.

In ancient Egyptian mythology the cobra represents a guardian of the underworld, and in Hinduism it serves as a protector of Shiva. But it is the appropriation of the symbol in the western traditional style that gives it the associations described above, best rendered in powerful bold line and bright colours.

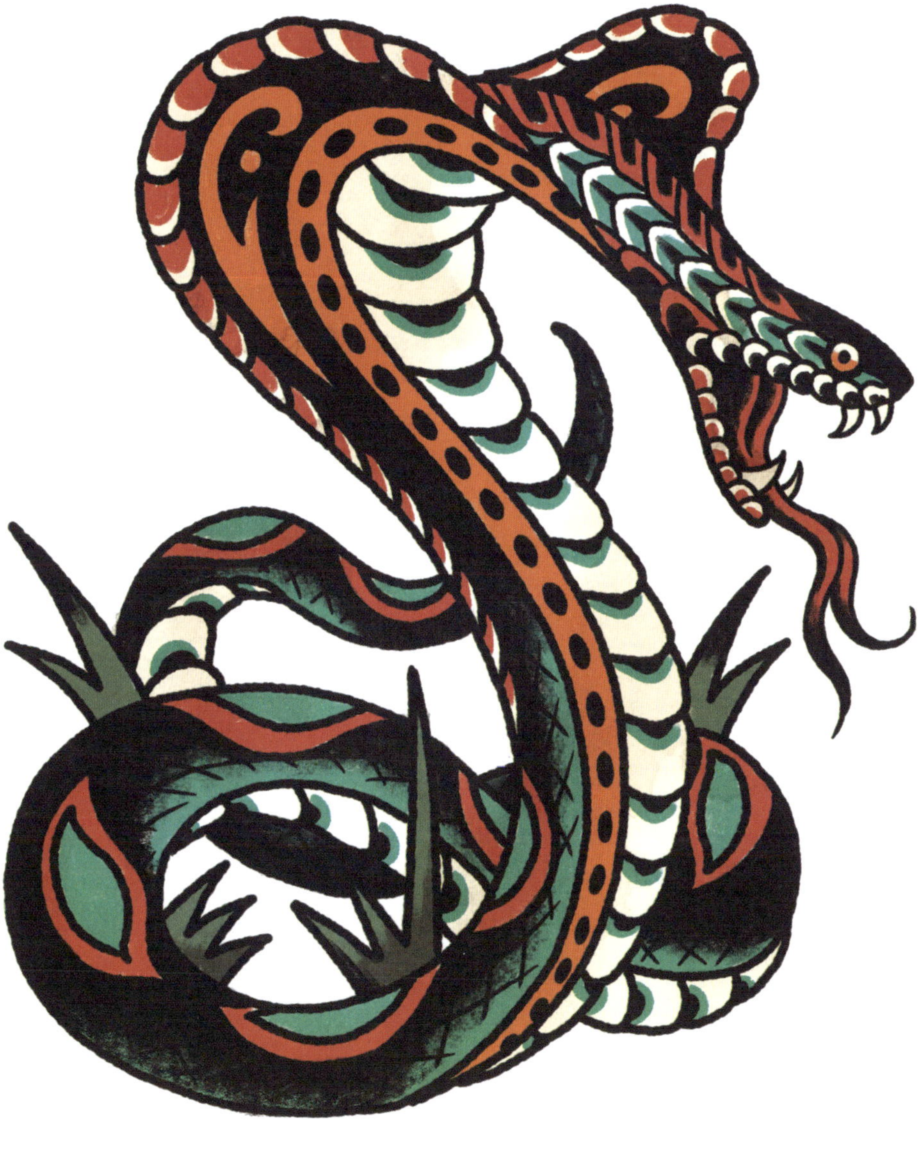

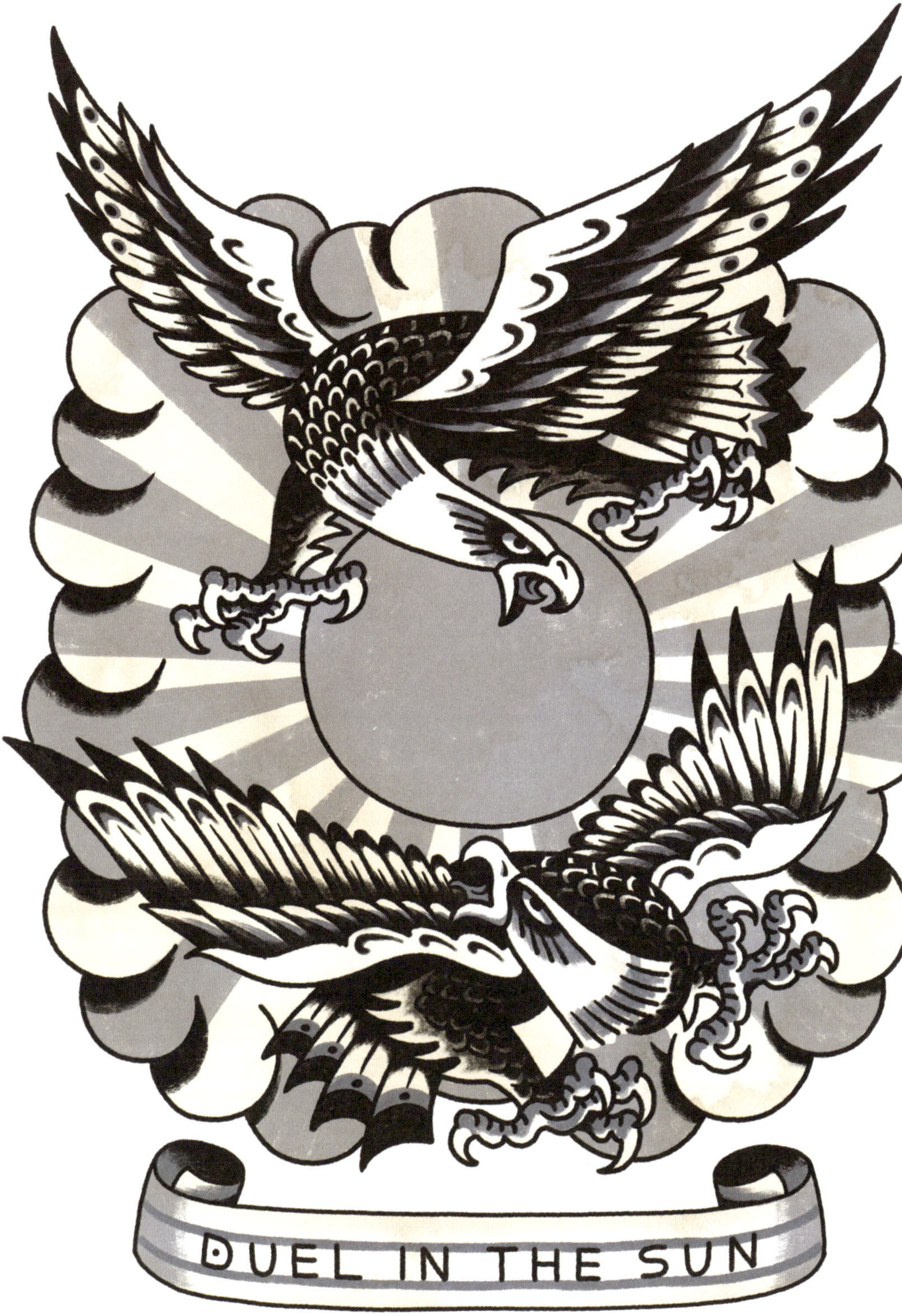
DUEL IN THE SUN

Duel in the Sun

A tattoo with a brilliant legacy, the 'duel in the sun' is well known as part of legendary Lyle Tuttle's body suit. Covering Tuttle's back, the work was inked by Bert Grimm from a drawing by Brooklyn-based Joe Lieber. Much like the battle royale, the composition brings together Japanese and western traditional styles to form an image unique to American tattooing.

The components include a radiating sun (Lieber's version bares resemblance to the now-controversial rising sun flag of the Japanese Imperial Army) and two eagles engaged in combat. Bald eagles, which are fiercely territorial, do indeed tussle. The meaning of the tattoo itself is not explicitly tied to this type of dispute, but may convey a willingness to take a sharp stand and hold ground.

Sword

Generally speaking, the sword is a symbol of power. As an image, the sword evokes authority, strength and courage – all characteristics that speak to overcoming obstacles. In history and in myth, swords are granted to protagonists (such as Perseus) who are preparing to face challenging foe (in Perseus's case, Medusa).

Western-traditional tattooing has no shortage of sword-related imagery. Rendered alone, with crown or skull hilt, or piercing anything from flowers to, playfully, the skin itself, the sword follows similar composition to popular dagger images. However, the difference between the two comes in a subtle elevation of the sword as emblematic of intellect and valour. This consideration shifts the association with strength beyond an individual to encompass broader community or cultural value structures.

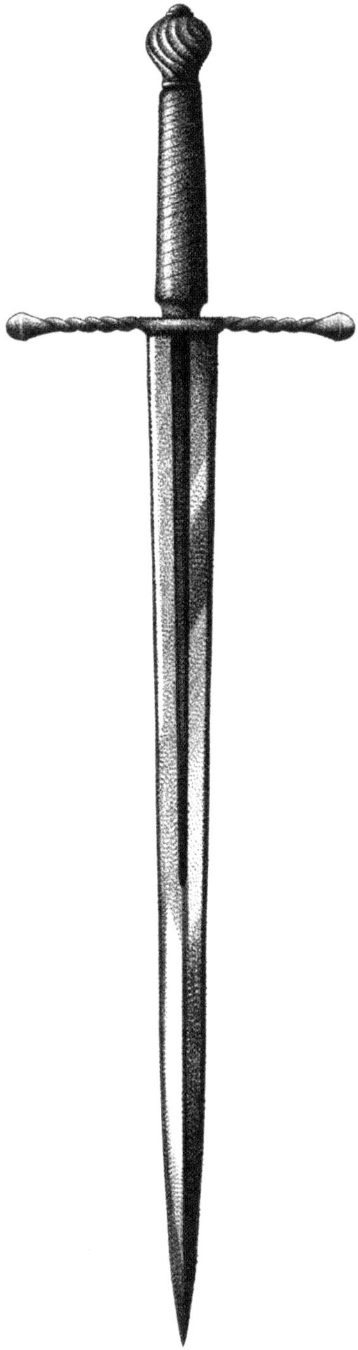

Snake and Sword

In the caduceus or Rod of Asclepius, a snake wrapped around a staff conveys a balance of strength and life. However, that association shifts dramatically when the snake is wrapped around, and pierced by, a sword. In this composition, the will of good versus evil plays out and is particularly potent as a visualization of Christian belief.

Positioning the blade in triumph over adversity augments the general reading of a sword tattoo and gives narrative to the wearer – whether one is sharing pride in overcoming a challenge or strength in the face of trouble.

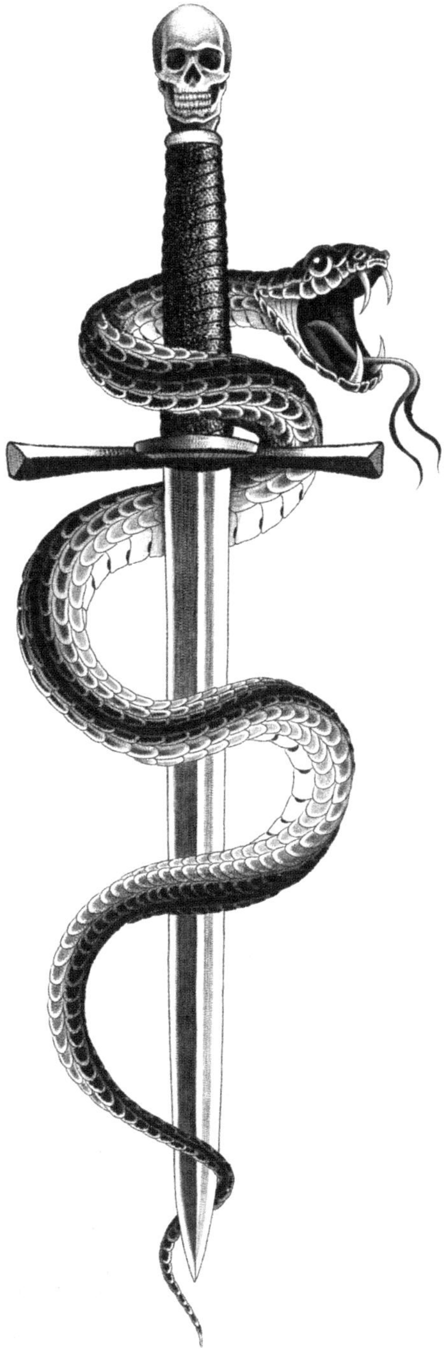

Anvil

The anvil, depicted with or without a hammer, symbolizes hard work and dedication. Overtly, there is connection to the blacksmith – and thus to craft – subtly allowing for consideration of strength and longevity.

As a tattoo, the anvil primarily features in the western traditional style. There remains a pleasing connection between the anvil, the circus, the strongman and tattooing, due to prevalence of the weighted object as a prop in shows. A few posters from the golden age of the circus show a strongman, often tattooed, lifting an anvil from chest piercings. Other images depict a strongman anvil on abs, taking hammer blows from an accomplice in an effort to relay extreme might.

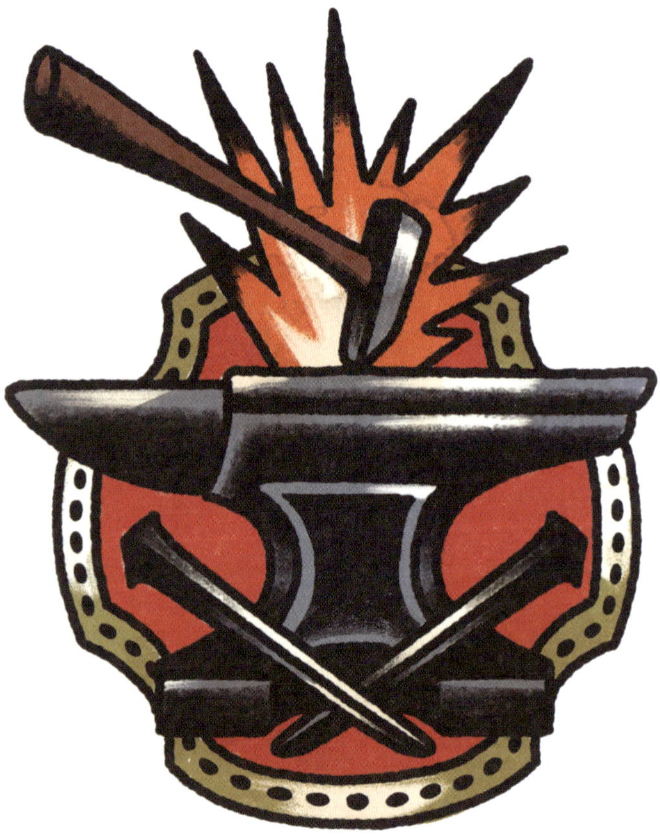

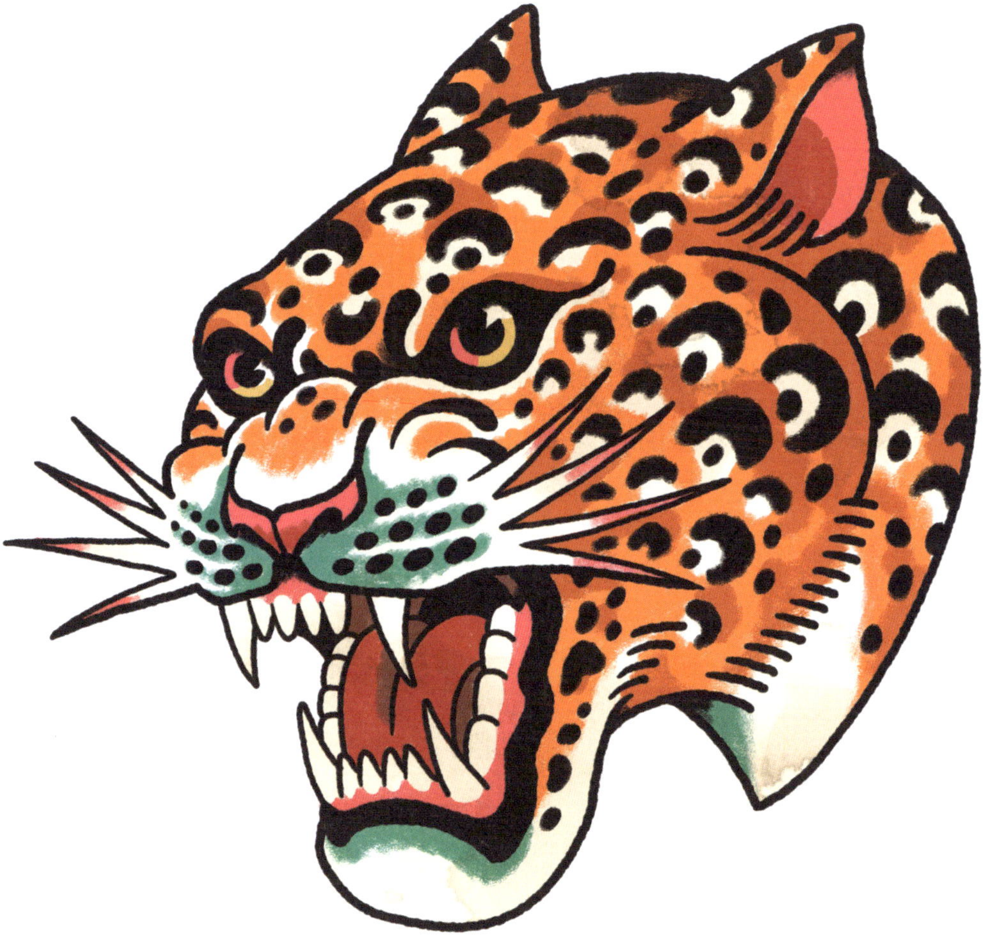

Leopard

Nocturnal and solitary, the leopard is famed for its rosette-marked fur. This animal is one of five extant species in the genus *Panthera*, which includes the lion and tiger. It is notable for its short legs and broad skull. Creative licence allows for the isolation of physical elements, such as using the rosette form as a standalone pattern, which makes for a potent design that represents characteristics of strength, such as ferocity, inner power and more.

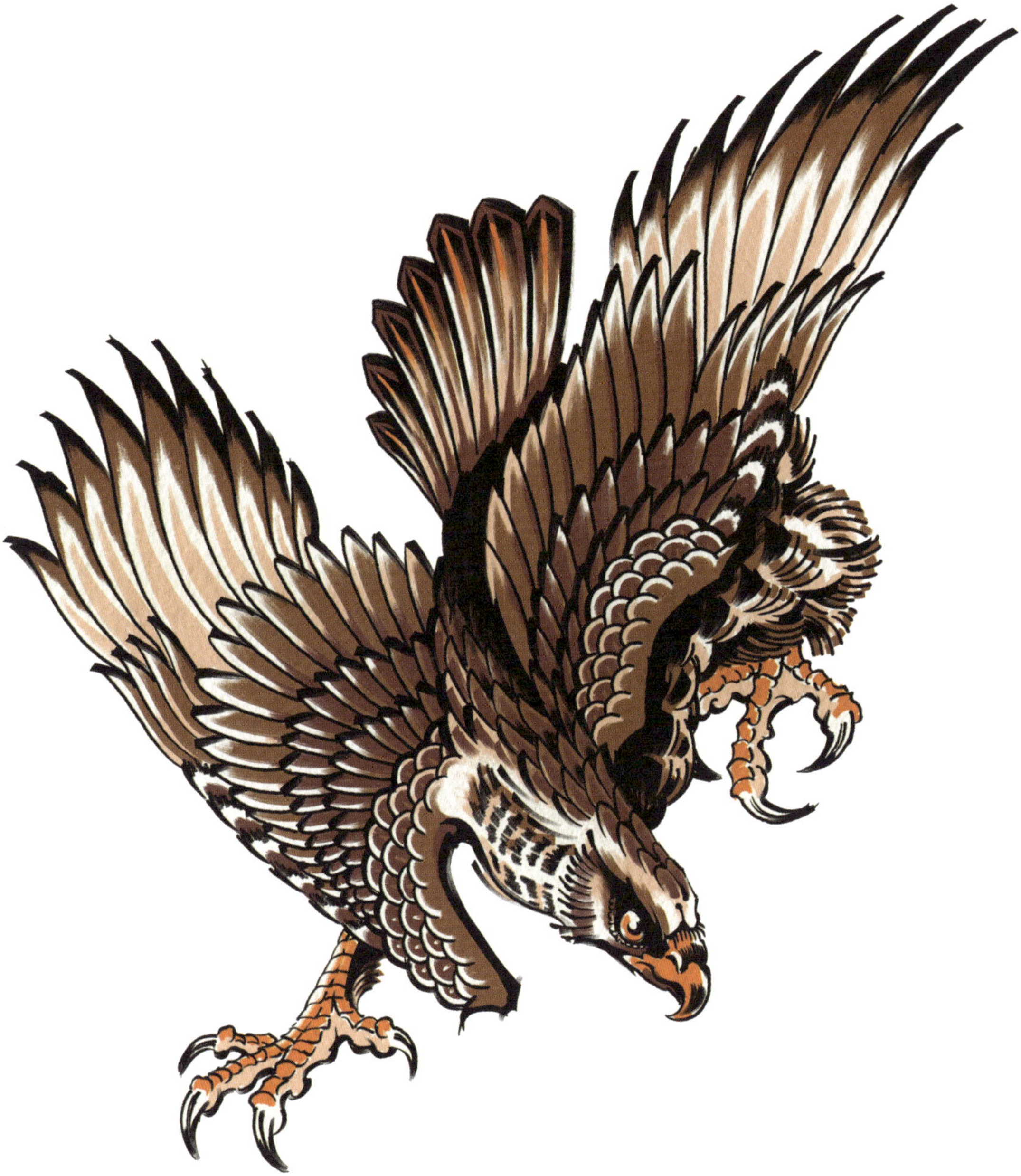

Taka

Within Irezumi, depictions of the taka, or hawk, commonly find the bird perched on a rock or a branch. There, the taka is in position to seek prey but not actively to hunt – significant as a subtle reminder of its power. Power, whether in those common compositions, or in association with the samurai, is key to the significance of the taka. Falconry became associated with the Japanese nobility in the Heian period, and the ferocity of the bird was prized through the Edo period, when shoguns created an influential role in their ranks: master of hawks. However, taka do not exclusively represent an absolute force. Balancing the taka and a cherry blossom branch, for example, forms a more complex narrative of transient power.

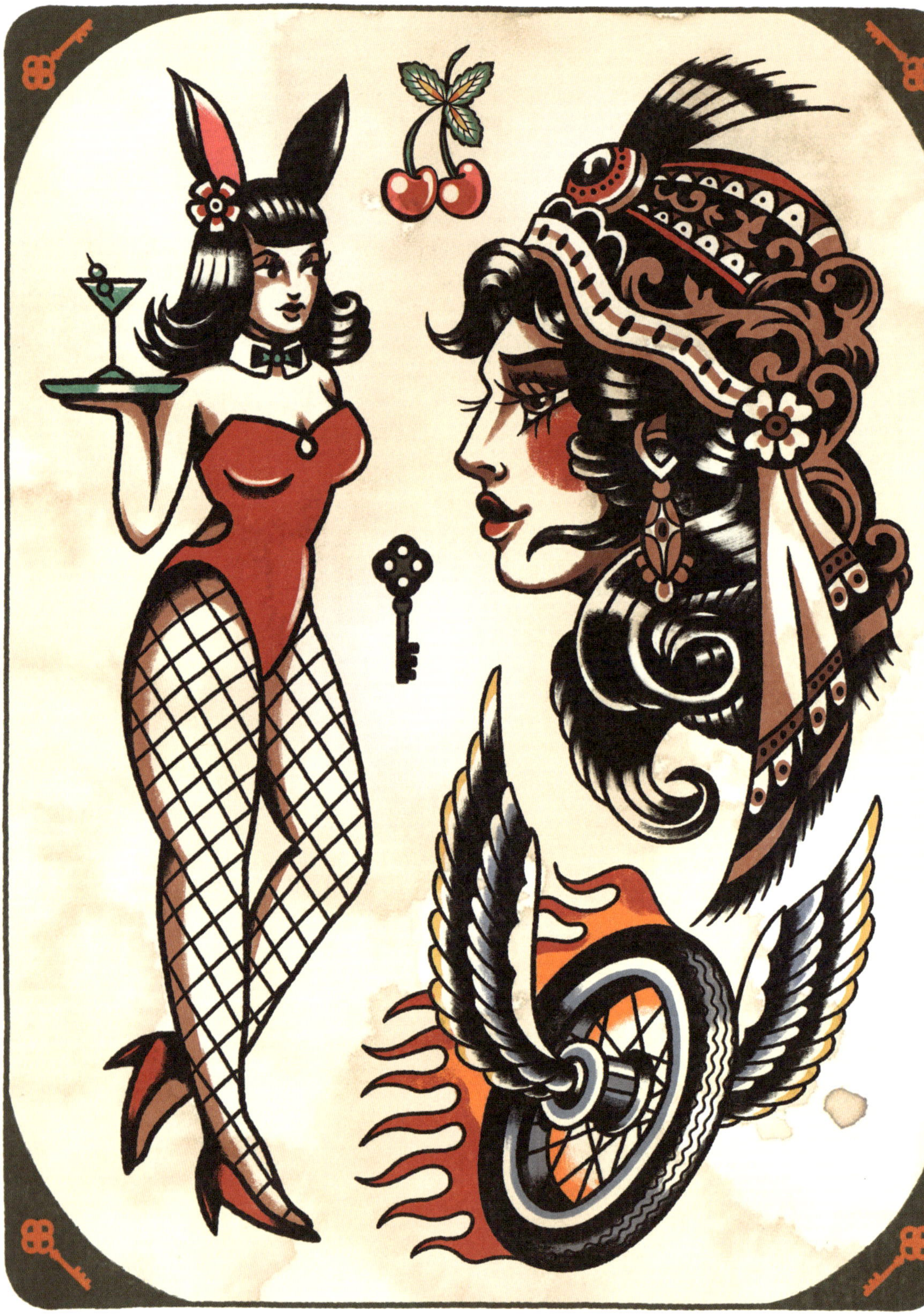

7

DESIRE

The sex, drugs and rock 'n' roll aspect of the tattoo cannot be underestimated. Neither should its close cousin wanderlust be overlooked. Tattoos related to desire celebrate vice, they champion exploration and they honour risk-taking. Many symbols also represent the pitfalls of lust. In both Japanese and western traditional vernaculars, there are tattoos that cover the duality of desire – joy and pain.

Some narratives related through these designs rely on the 19th-and 20th-century mythologizing, and later Hollywoodization, of certain lifestyles, and characterizations celebrated through the travelling carnival. Others connect to, and draw on, the history of erotic drawings – from Japanese *shunga* to the work of Tom of Finland.

Regardless of the exact choice of design, a symbol of desire reflects a willingness to become immersed in life's exciting possibilities.

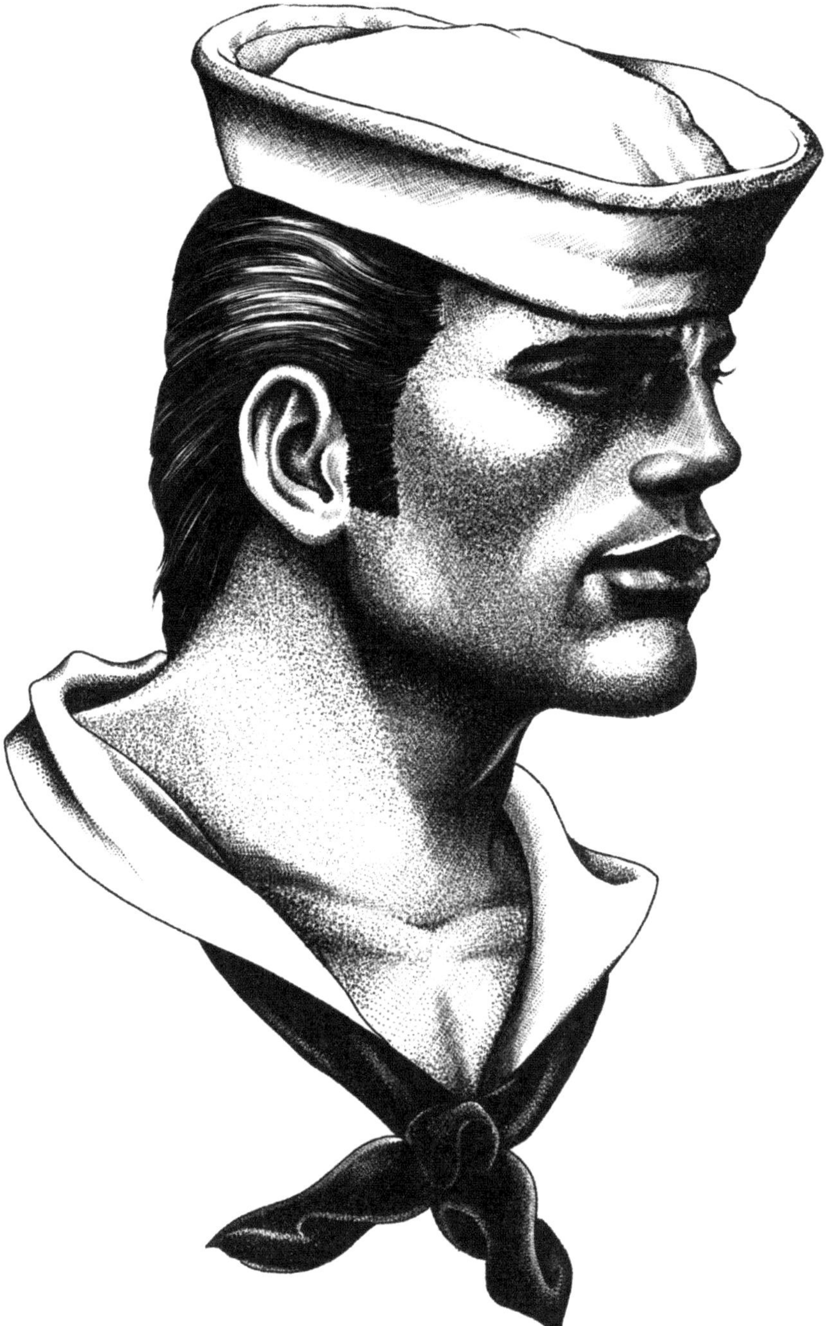

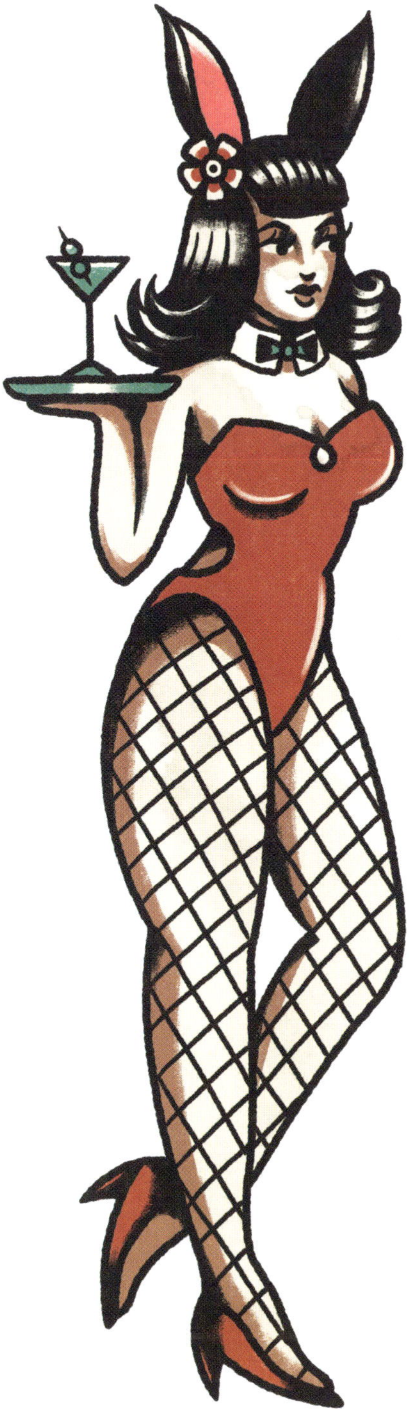

Pin Up

While the term 'pin-up' was coined in the 1940s, the origins of the mass-produced, sexualized female image dates back to the 1870s and 1890s, with the advent of the Gibson Girl in the United States and magazines featuring burlesque dances in Europe. It's no surprise, then, that tattoo culture embraced the idealized figures as part of its visual vocabulary, with flash books from the turn of the century devoting at least a few pages to articulating a certain vision of buxom beauty.

The pin-up received a boost between 1900 and World War II, when images were placed on ships, planes and, of course, newly enlisted servicemen. Wearers inked with such 'morale-boosting' reminders of the fun at home were sometimes rebuked and forced to give the figures a little more covering. As early as 1908, the United States Navy prohibited nude pin-ups, with several tattooists, including New York's Charlie Wagner, stating that the dictum brought in a sizable business of touch-ups.

Today, the highly stylized western traditional pin-up girl remains popular, with neo-traditional styles inviting more flexible definitions of beauty. It is important not to overlook 'beefcake' designs, some of which follow from the stylized masculinity of Tom of Finland. Furthermore, other designs capture a range of kink and push the pin-up idea to more nuanced territories.

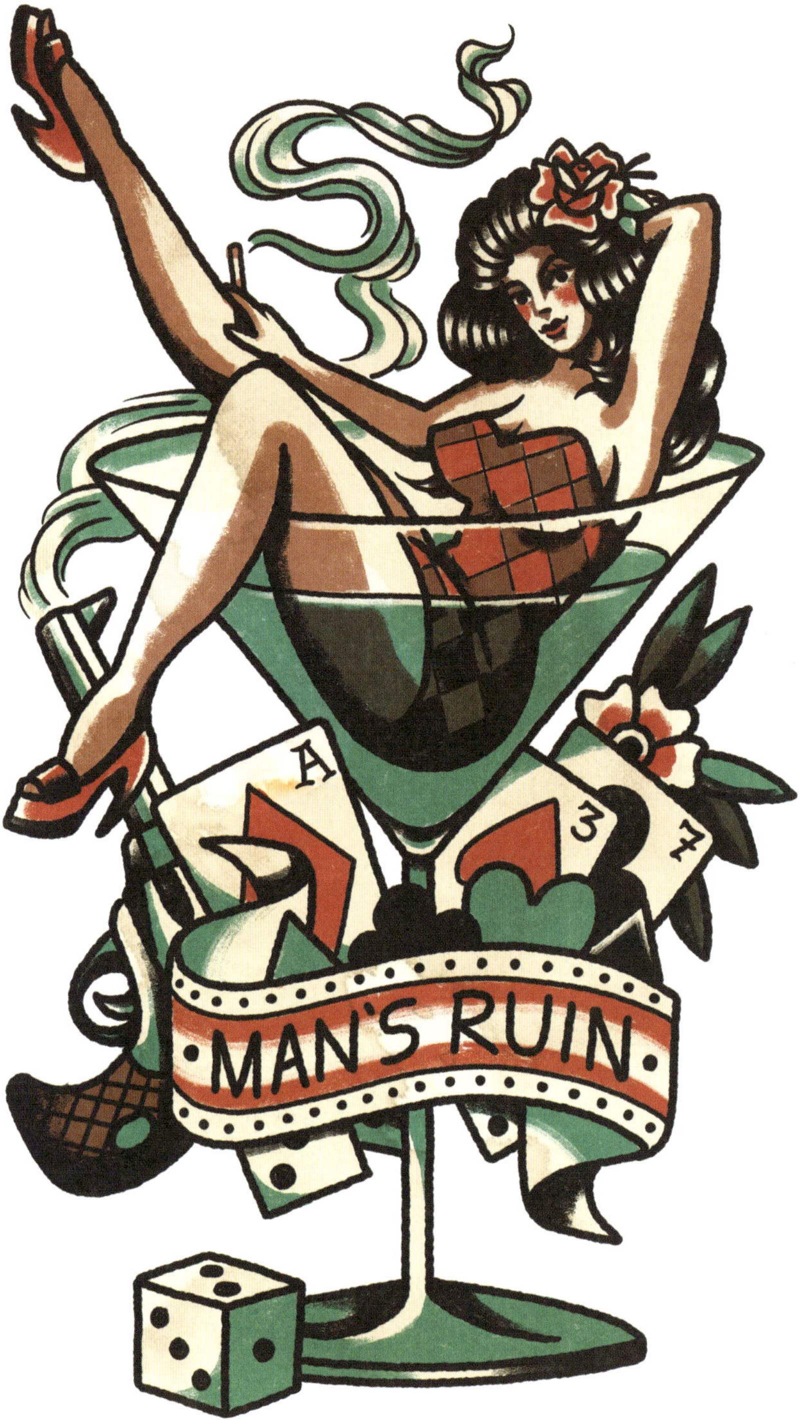
A
3
7
MAN'S RUIN

Man's Ruin

A compilation of vices, 'man's ruin' reflects tattooing's bawdy, predominantly heteronormative, 20th century history. Common elements include booze, gambling ephemera and a woman – the chasing of each having potential to 'ruin a man'. The design, especially at its most base, allows the wearer an embrace of debauchery. Drawing a little from the tongue-in-cheek origins, and personalized for one's own perversions or preoccupations, the conceit becomes a more universal exploration of the perils (or joys) of desire.

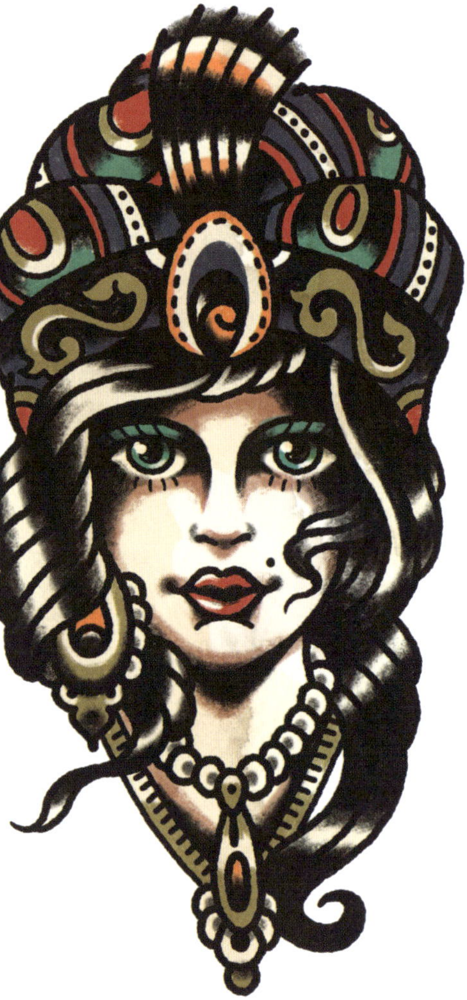

Gypsy Head

The gypsy head, or girl head, owes its development to a very particular time in popular culture. Circus attractions, penny arcades and all the hustle and bustle of burgeoning, cheap urban entertainment in the 19th century relied on several commoditized attractions, among which were the heavily tattooed man and woman. Another was the gypsy fortune-teller. While the former no doubt helped to spread standard tattoo images, the latter inspired, to a degree, a now common design.

Flash books of the 1920s and 1930s shared various styles of girl head, each displaying an unbridled feminine power. Representing fortune, opportunity and risk, these designs (despite being stereotypical and problematic today) largely carry positive association. Contemporary wearers may wish to convey a certain optimistic wanderlust. The composition, which can include specificity to adornments, remains a western traditional classic.

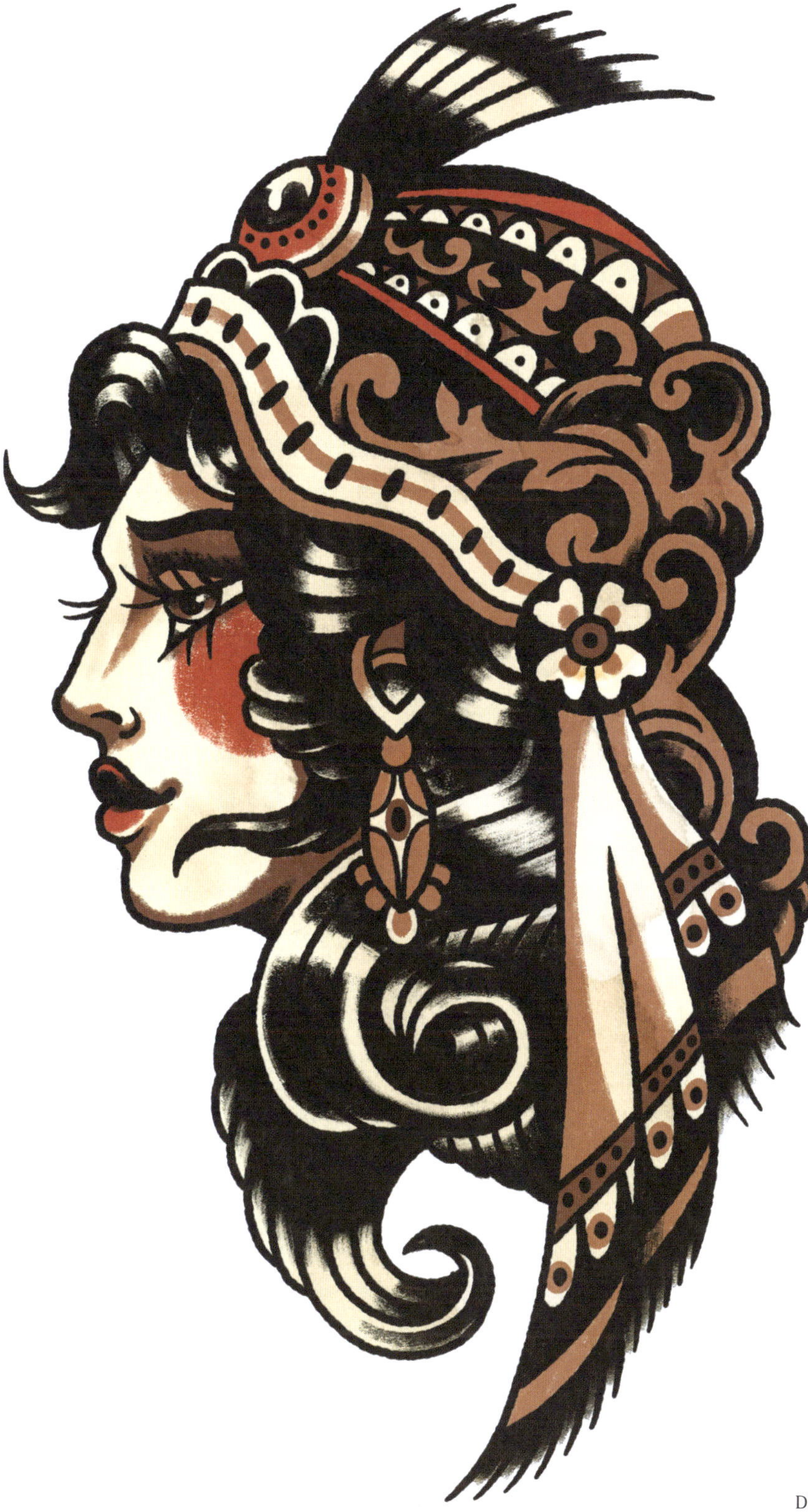

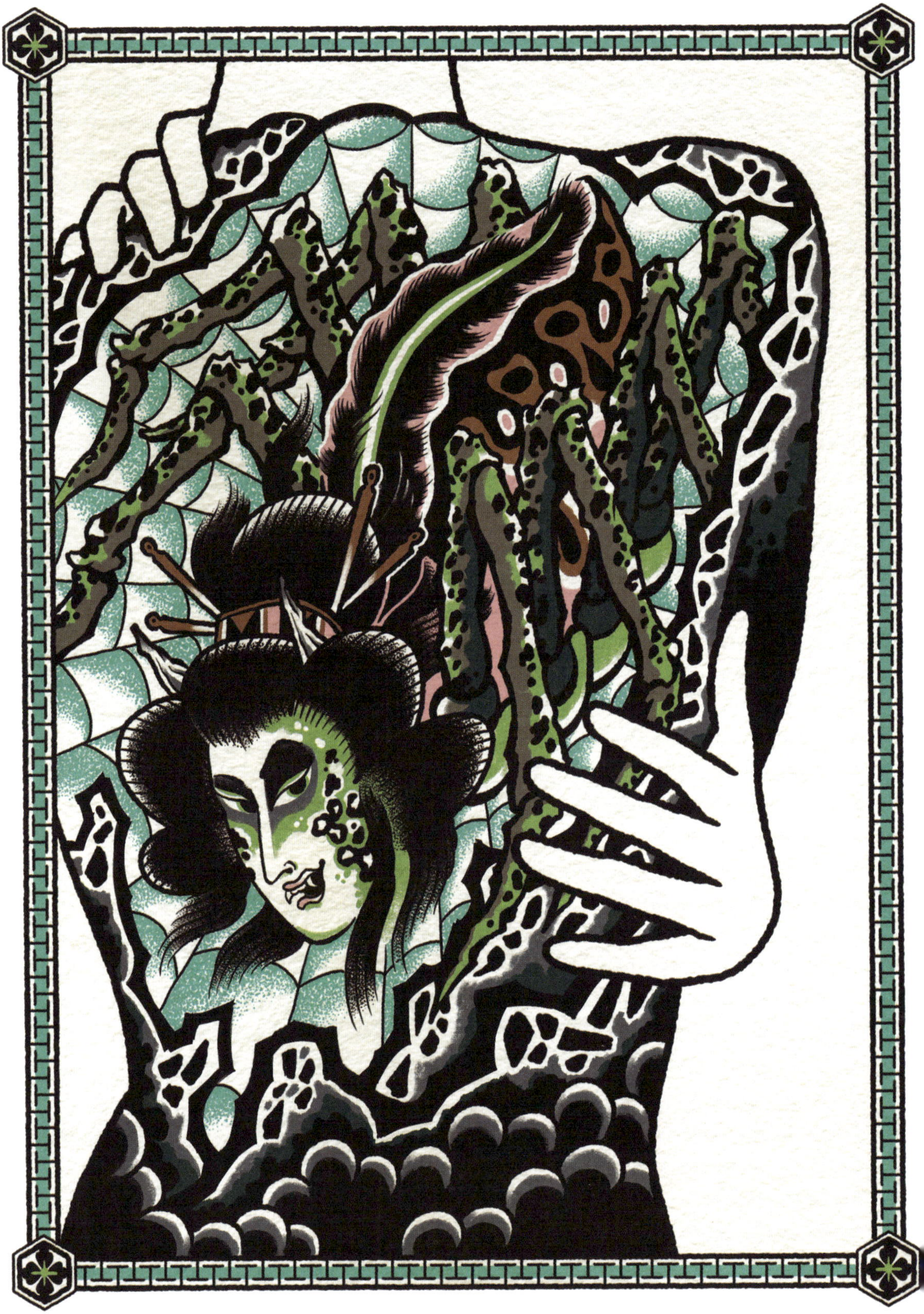

Jorōgumo

The jorōgumo, woman spider or binding bride, is a shapeshifting *yōkai* (Japanese folkloric goblin), that entangles men with false charms. Its figure, the body of a spider with a beguiling human face (often depicted as a geisha), makes it one of the most visually intriguing motifs in the Irezumi vernacular. It represents the dangers of a universal human weakness – that of succumbing to overwhelming, instantaneous desire.

As an idea, lovesickness finds expression in many cultures, from the tales of eros to contemporary pop songs. As a tattoo, through the jorōgumo, the notion becomes a visceral image. In one particular myth, set at the Jōren Falls of Izu in Japan, despite her destructive side, the jorōgumo also carries the power to ward off disaster. That duality serves the tattoo well, acting as a reminder that recognition of risk predetermines security.

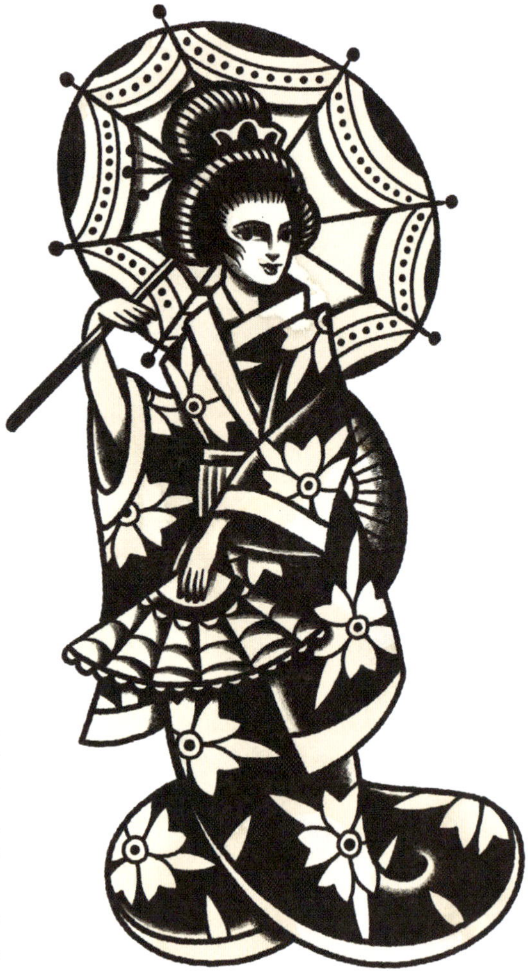

Geisha

Closed to the West until 1853, the opening of Japanese ports to international trade prompted a period of intense interest in the country's art. Luminaries from James McNeil Whistler and Edgar Degas to Claude Monet and Mary Cassatt were entranced by masterful woodcut prints. Through the late Victorian and early Edwardian periods, fascination in the Japanese aesthetic and craft permeated all visual arts, influencing architecture and interiors (as evidenced in the work of New York's famed Herter Brothers), as well as bringing a perceived exoticism to mass-produced goods.

Among the popular forms were Westernized images of geishas – Japan's famed professional artisans. Face framed by a parasol, the motif was quite familiar by the 1880s, appearing as bronze statuettes and teapots, ceramic figurines and, as produced by New Haven, Connecticut's Russell & Erwin, distinctive doorknobs.

Geisha designs were adopted by tattoo artists as well, taking root in the late 19th century and continuing to formalize through the 1910s. The influence of Japanese imagery on tattooing, blossoming in this period, ensured that several key designs – the dragon and the geisha among them –became ubiquitous in flash sheets and books.

A particularly striking example appears on a flash sheet painted by Edward Smith in 1911, where it appears alongside a large-scale pharaoh's horses design (see page 132), illustrating the cross-cultural pollination that informed tattoo vernacular at the time. Contemporary geisha designs are, undoubtedly, remnants of the 19th-century visual culture. Meaning derives from associations with beauty and mystery, and the image continues to relay an untouchable grace and feminine power.

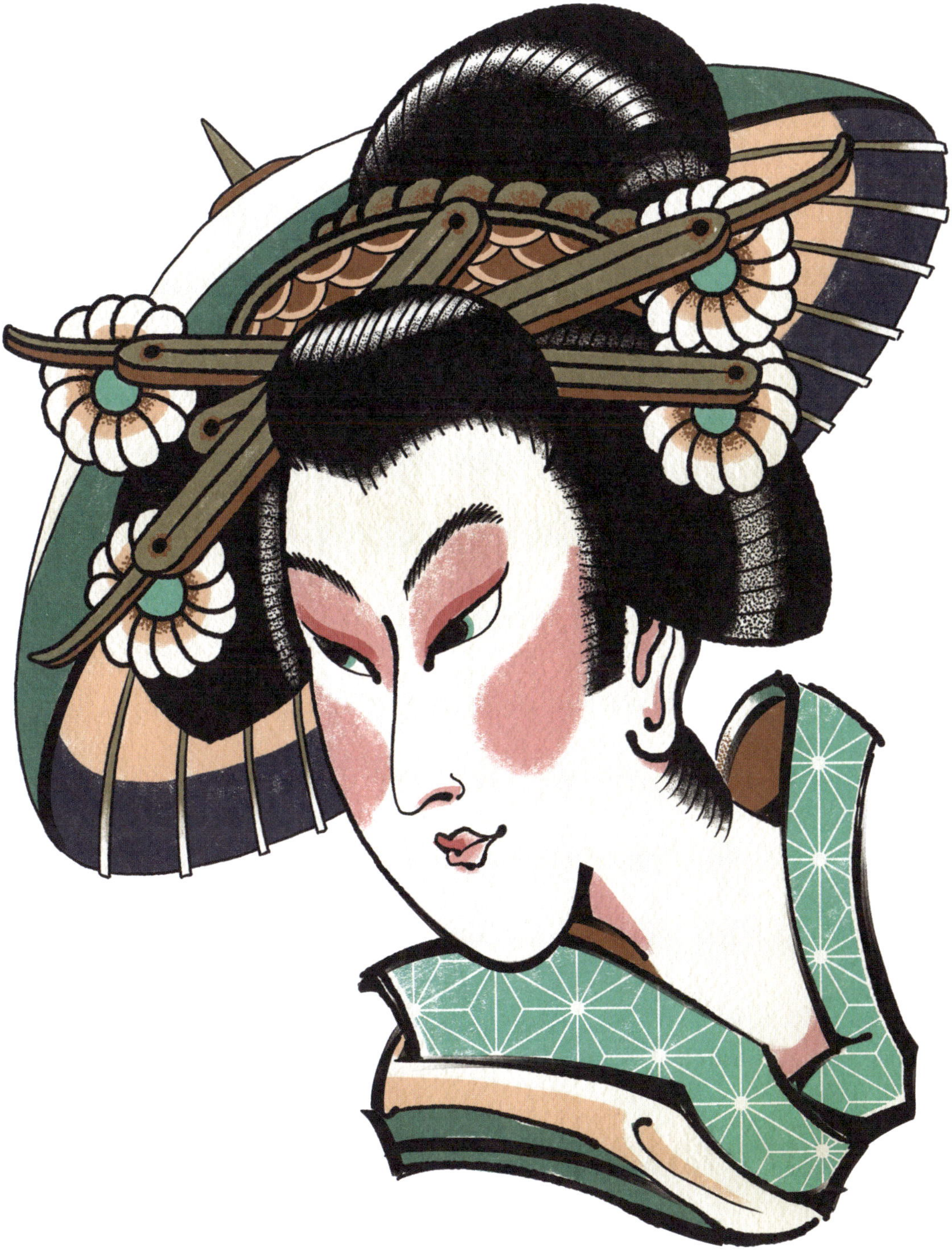

Cowboy

As with the cowgirl (see overleaf), the popular image of the cowboy blossomed with the swell of Victorian popular entertainment. A hallmark of the Wild West, the cowboy represented less the multicultural assemblage of people working the region and more an idealized personification of freedom.

The 19th century witnessed the rise of cowboy stars, such as Buffalo Bill, as well as renowned outlaws. These characters helped shape the tone of the image but, unlike the cowgirl, it was not a prevalent design in early 20th-century tattooing. However, within the neo-traditional style, celebration of the cowboy as a metaphor for free living is clear and constant.

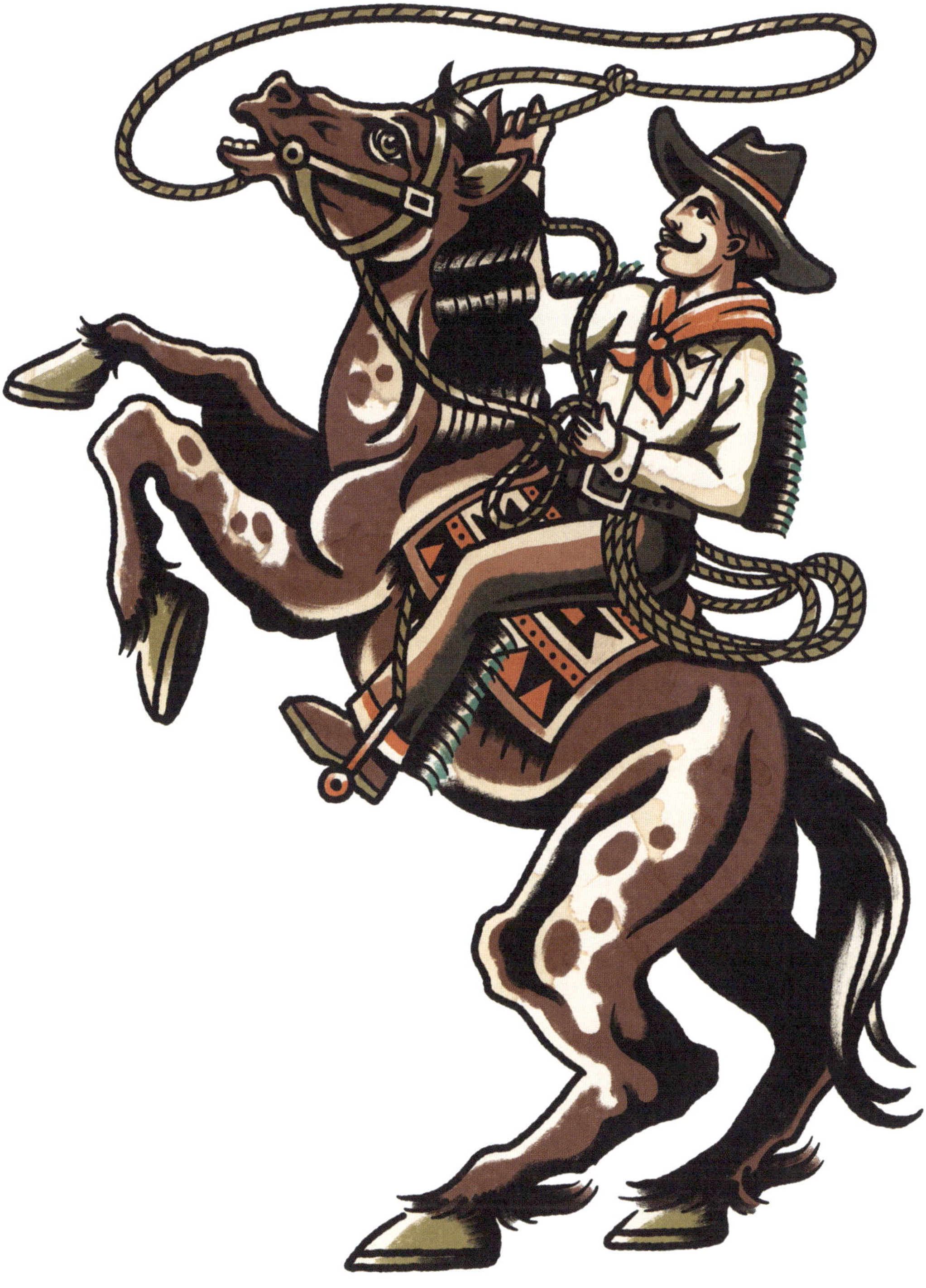

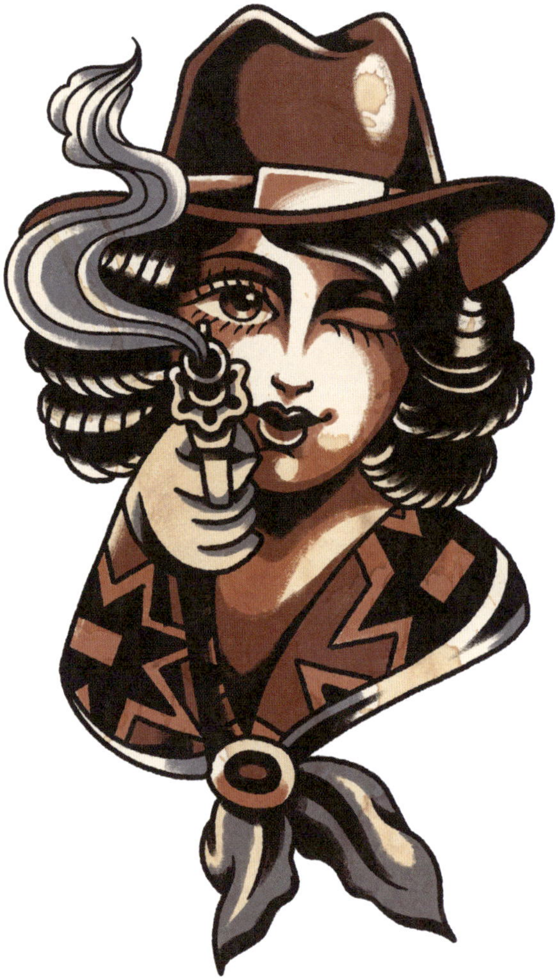

Cowgirl

During the final third of the 19th century, idealization of the cowgirl gained traction in the popular imagination through the sensational press coverage of tours such as Buffalo Bill's *Wild West Show*. Tough, beautiful women depicted sharp with pistol and rope helped form the standard image of a stunning figure adorned with brimmed hat and a bandana around the neck.

This vision of the cowgirl spread from papers and posters to flash sheets – where they remain consistent today. As with the pin-up (see page 156), these female-focused designs express desire. However, nuance comes in combination with the free-living stereotype of the Wild West outlaw, granting a more unbridled lust (for life, at least) to the image.

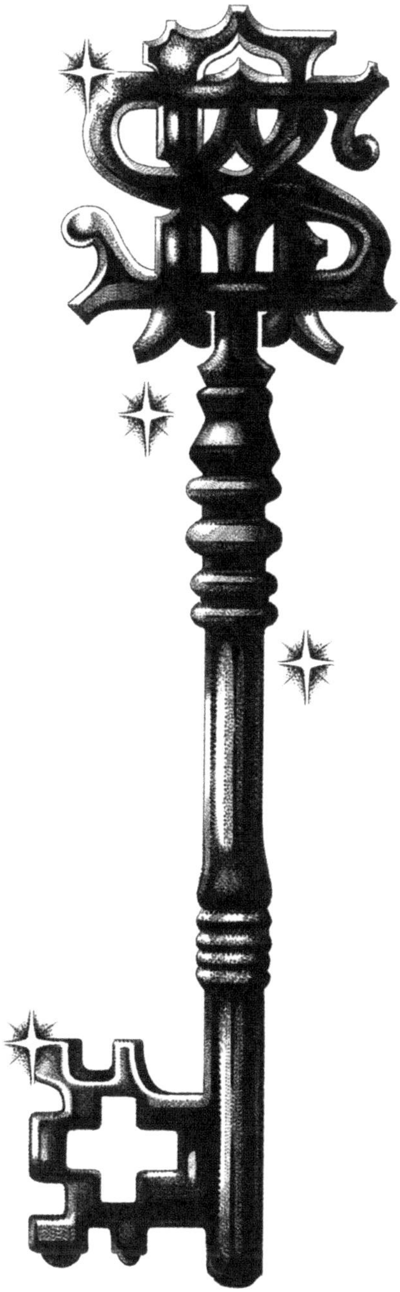

Key

The key represents, naturally, the ability to unlock potential. Tie that idea to freedom, and the key becomes a brilliant conduit for expressing a broad, bold vision of desire.

Stylistically, many key tattoos are modelled on Victorian skeleton keys, in which much exploration and variation of the bow (the bulbous portion of the key's anatomy) is evident. Designs range from simple ovals to hearts and build in complexity with ornate interlockings.

Mermaid

Mermaids are a natural fit for the western traditional style. Embodying all the mystique and visceral lure of the sea, the symbol conveys a thrilling combination of sensuality, freedom and independence.

The mermaid has origins in ancient mythology, as a charmer of seafarers with both beauty and song. Depicted in the visual arts since that time, mermaids appear as tattoos at least from the mid-19th century. One clear example was catalogued in naval records pertaining to Philadelphia-born sailmaker James Forten Dunbar, who was documented in 1863 as having a mermaid on his right forearm. As the tattoo design matured, similarities with the pin-up reinforced the connection between the charms of the ancient siren and sailor lust.

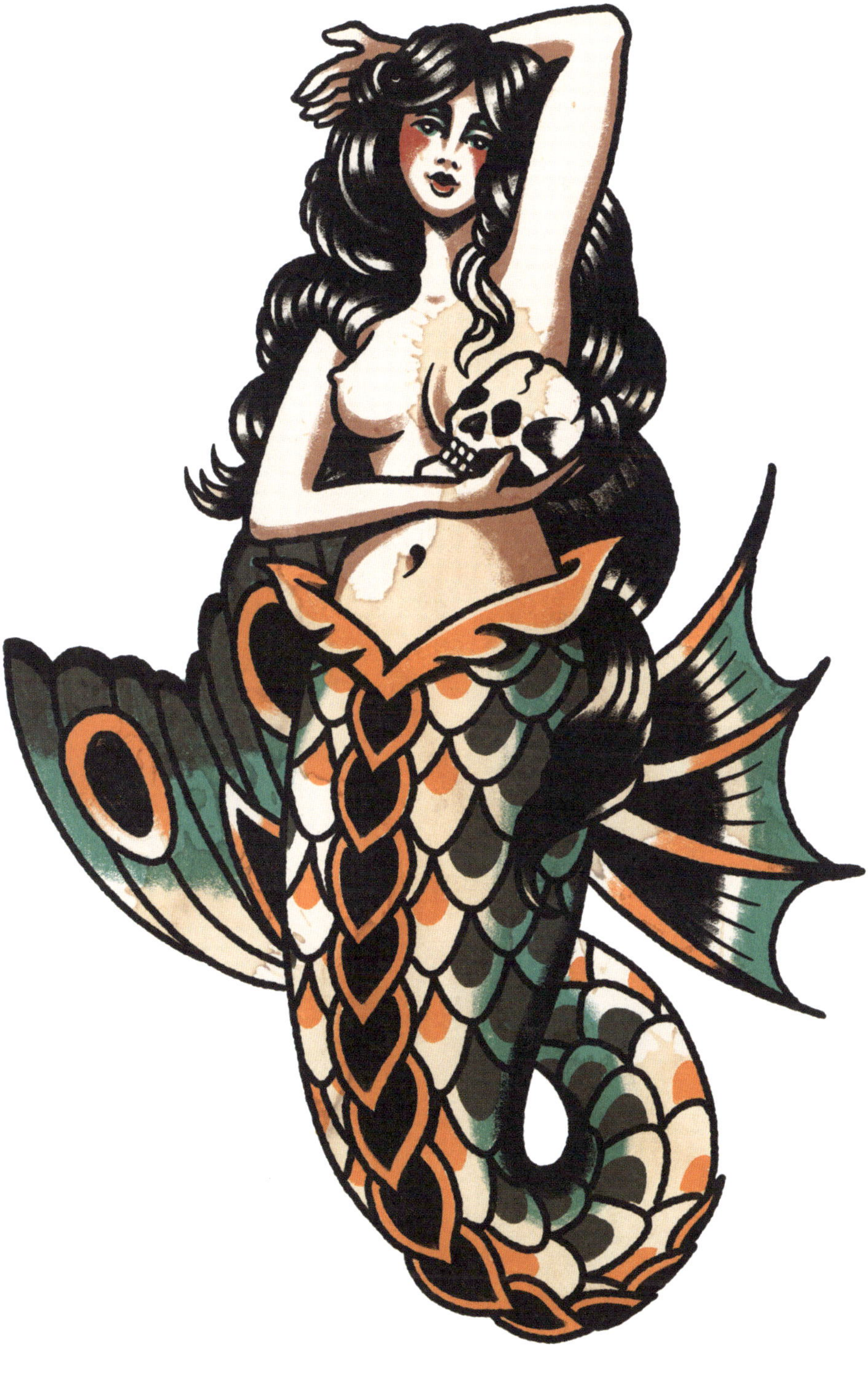

Cherry

The classic western traditional cherry tattoo carries strong sexual connotations: desire, lust, innocence, femininity, fertility and more. The aesthetic, a pop-driven pseudo-realism, follows from use of the cherry as a printed motif in fashion from the late 19th century onwards. By the 1940s and 1950s, the cherry had leapt from fabrics to Bakelite and flourished as celebrated mid-century kitsch.

Rockabilly nostalgia is one conduit for the enduring appeal of a cherry, too. The design is a revival of a certain '90s ebullience; the vibe of the eras common flash sheets, from Cheery Creek, rediscovered. While meaning ascribed to the cherry may not retain the same cultural reading as over a century ago, fresh societal nuances steady the core tenor (again, that sexual charge) with new opportunity.

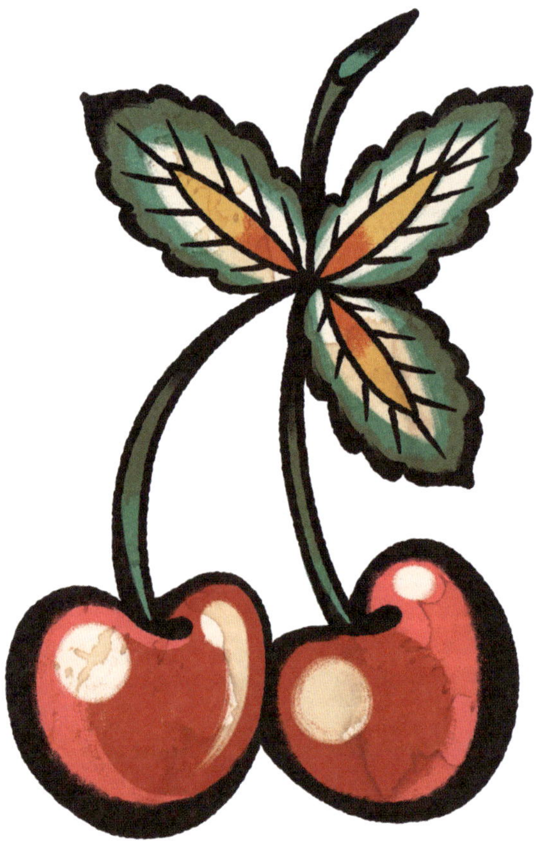

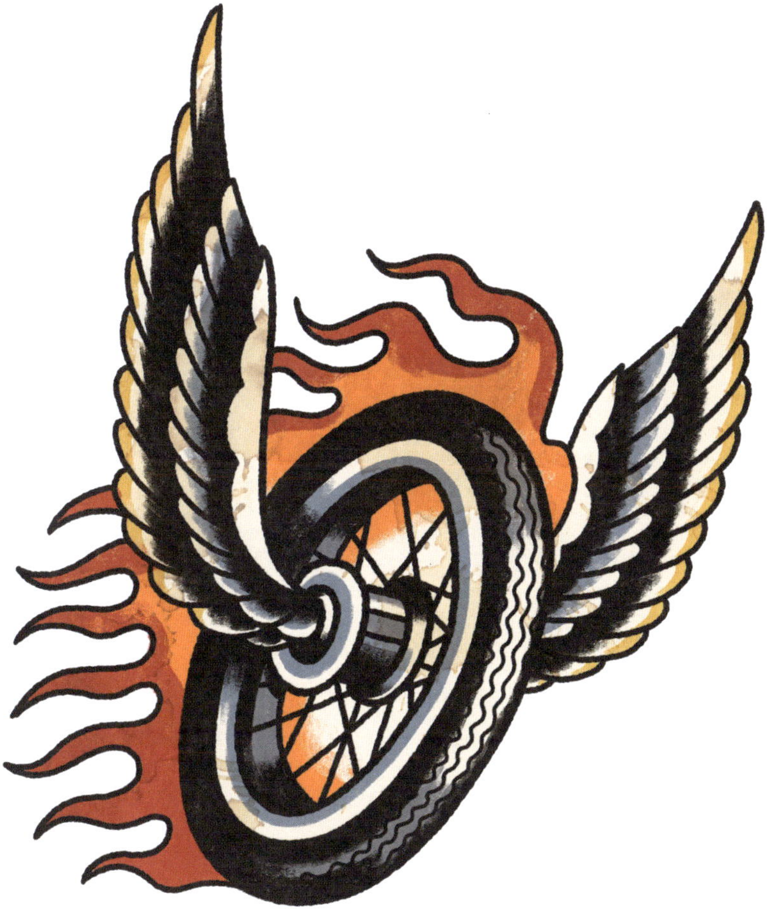

Flaming Motorcycle Wheel

Taking inspiration from the winged wheel, with its origins in Mesopotamia and links with the Greek god Hermes, cycling clubs and railway guards, the flaming motorcycle wheel speaks to deep burning passion and desire. Inherently, the design assumes movement. And, in practice, it represents a type of blazing wanderlust represented by motorcycles, the open road and all its inferred rebelliousness.

Such images are rooted in both the popular culture and tattooing of the 1940s, 1950s and 1960s, especially following films such as *The Wild One* (1954) and *Easy Rider* (1969). The association, stereotypical or otherwise, between outlaw and biker, was a significant theme within early tattoo magazines, where magazines dedicated to motorcycle culture featured tattoos, helping create some of the modern associations for the practice.

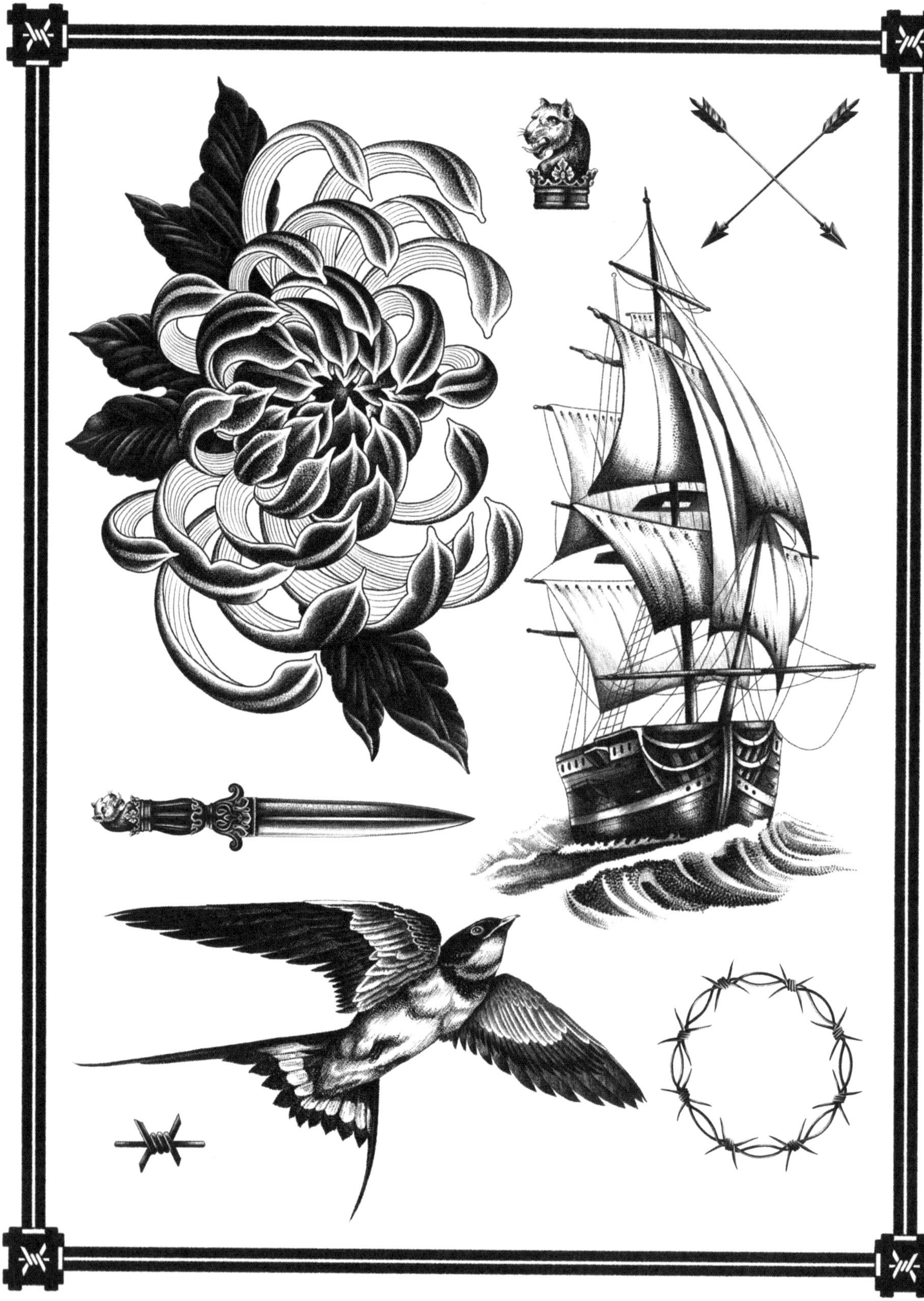

8

RESILIENCE

Toughness comes in various guises, particularly when it comes to tattoo-related symbols. While there are scores of designs and motifs representing strength, there far fewer specifically signifying durability of spirit.

Tattoos that acknowledge resilience generally split into two camps: those that validate the impact of a challenging journey and those that serve as talismans against a formidable experience. Both are important to tattooing's rich vernacular, expressive of, in the case of the koi, an honouring of century's rich mythology and, as with the boxer, the capacity to create an endearing and multifaceted symbol.

Western sailors made a high percentage of the symbols shared here famous – from the swallow to the glorious Homeward Bound composition. As tattoos, the endurance of these designs speaks to the centrality of client design to convey resolve over the decades, centuries and, perhaps, millennium. Adoption today shares not only the stickiness of the graphic integrity of the designs, but also reminds that symbols within tattooing continue to be adapted by successive generations.

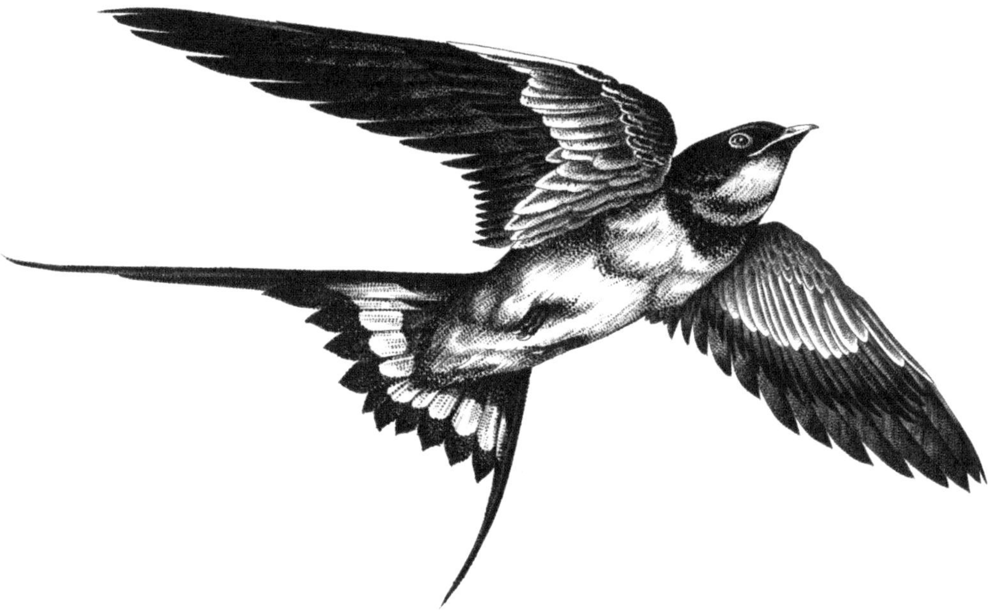

Swallow

The swallow tattoo is indebted to sailor lore. Several legends pay homage to the swallow's monogamy, migratory mates returning to the same breeding ground year after year. Sailors also associated the swallow with experience and tattooed themselves with the bird as testimony to their success in travelling long and dangerous distances: a single swallow denotes 5,000 miles (8,000 km) sailed; a pair 10,000 miles (16,000 km). The typical location of the swallow tattoo, on chest, hand or neck, follows sailor tradition, too. One further legend, from the British navy, suggested a swallow tattoo between thumb and forefinger upon the rounding of Cape Horn.

Today, the swallow tattoo appeals to those wishing to commemorate a journey or voyage. It has become a universal symbol of resilience and is one of the most recognized designs in the western traditional style.

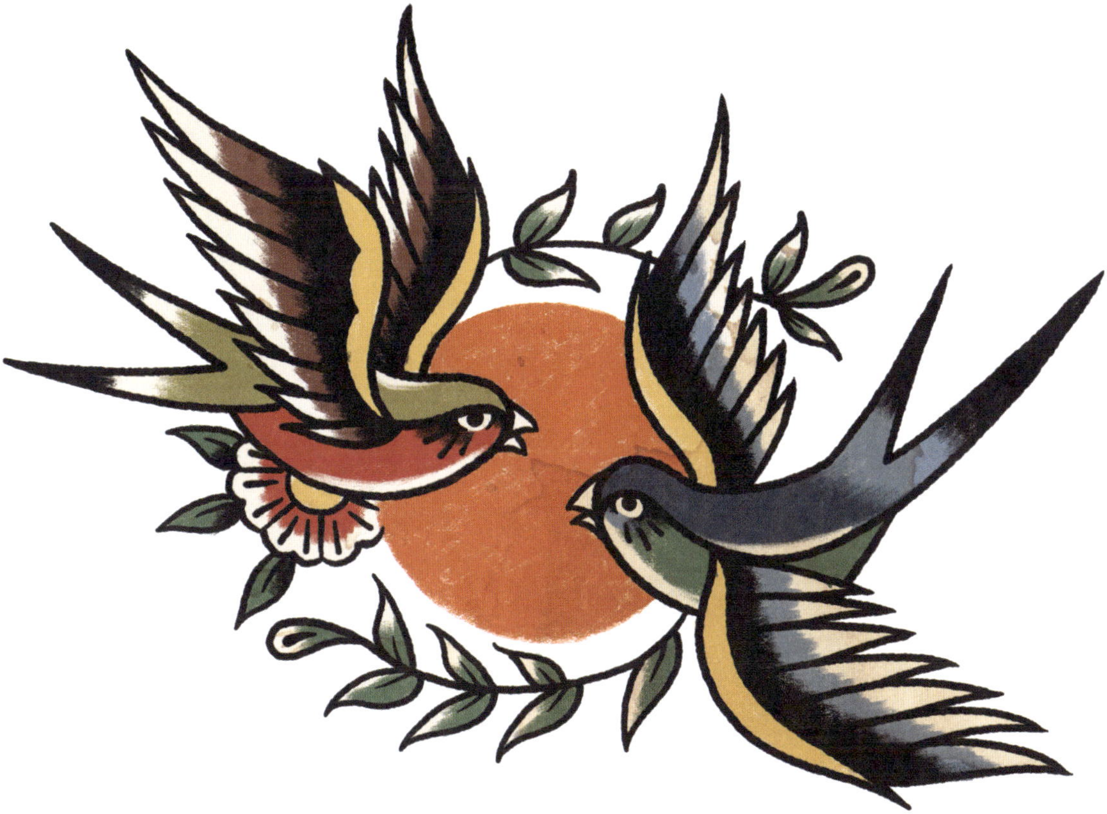

Boxer

Classic boxer tattoos epitomize toughness and resilience. Designs in the western traditional style take a cartoon-like stance, the idea being to exaggerate the (primarily) male physique and play up the wearer's inner strength by bolstering their outer strength.

The boxer conveys a 'life can't knock me down' message, although combining figures with banners of text allow for more literal proclamations. Additionally, the body of the boxer itself may be decorated with tattoos, layering meaning, and giving the design both a personal and a playful punch.

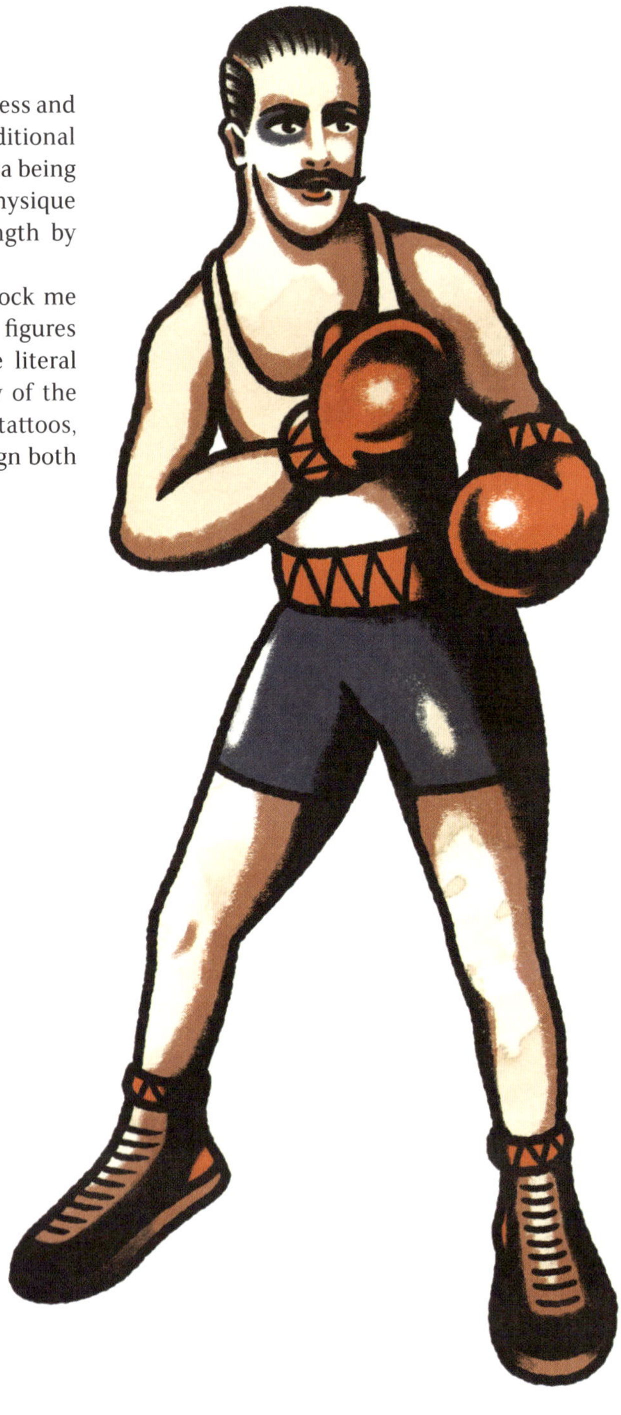

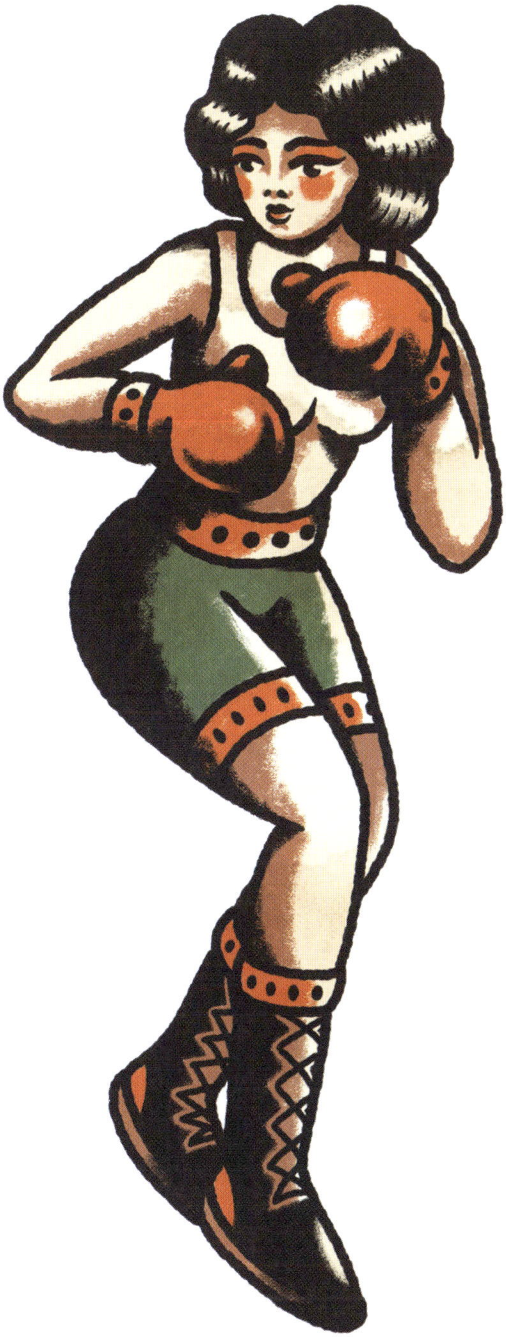

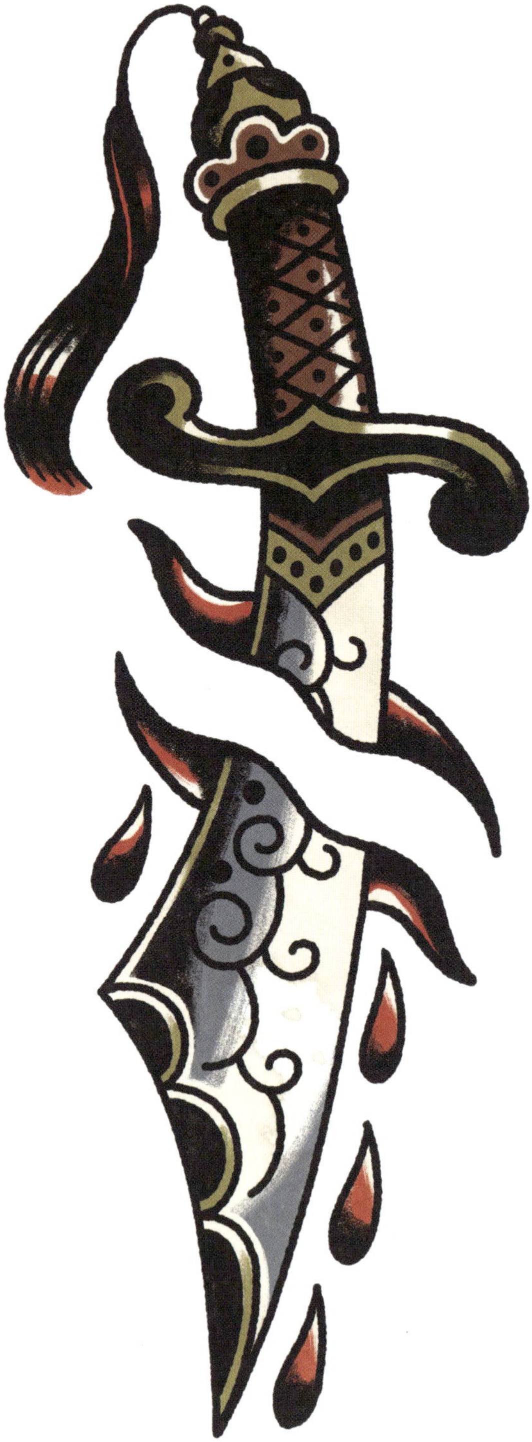

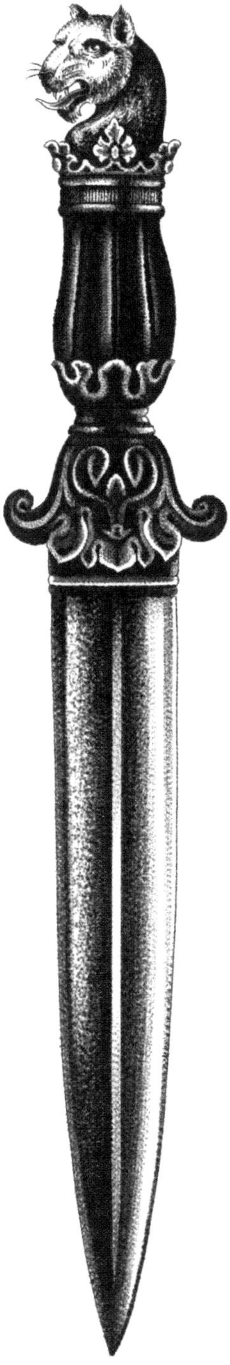

Dagger

The traditional dagger tattoo conveys the fighting spirit of the wearer. As with the swift, brutal use of the weapon in combat, as a symbolic device, the dagger is suited to strong, blunt statements.

Many designs embrace it as a device for celebrating protection and sacrifice. Paired with a rose, for example, a dagger expresses a willingness to defend the vulnerable. Adorned with a banner reading 'Too Tough to Die', the dagger signifies bravery in facing one's mortality. Positioned with a heart, the dagger represents the polarities of love (beauty, pain and loss). These examples explore a specific potential for dagger tattoos, one in which the composition allows the wearer to explore opposing life forces specific to their individual journey.

Homeward Bound

A full-rigged clipper, its bow splitting waves, and a triumphant banner reading 'Homeward Bound' stands as one of the most iconic images of western traditional tattooing. The design's immediacy emphasizes the potency of its narrative, and it serves as an amulet for sailors aware of dangerous and lengthy voyages that lie both in the past and in the future. In sailor lore, homeward bound tattoos are associated with 'rounding the Cape' or 'rounding the Horn', navigating the crashing waves and heavy currents where the Atlantic and Pacific Oceans meet above the icebergs of Antarctica. Recording one's escape from the clear threat of danger, and the risk of succumbing to a watery grave, was paramount.

Compositionally, the homeward bound design was crystallized in the early 20th century by legends such as Bert Grimm, often appearing on fully covered bodies. The clipper might be augmented by clouds and rippling water. It might also be framed by fish or sit atop an eagle. Contemporary deviations might place the clipper in a bottle. Regardless, the power of the image derives from its resolute spirit and a belief in overcoming challenge.

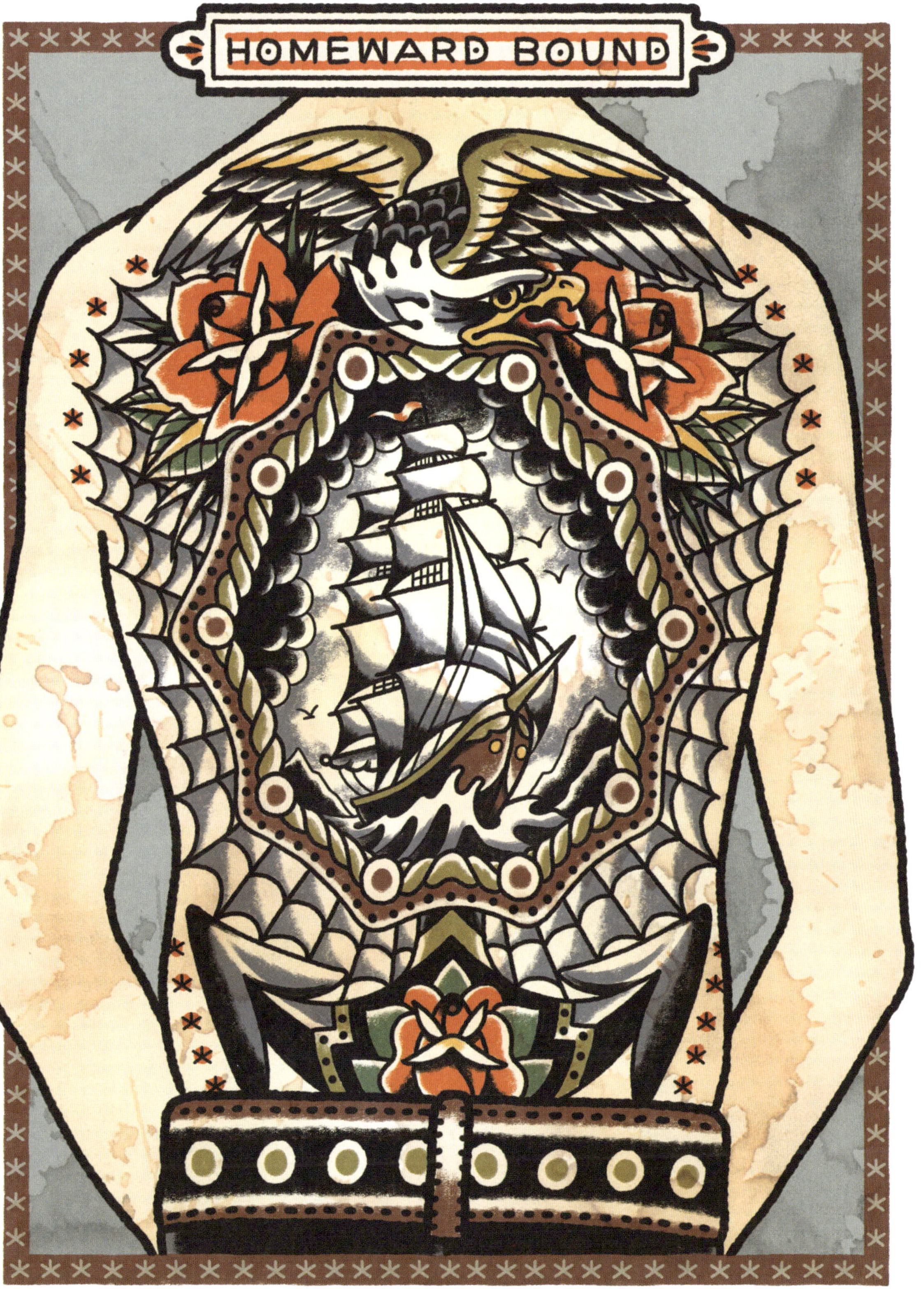
HOMEWARD BOUND

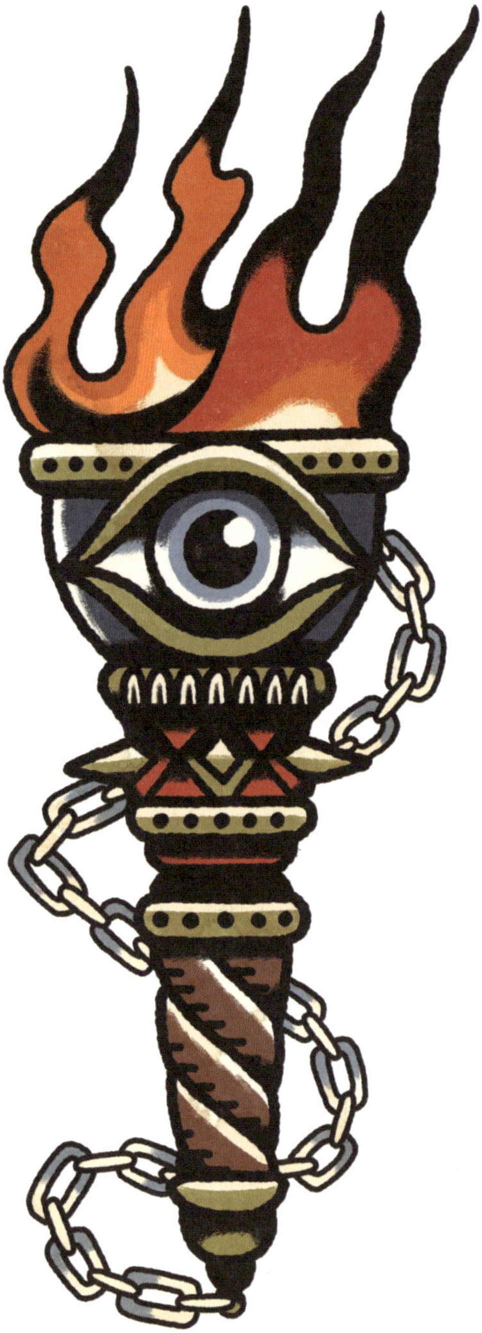

Torch

Popular in 19th-century funerary symbolism, the inverted torch with burning flame, represents eternal life. The symbol derives from Greek and Roman mythology (specifically the gods Thanatos and Mors) and additional motifs, such as wreaths and wings, evidence the Victorian trend for reviving and formalizing perceived pagan ritual.

Depicting the inverted torch with a wreath denotes victory over death; wings suggest a smooth journey into the afterlife. Employment of an inverted image may also serve as a reorientation of life, of putting one stage to rest and setting forth on a new chapter.

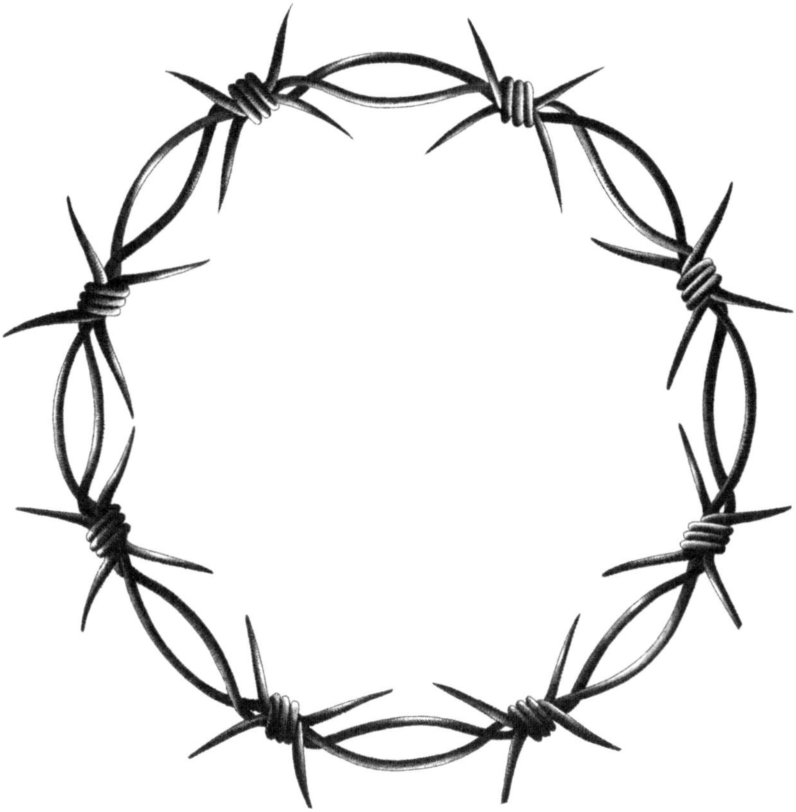

Barbed Wire

Patented in the 1860s, the use of barbed wire to define controlled spaces spread quickly in the late 19th and early 20th centuries. The characteristic barbs are harrowing, striking, visceral – characteristics that serve tattooing well. For those who came of age in the 1990s, barbed wire tattoos carry cringe-inducing associations with mass-market cool. Produced as bicep bands, loosely mimicking the era's watering down of neo-tribal style, barbed wire adorned the bodies of Hollywood A-listers and professional athletes alike.

Despite the numbing ubiquity of the design at that time, barbed wire tattoos symbolize faith during struggle. There is a Christian connection to Jesus' crown of thorns, and, more universally, the wire represents strength and perseverance. Wrap a heart with barbed wire, and the composition speaks to redemption. Connect with a rose, and a story of peace overcoming danger blossoms. Each of these options, and several more interconnected barbed wire designs, confirm resilience in the face of challenge.

Arrow

The arrow is one of the most adaptable symbols in tattooing, where popular associations with love (and cupid) abound. The most potent connections, however, derive from Native American tradition. Arrows are tools for sustenance, through hunting, and for protection. Crossed arrows represent a truce, or alliance, while a broken arrow signals harmony and peace.

Adaptations relate to a central theme of triumph over struggle, of finding calm and moving confidently into a new phase of life. For many contemporary wearers, the arrow signals positive direction.

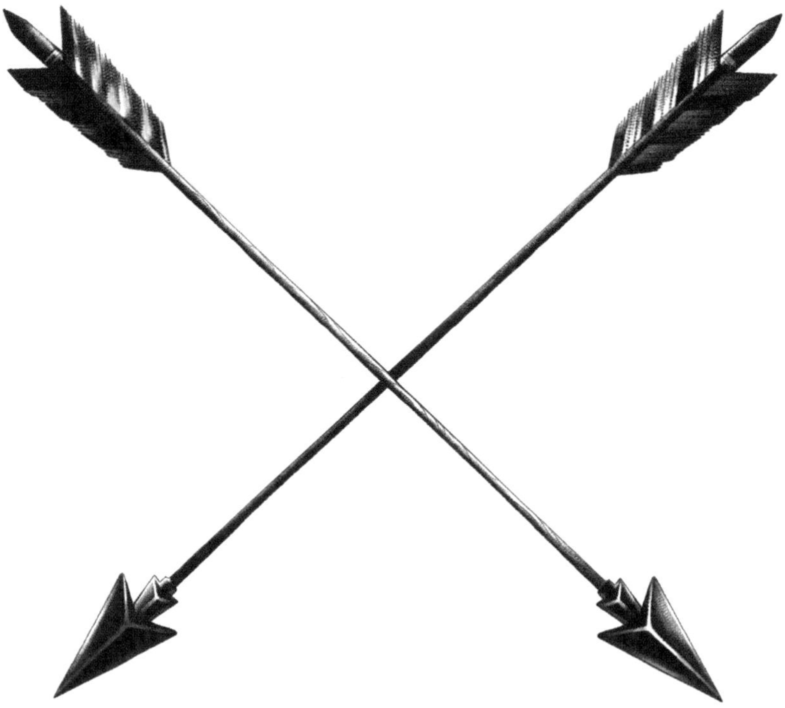

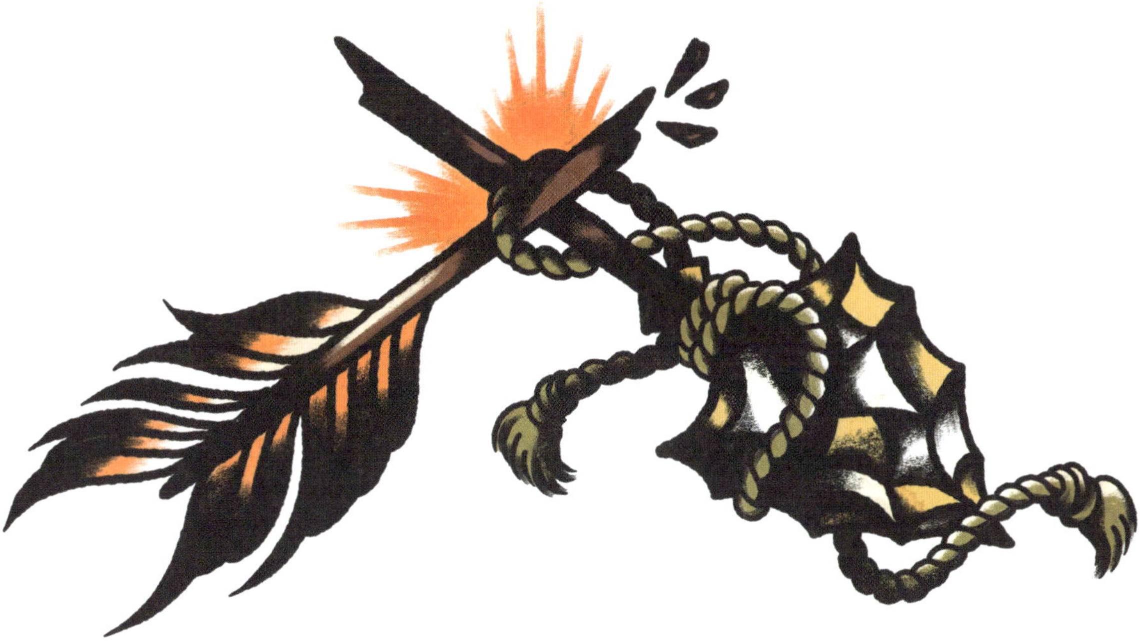

Ship

Sailors' have worn ship tattoos for centuries. In fact, numerous American seamen documented by Sailor Protection Certificates (which protected carriers from forced foreign naval service) in the late 1700s included notes on tattoos. The certificates themselves were employment-related, as were the tattoos in many cases, including anchors, wheels and vessels, and similar association between the ship and safe return is achieved by pairing a boat with a compass.

While the origin of the ship tattoo is firmly entrenched in seafaring lore and community, contemporary depictions stretch the mystique to an all-encompassing celebration of life's journey. A ship can represent a spiritual awakening towards a new beginning.

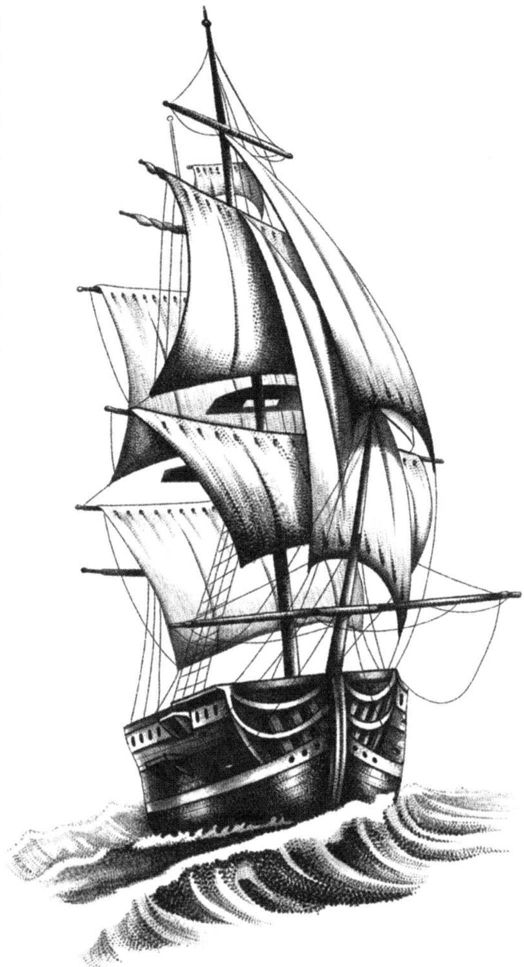

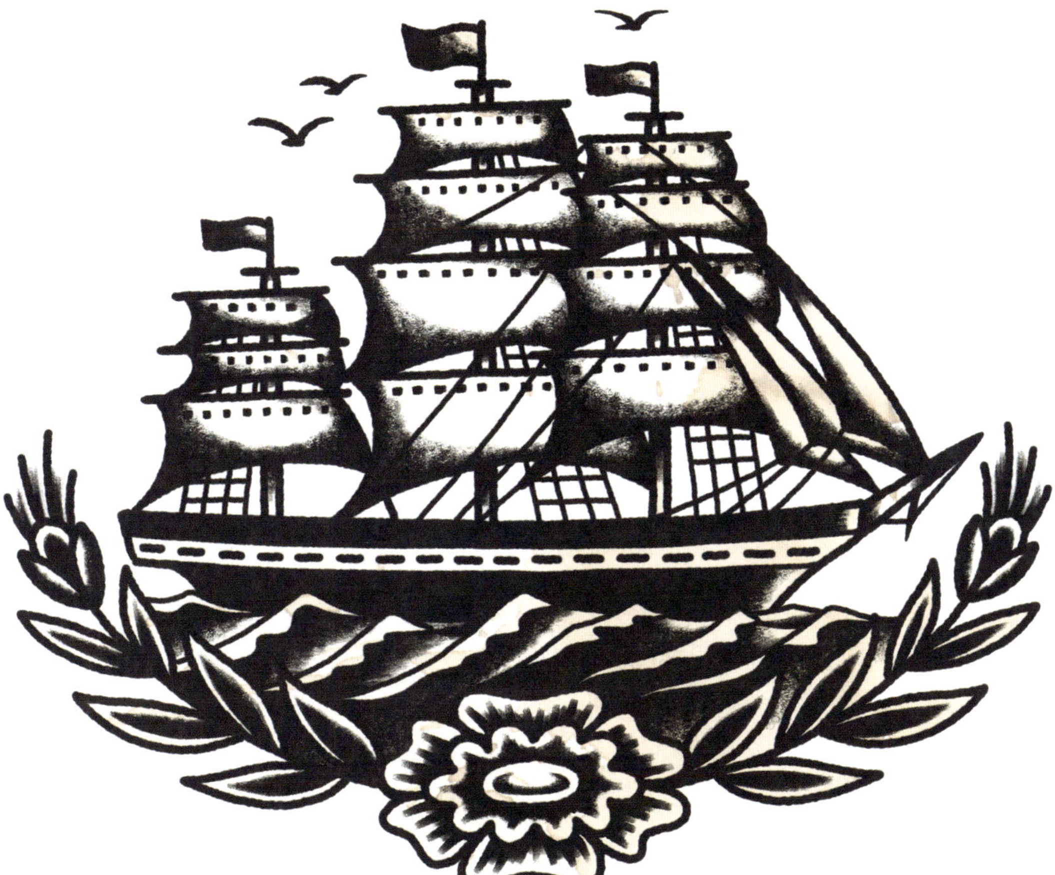

Chrysanthemum

Blooming in autumn, the chrysanthemum's cycle brings beauty despite the oncoming winter. It is one of the most cultivated flowers in the world, with more than 20,000 different cultivars identified, and as such carries nuanced meaning across different cultures. For example, in parts of Europe, the flower is given to express sympathy and is specifically associated with death. However, in Asia, the chrysanthemum symbolizes a long and happy life. This is the meaning most frequently represented in tattooing, where the chrysanthemum stands for longevity and devotion.

In Irezumi, the chrysanthemum motif is associated with the imperial family, symbolizing perfection and chivalry. These characteristics underscore the longevity and joy required to maintain harmonious order in society. Chrysanthemums also figure in tattoos that honour recovery – whether from illness or some other challenge – extending the core meaning and more overtly referencing a resilient spirit.

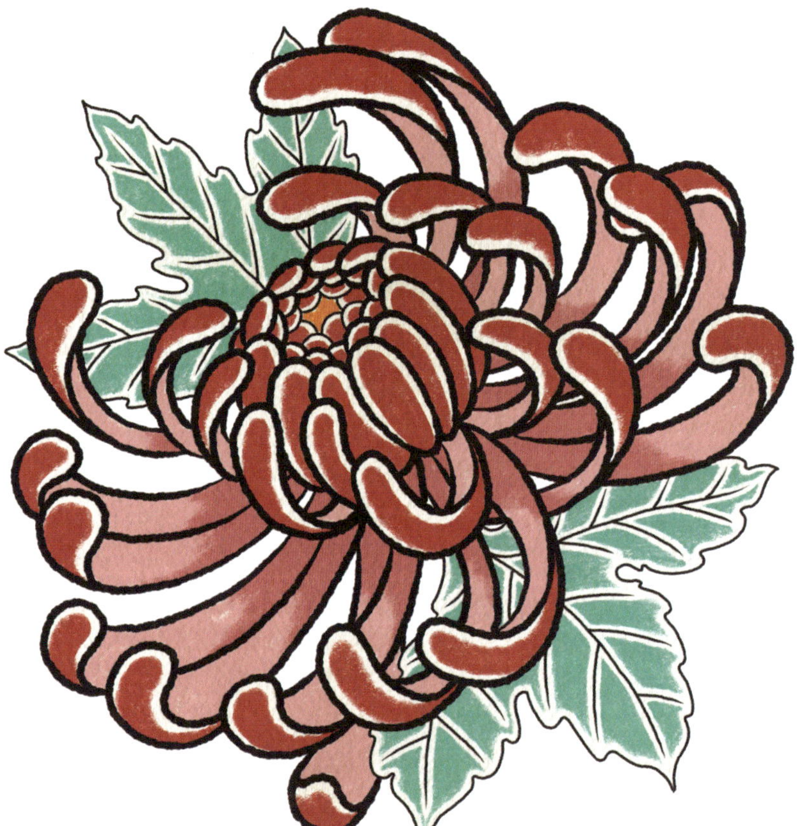

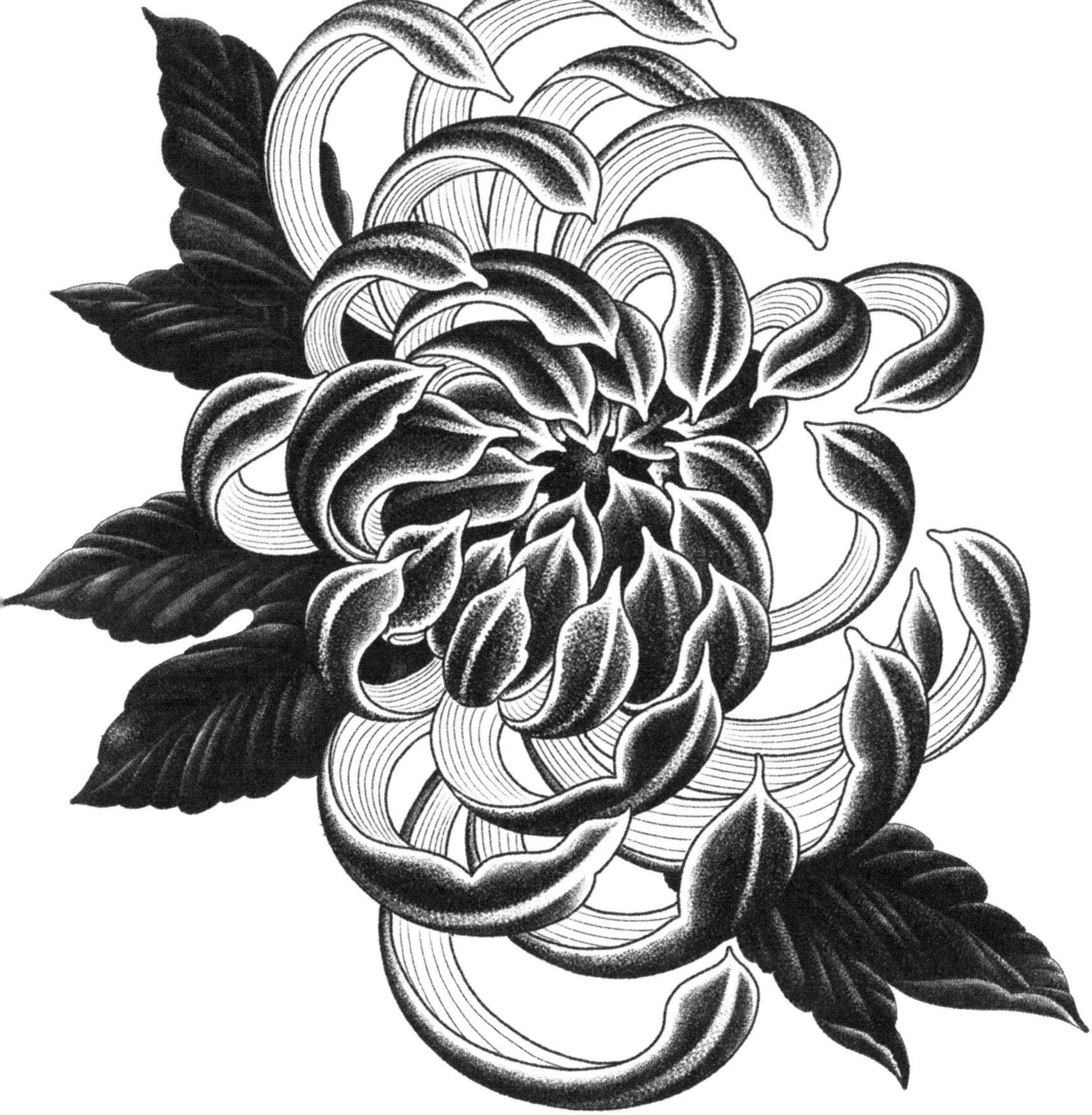

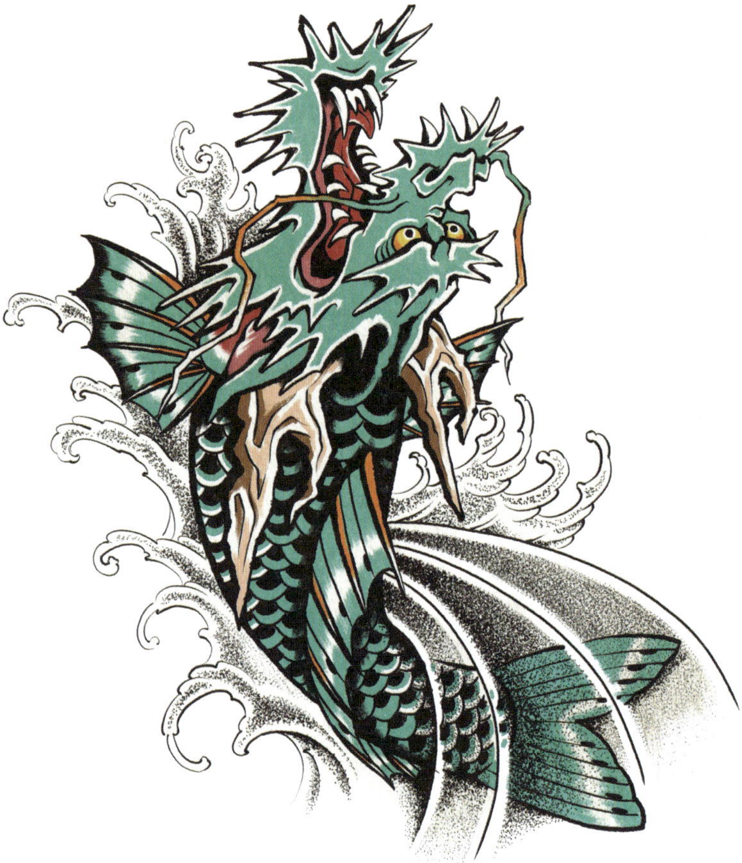

Koi

Most simply, koi – an ornamental variety of carp – stand for courage and perseverance. In both Chinese and Japanese legend, the fish stars in tales of overcoming insurmountable challenge. The most famous myth finds the koi tirelessly progressing upstream, pushing beyond rapid currents before reaching a waterfall. Undeterred by repeated failures, as well as mocking by onlooking demons, the koi finally reaches the top and transforms into a magnificent dragon. The koi's resilience thus allows it to become an even greater creature.

In tattooing, compositions of koi commonly depict the fish moving upwards in recognition of the myth and its powerful symbolism. A koi depicted downstream is by no means representative of failure. In contrast, it relays that the wearer has reached a tranquil place – years of resilience in overcoming obstacles now allowing for a period of calm. Colour choice is also significant: a black koi is associated with overcoming challenge, red with intense love.

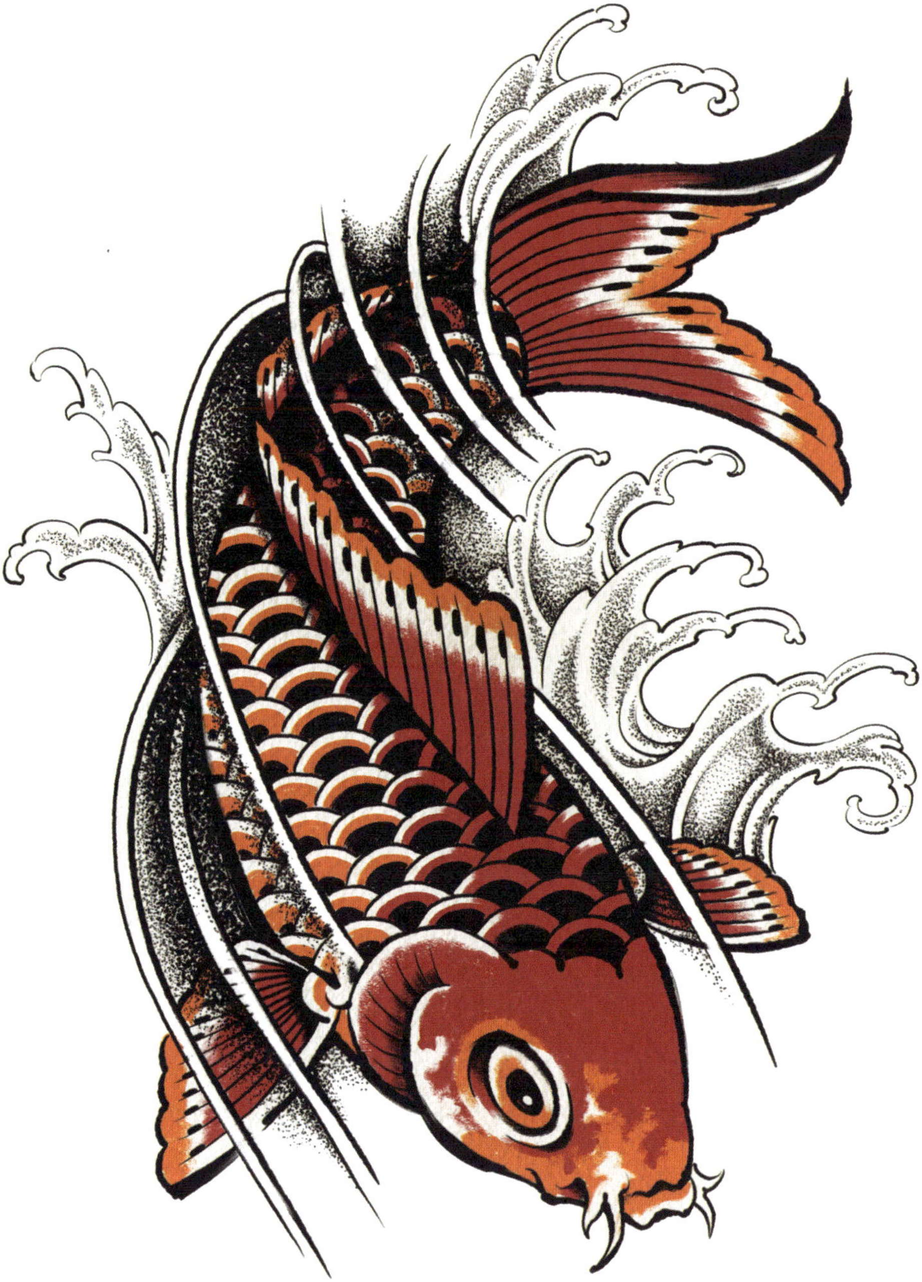

Bulldog

Many popular designs entered the tattoo lexicon during war time. Among those is the instantly recognizable United States Marine Corps (USMC) bulldog, or 'devil dog', which was born during World War I and has continued to relay a specific resilience ever since.

The composition, which features an English bulldog in battle helmet, stems from a 1917 USMC recruitment poster. Reading 'Teufel Hunden' (devil dogs), the poster refers to a German nickname for US Marines, granting it a tough, jowly and unforgettable image. The bulldog became the USMC's unofficial mascot, with a string of famous enlistees joining from 1922.

In contemporary tattooing, associations with determination and stubbornness to challenge remain tied to the bulldog. Its image, now in a wide variety of western traditional articulations, is not only a common one on flash sheets, but also an ever-popular design.

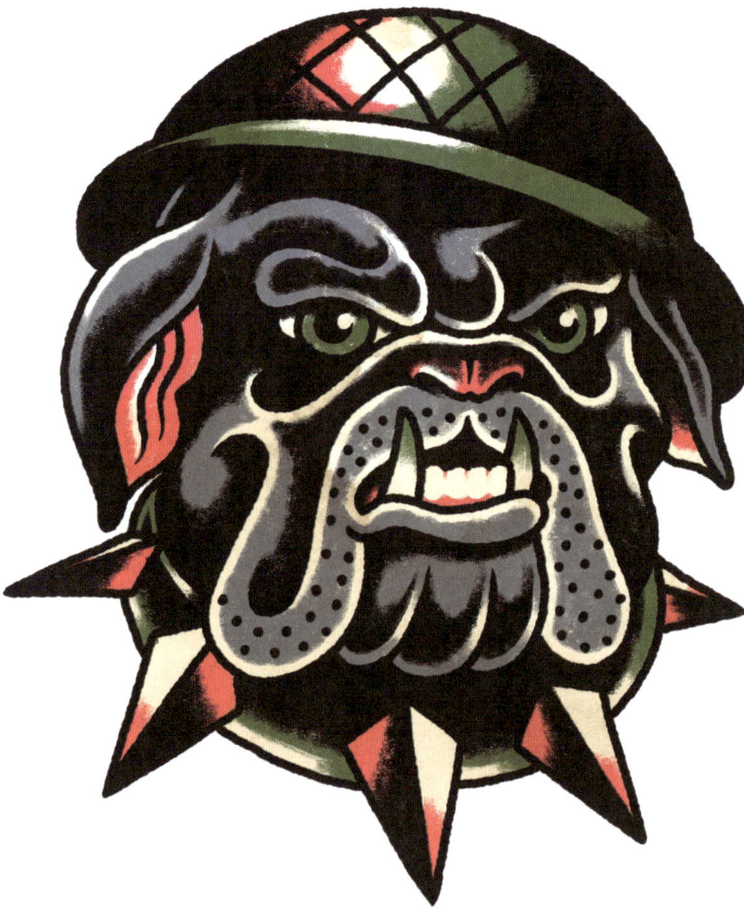

Death Before Dishonor

The phrase 'death before dishonour' says it all: a privileging of upright service above all else.

Historically, variations of the idiom flow from the Bushido code of the Japanese samurai and through centuries of European military units. Another relation to the phrase derives from the ancient Roman story of Lucius Verginius, who killed his daughter, Verginia, rather than have her virtue taken by the corrupt Appius Claudius. This tale, along with the phrase 'death before dishonor', appeared in the pages of *Harper's Weekly* in 1844, depicted by cartoonist Thomas Nast, and would have been easily read in relation to 19th-century honour culture. Elements of these beliefs are further disseminated in 20th-century comic books.

Most commonly, death before dishonour tattoos include strong graphic elements, such as daggers, or symbols of national pride, such as the eagle. The words of the phrase are elevated above the graphic elements in a flowing banner. And while there is clear connection today with military service, particularly the US Marine Corps' *Semper Fidelis* (Always Faithful) motto, the application for anyone wishing to convey a life lived without compromise rings strong.

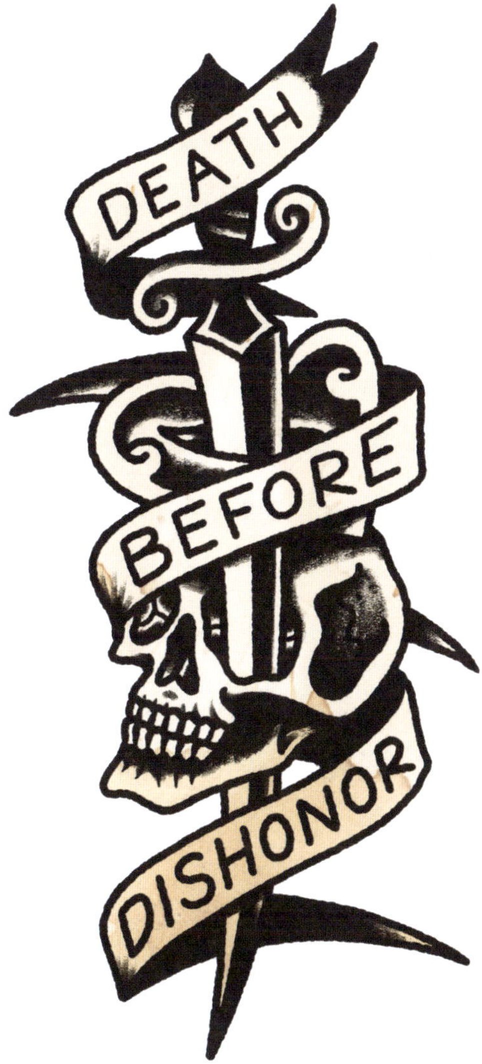

Cockerel

One of the prevailing interpretations of a rooster, or cockerel, in tattooing derives from maritime folklore. Housed in wooden crates on deck, roosters and pigs were believed to have a high rate of survival in the event of a shipwreck. The duo formed a tattoo conceit – pig and rooster – with the rooster on the top of the right foot and pig on top of the left. Together, they offered luck against tragedy.

Cockerel tattoos are, however, not defined by this association alone. As with many tattoo designs in the Western cannon, rooster and cockerel images have 20th-century meanings. The bird's inherent courage and fight (celebrated from World War I as an unofficial symbol of France) primarily serves as a reference to toughness and masculinity. A self-confident and, ultimately, resilient attitude is imbued within designs featuring the rooster.

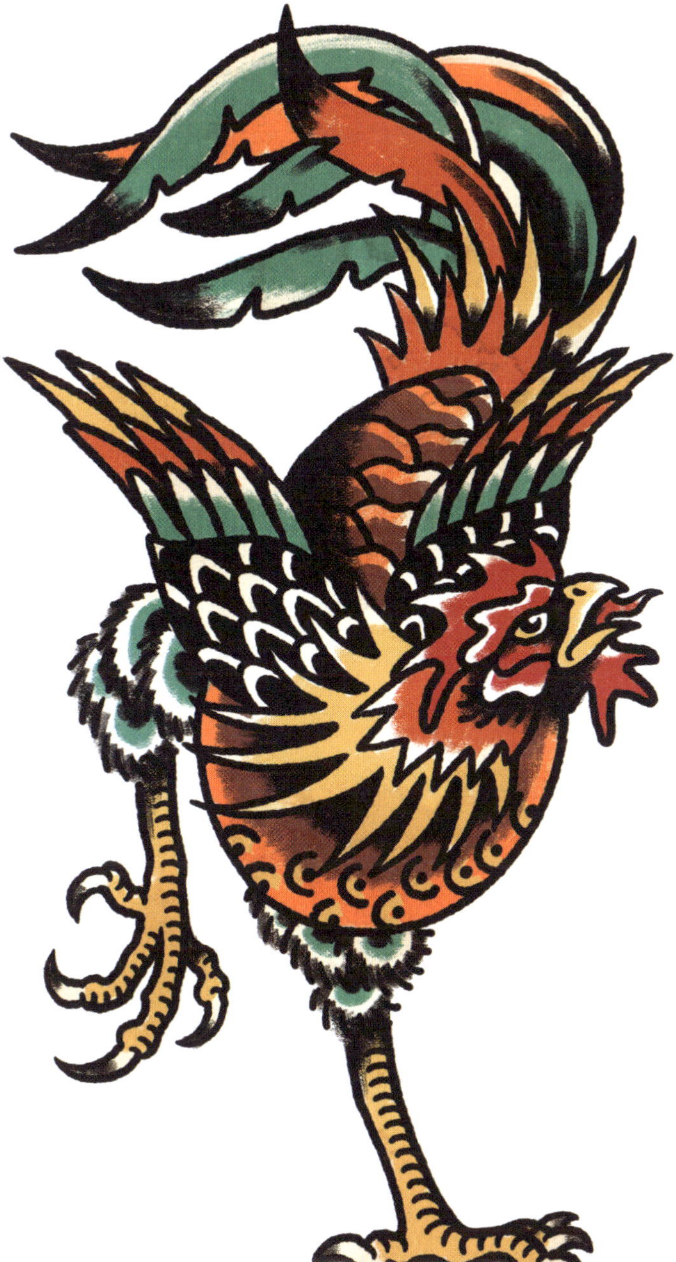

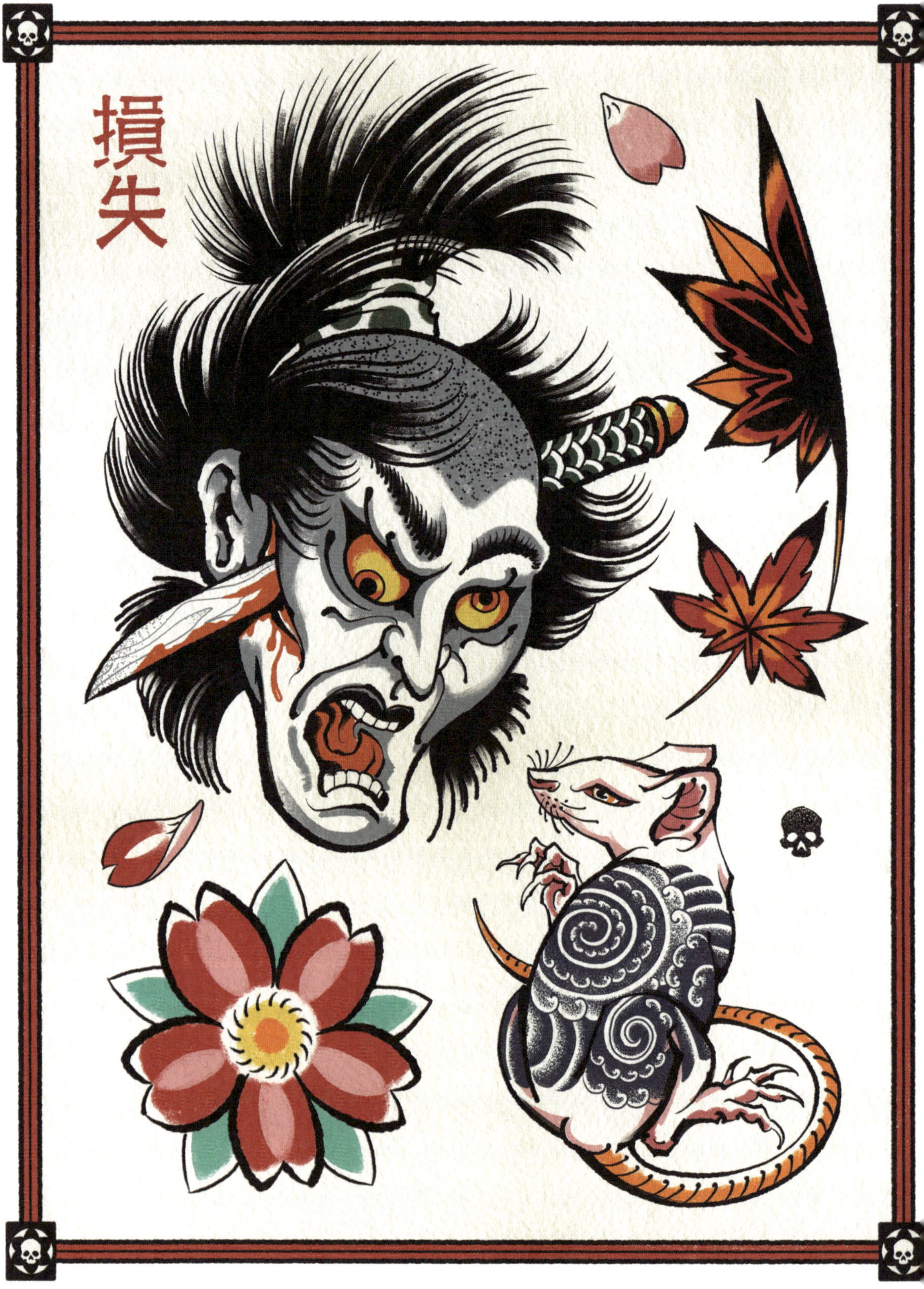
損失

9

LOSS, MEMORY AND TRANSIENCE

The spectre of death, and of finality, looms large. In tattooing, issues of loss and memory, and of transience and death, are natural subjects. Even if they do not address mortality directly, they reflect associations of time spent or passed.

The fact that tattooing and death ritual began to commercialize at roughly the same time may account for the prominence of mourning art in 19th-century flash sheets. Weeping willows, tombstones, grieving sons – all are common. Elaborate, almost prescriptive customs made commemoration of the dead a defining activity of the era. It held a thoroughly sombre tone, with death embraced as a moment to linger on loss itself.

Even older symbols, such as those derived from Roman tradition, carry a deep darkness. Mid-20th-century favourites like the firecracker cat, are an almost tongue-in-cheek revival of that ancient macabre. Meanwhile, the neo-Edwardian flare of some 2000s designs gives space for play on time-keeping and time lost.

Symbols like cherry blossom encourage a celebratory embrace of ephemerality. Similarly, Day of the Dead iconography shares a more exuberant perspective on death as compared to Victorian behaviours. And even the grim reaper, as terrifying a figure as any, can convey a positive sense of the wearer's hold on time.

Rat

The rat has an unshakable association with plague, blamed as it was for spreading the Black Death during the 14th century. And while scientific evidence for this is lacking, rats continue to be linked with disease and death.

More potent, however, is this creature's association with fertility and resilience. These characteristics are clear in Chinese zodiac symbolism, where the rat is championed for ambition and intelligence.

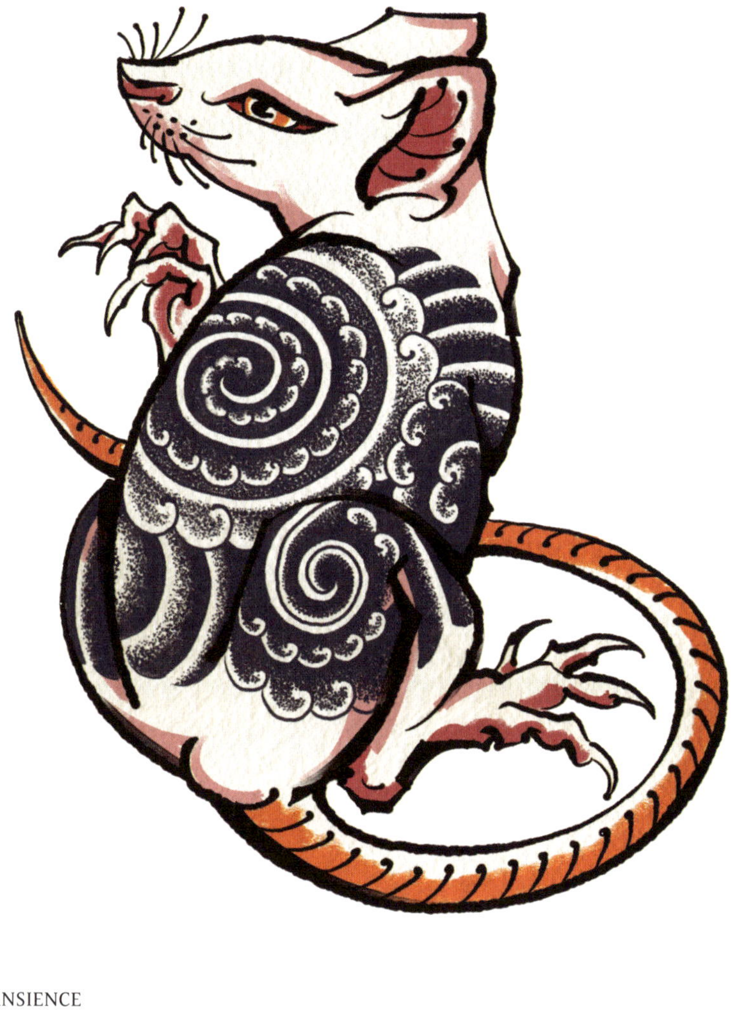

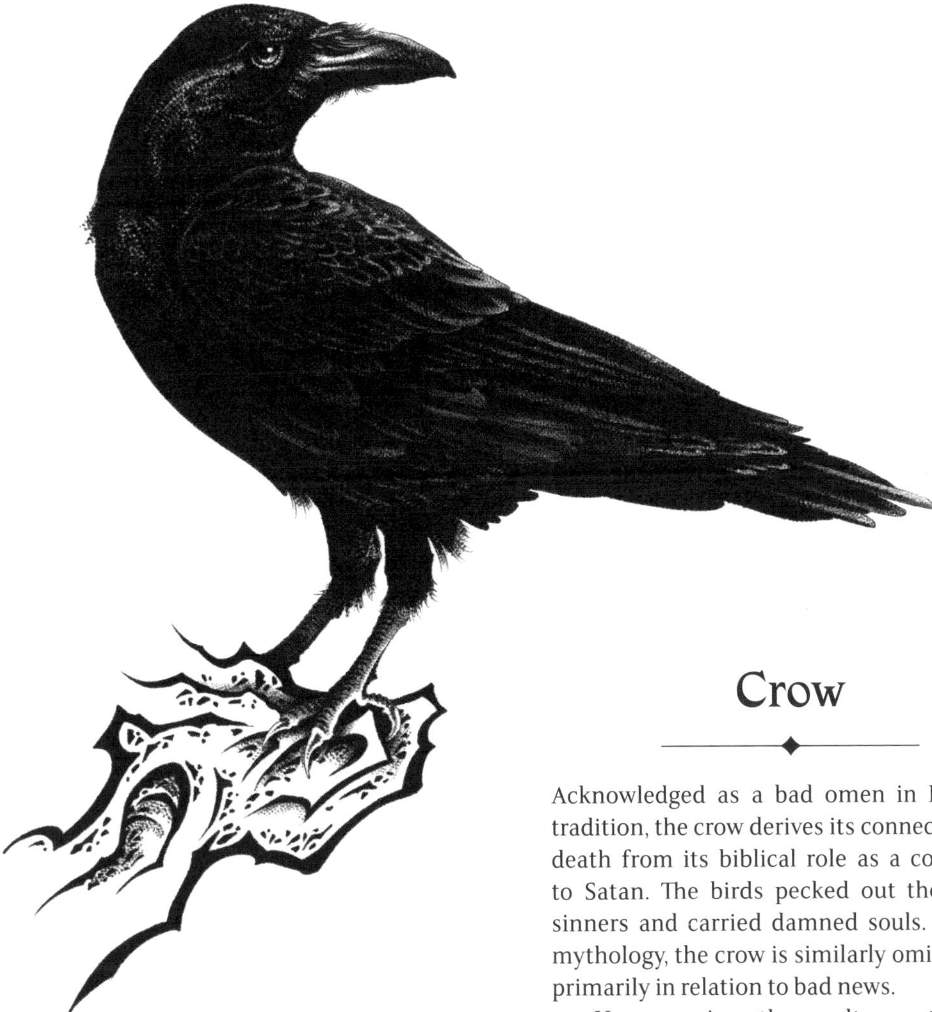

Crow

Acknowledged as a bad omen in European tradition, the crow derives its connection with death from its biblical role as a companion to Satan. The birds pecked out the eyes of sinners and carried damned souls. In Greek mythology, the crow is similarly ominous, but primarily in relation to bad news.

However, in other cultures, the crow carries more positive associations with transience. Shinto tradition treats the crow (*karasu*), in particular the three-legged Yatagarasu, as a divine intervention guiding luck and decision making. Native American cultures view the crow as a mediator between the land of the living and land of the dead.

This breadth of association allows some diversity in representation. But alignment with the 'in-between' gives the crow a versatility in designs driven to explore transience and monumental shifts.

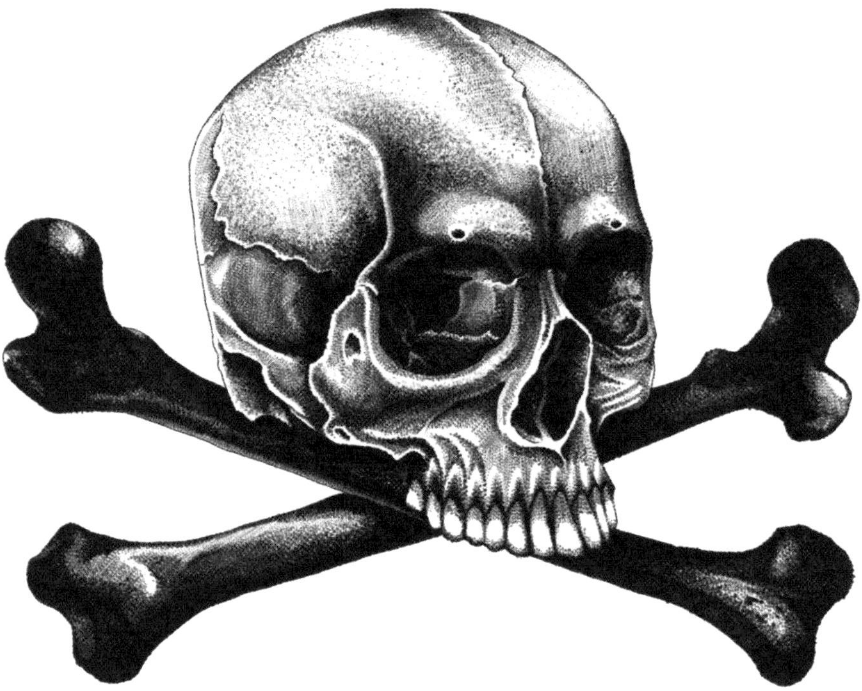

Skull and Crossbones

Many point to the Capuchin Crypt in Rome as home of one of the original skull and crossbones symbols. There, the icon lives in eternity alongside 4,000 resting souls of the order's monks. The crypt stands as a visceral, powerful memento mori and the skull and crossbones is now a universal emblem of death, used as a standard warning sign against hazards since the 1880s.

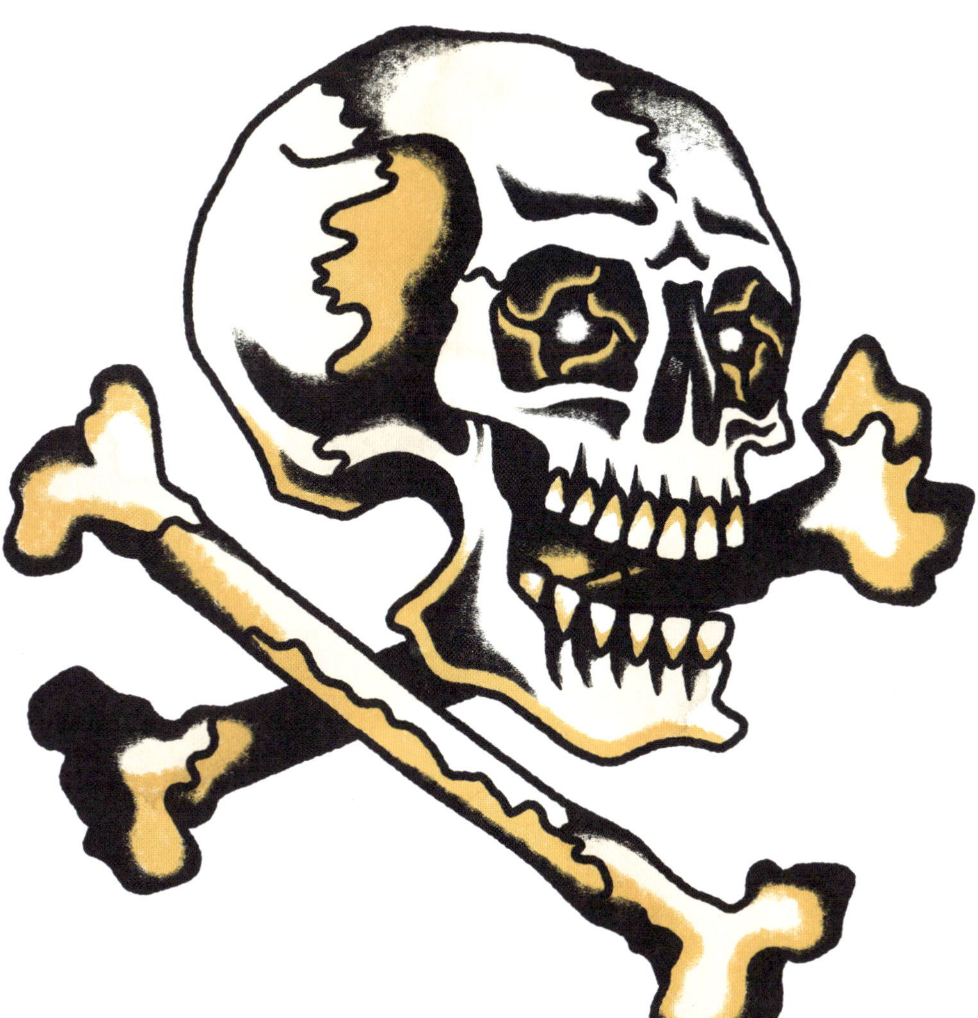

Calacas

Commonly decorated with flowers and butterflies, the colourful *día de muertos* skull (or candy skull) references Mexican tradition in honouring the dead. The creation of wooden skulls, known as *calacas*, correlates to the celebration of All Saints' Day and All Souls' Day at the beginning of November, which gained popularity after the Mexican Revolution. During the festivities, the skulls are given as gifts to both the living and the dead. As tattoos, they reference strength in familial lineage and celebration of life.

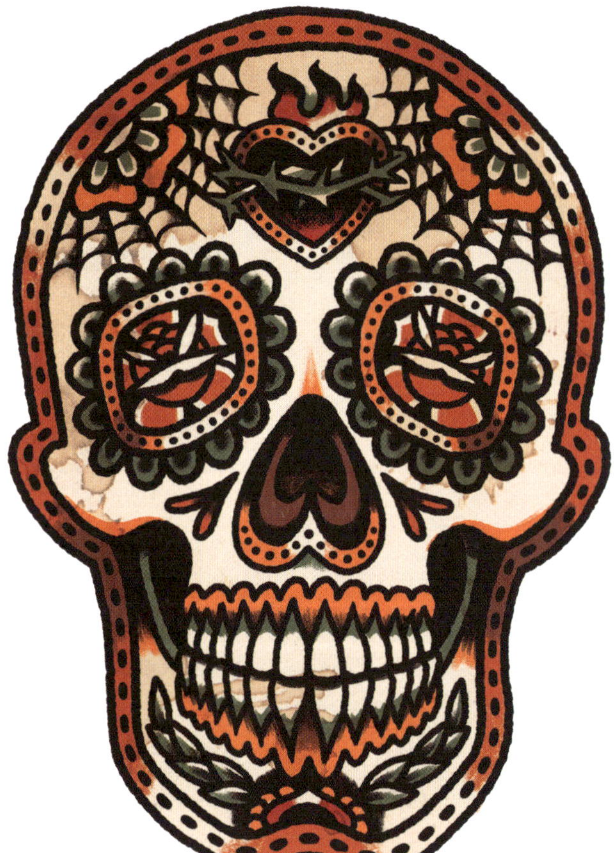

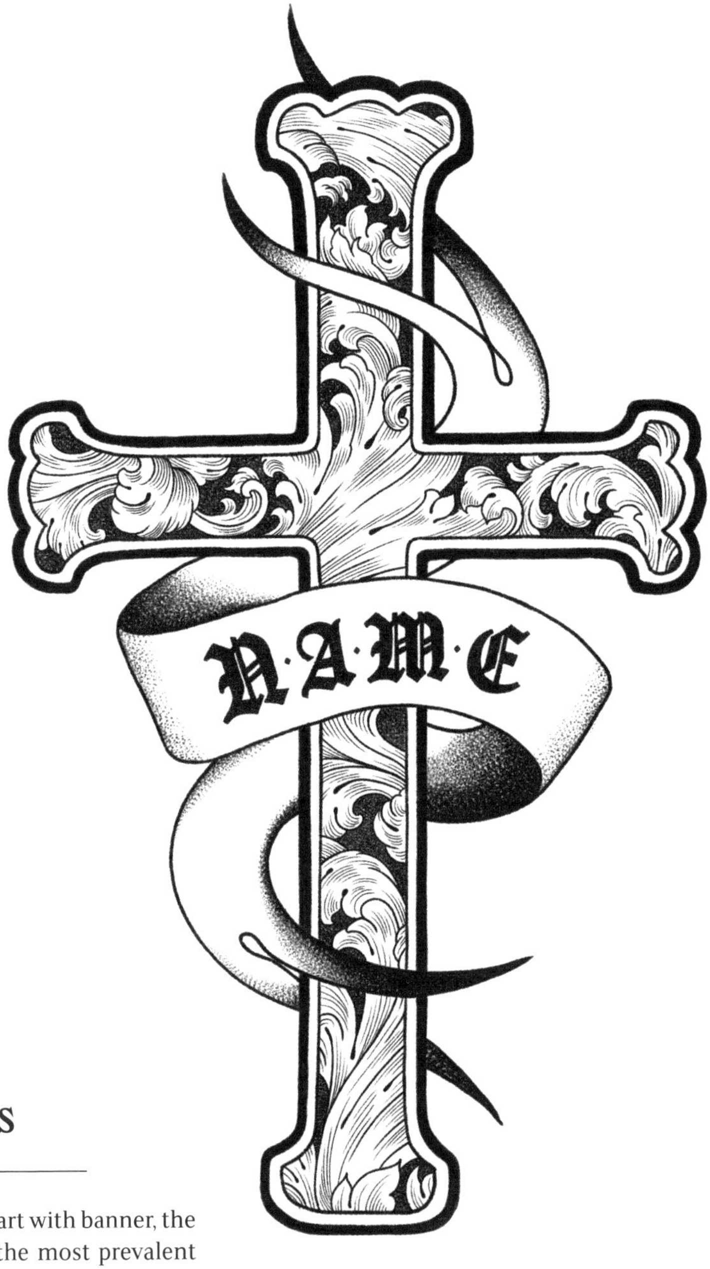

Cross

The visual antonym of a heart with banner, the memorial cross is one of the most prevalent symbols of loss in contemporary tattooing. With origins in mourning imagery of the 19th century, the standalone cross with banner follows from tombstone depictions ('In Memory of Mother/Father') and finds best form in the three-dimensionality afforded by the black and grey style.

Tombstone

Employment of a tombstone in memorial tattoo designs owes much to the mourning traditions of the Victorian era. This period, spanning 1837 to 1901, was marked in the West by swift spread of disease and high infant mortality, the American Civil War and, generally, a low life expectancy. Together, these factors made mourning not only a regular part of daily life, but a very public one. As such, a robust industry of memento making arose – funeral cards, etchings and lithographs — expanding the visual culture of death and transforming conventions related to displaying grief. As with several other, now classic, tattoo designs, including the formidable 'rock of ages', the image of family members grieving beside a tombstone (both with and without a background willow) shifted easily from print to tattoo culture. Tattoo flash books of the 20th century regularly included a few articulations of the idea, and as the western traditional style – with its characteristic heavy line and strong shading – matured, standalone tombstones took on a new design integrity.

Today, tombstone tattoos remain a popular way to reflect on loss. Whether in the western traditional or rendered in the black and grey style, the symbol serves with or without further decoration. However, the incorporation of other symbols – doves, keys, roses – often augment the image and add depth to its story.

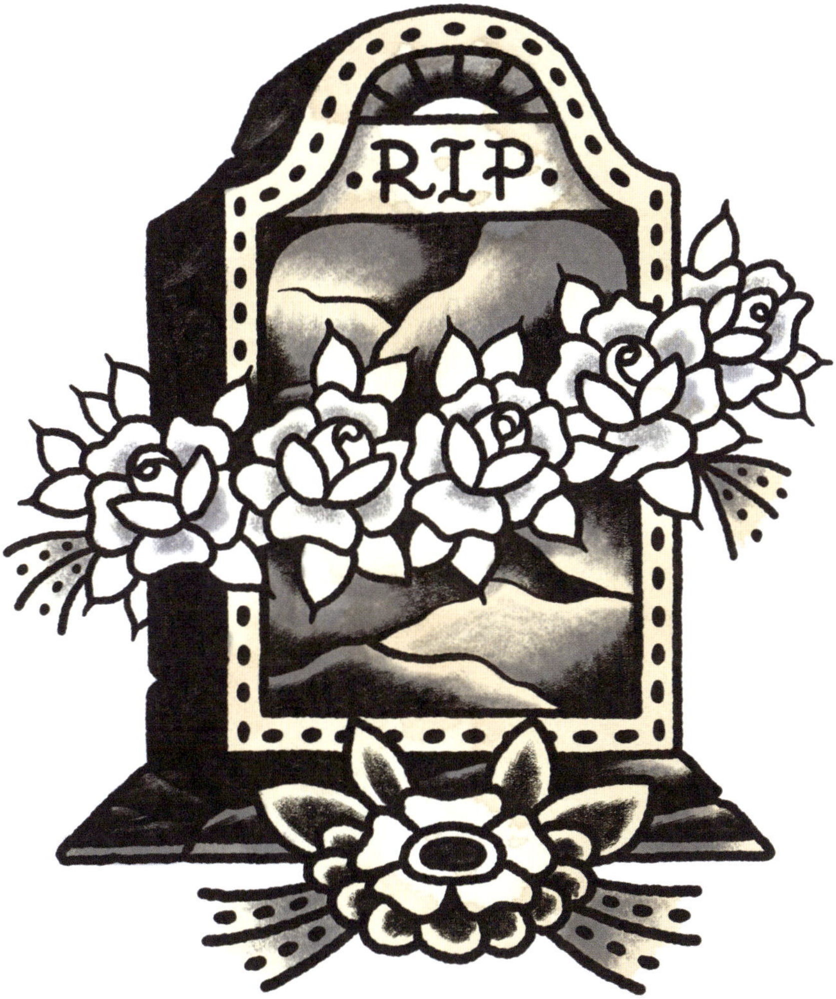
RIP

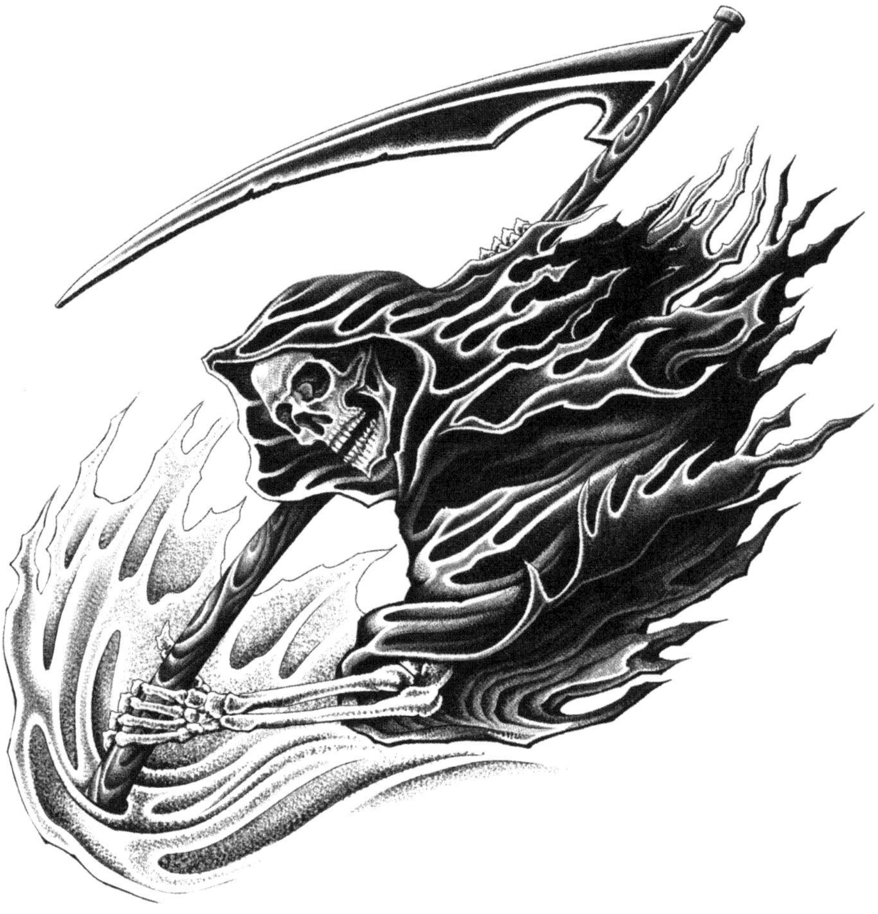

Grim Reaper

If candles, clocks and watches relay transience of time, the grim reaper carries with it an abrupt impermanence. As a symbol, it is commonly understood as the personification of death. The notion of the figure, complete with scythe, may have emerged in popular imagination during the Black Death, which swept Europe during the middle of the 14th century, but the name 'grim reaper' doesn't appear in English until the 19th century.

Of course, the grim reaper is not alone as a personification of death – a constant in all cultures, inclusive of the angel of death. However, the hooded skeleton with scythe makes for a powerful, agnostic tattoo articulating the inevitability of life's end. Wearers aren't just honouring their demise, but also reminding themselves to embrace life as lived.

Pocket Watch

As with the hourglass (see page 211), pocket watch tattoos mark the presence of time. However, in design there is greater opportunity for personalization. The watch face can be 'set' to mark important moments – birthdays, commemoration of life-altering events and even counterculture associations. Aesthetically, a pocket watch takes to the black and grey or western traditional style with equal vigor.

Pocket watch tattoos are among the motifs that became common through steampunk and other cultures pioneering a futuristic, Victorian-era look. Though not exclusively associated with that scene, the bubbling of corseted ladies, penny-farthings, sewing machines and other 19th-century paraphernalia at the turn of the 21st century, certainly elevated the place of the pocket watch in contemporary tattooing.

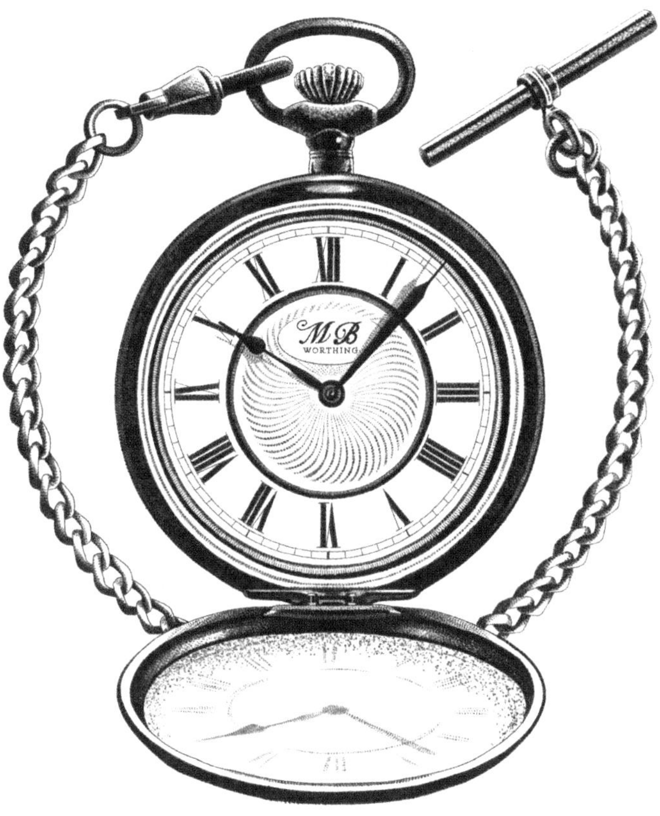

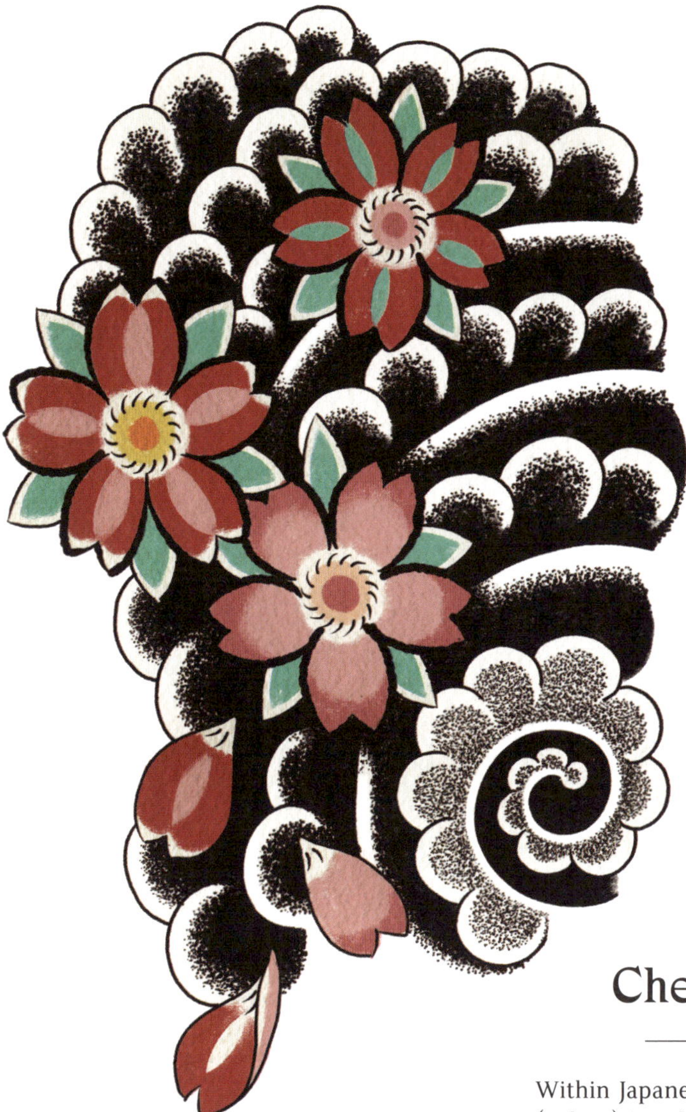

Cherry Blossom

Within Japanese culture the cherry blossom (*sakura*) is celebrated as a symbol of beauty and youth. Blossoming in spring, and falling quickly, the flower itself commands attention as a stern reminder that joy begats melancholy. Thus, given the fleeting nature of the *sakura*, images employing these blooms reconcile the tides of time in sensitive contemplation of transience. The notion connects to a specific concept: *mono no aware*. In essence, the embracement of ephemerality.

Hourglass

Symbols of time form a unique body of tattoo vocabulary. These range from the overt – a commemorative date inked on the wrist – to various representations of quotidian details. One popular articulation, the hourglass, can run the gamut, allowing for visualization of passing time at different scales. The hourglass was certainly cemented in popular culture in the 14th century, appearing in visual arts and gaining significant use across a variety of industries.

Though now obsolete as a central timekeeping device, the hourglass remains etched in our collective conscious. As such, the image of the hourglass serves well in tattoo compositions related to life, death and the spirit of human existence. The hourglass reminds of fleeting existence (punctuated when wings are included in the design) and the eternity of the soul.

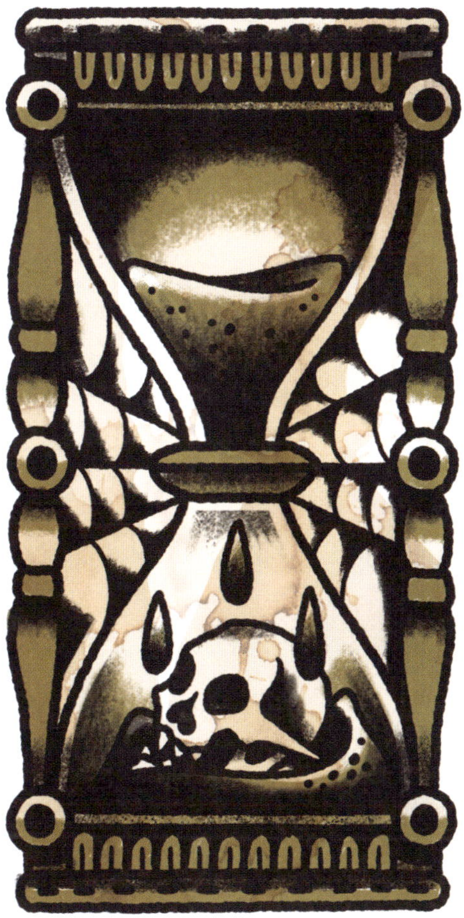

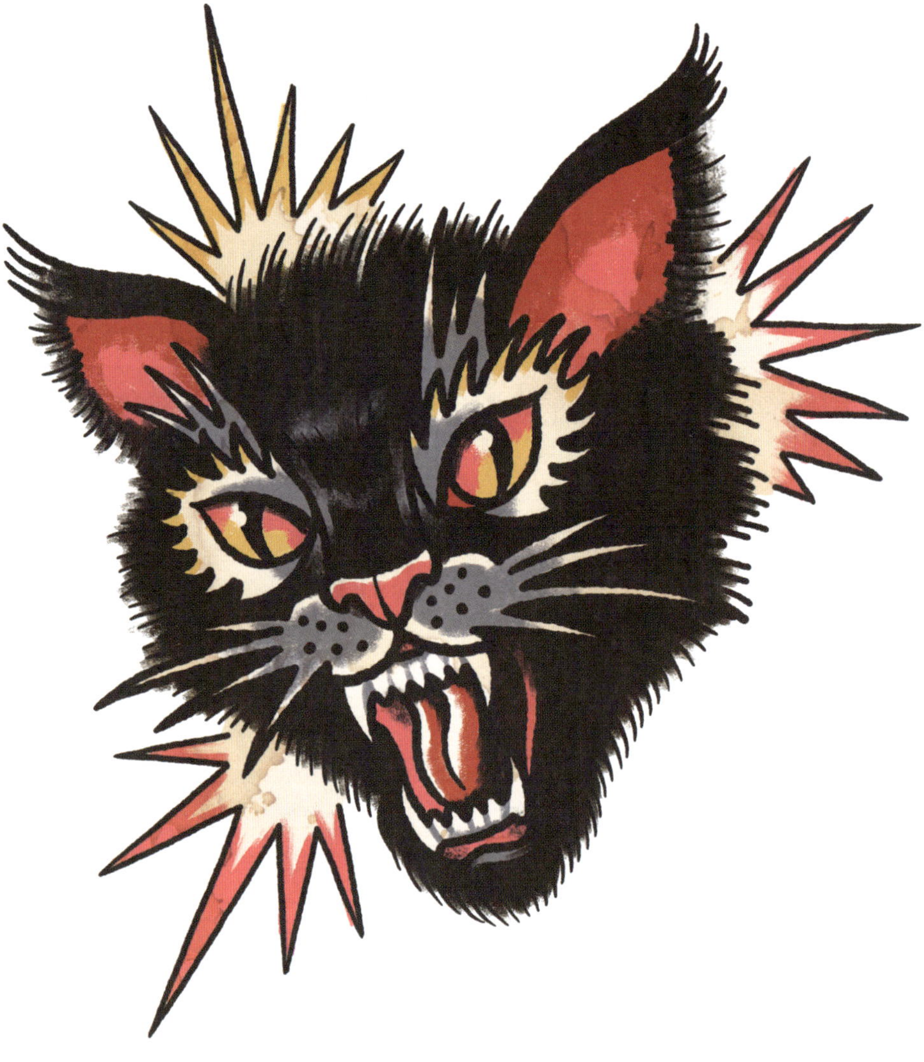

Firecracker Cat

There's a direct reason for the naming of this now ubiquitous image: the cat's head derives from the logo of a famed firework brand, Black Cat. With hissing mouth and piercing eyes, the firecracker cat forms an arresting image of fear and pain.

The Black Cat brand emerged in the United States in the 1940s, gaining a patent in 1952. It has since become the mainstay of any celebration involving fireworks. Disconnected from its origin, the firecracker conveys a pronounced era-specific macabre tone – all the mid-century creepy cat feels.

Maple Leaf

While the *sakura* blooms and dies in spring (see page 210), the spectacle of the maple leaf's transition to brilliant reds and oranges sparks moment to ponder the cycle of life in autumn. In Japanese tattooing, the maple leaf (*momiji*) is used as a symbol of life's transience – a vivid reminder that all things live and die – and a reminder of passing time. Leaves are often represented as flowing in water or floating in wind, augmenting their association with fleeting moments.

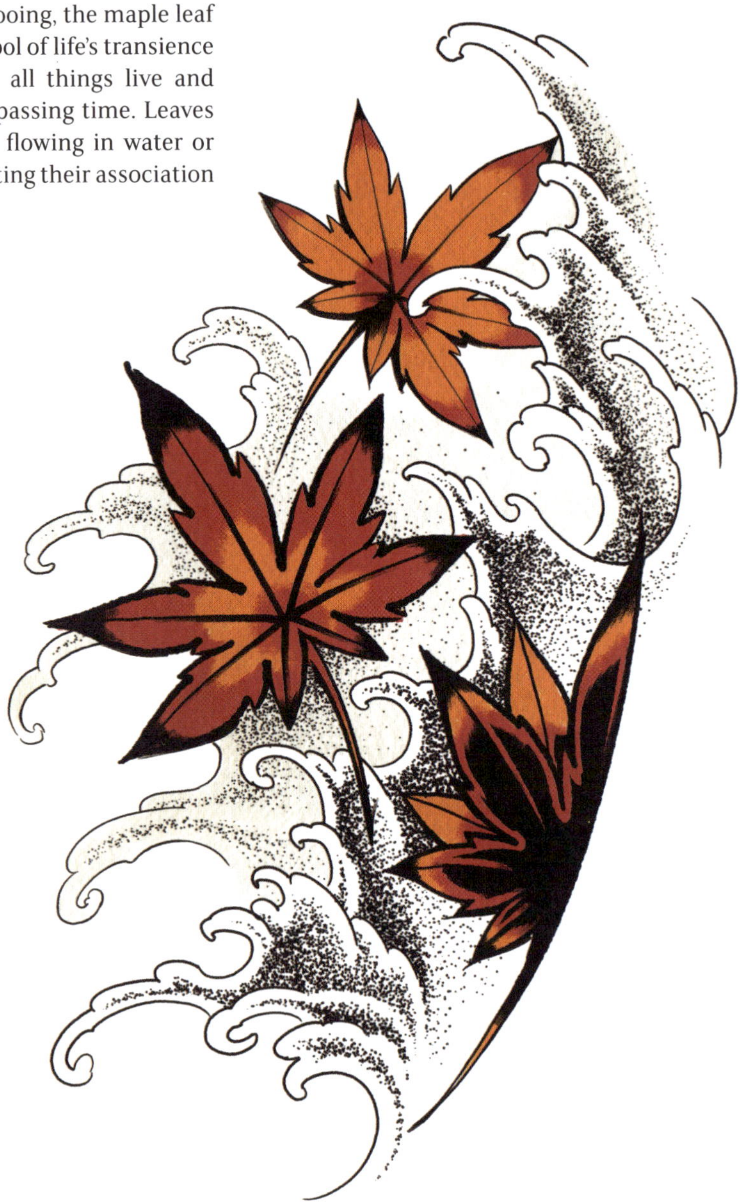

Candle

The candle's connection to death lies in its inherent impermanence. With the flame dancing, life abounds. Yet, blown out, the candle is diminished and spiritless.

Moreover, the candle embraces transience. The fleeting nature of the flame demands that the wearer considers life in the moment – living to one's fullest potential – and is especially potent when combined with other elements in memento mori or vanitas imagery.

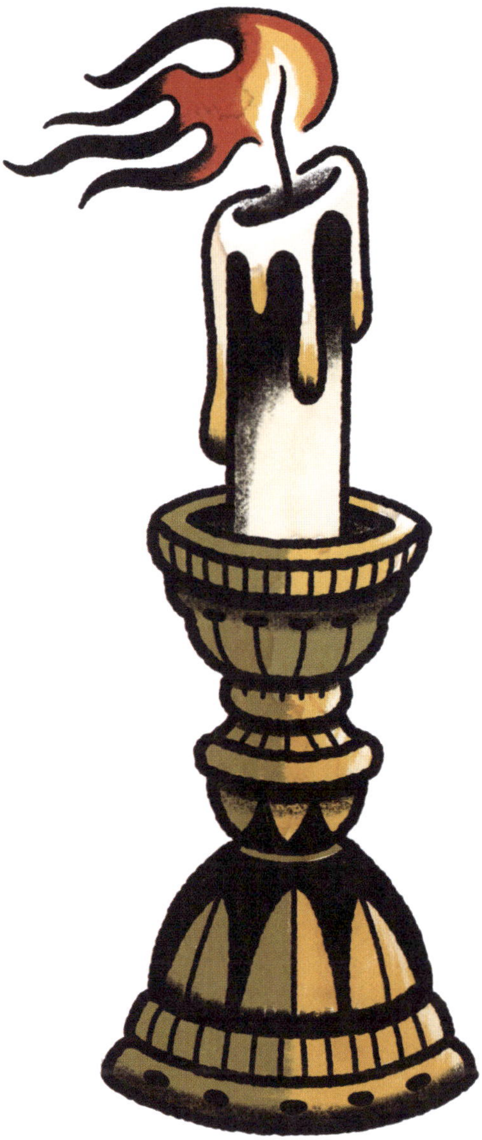

Coffin

The coffin is a direct, and rather overt, ode to mortality. In articulation, the design is best served up in the western traditional style – with or without colour. Flowing banners allow for direct personalization, either in memory of a specific individual or to carry a common idiom (for example, 'Sleep Well'). Alternatively, phrases combine with the coffin motif to lay to rest a bad habit and close off a phase of life.

Considering shape, the six-sided coffin – tapering from shoulder to foot – finds regular use in contemporary tattooing. Rails and other adornments, elements that became common with the commercialization of funeral ritual in the Victorian era, allow additional choices in how one might define the tone of the coffin itself.

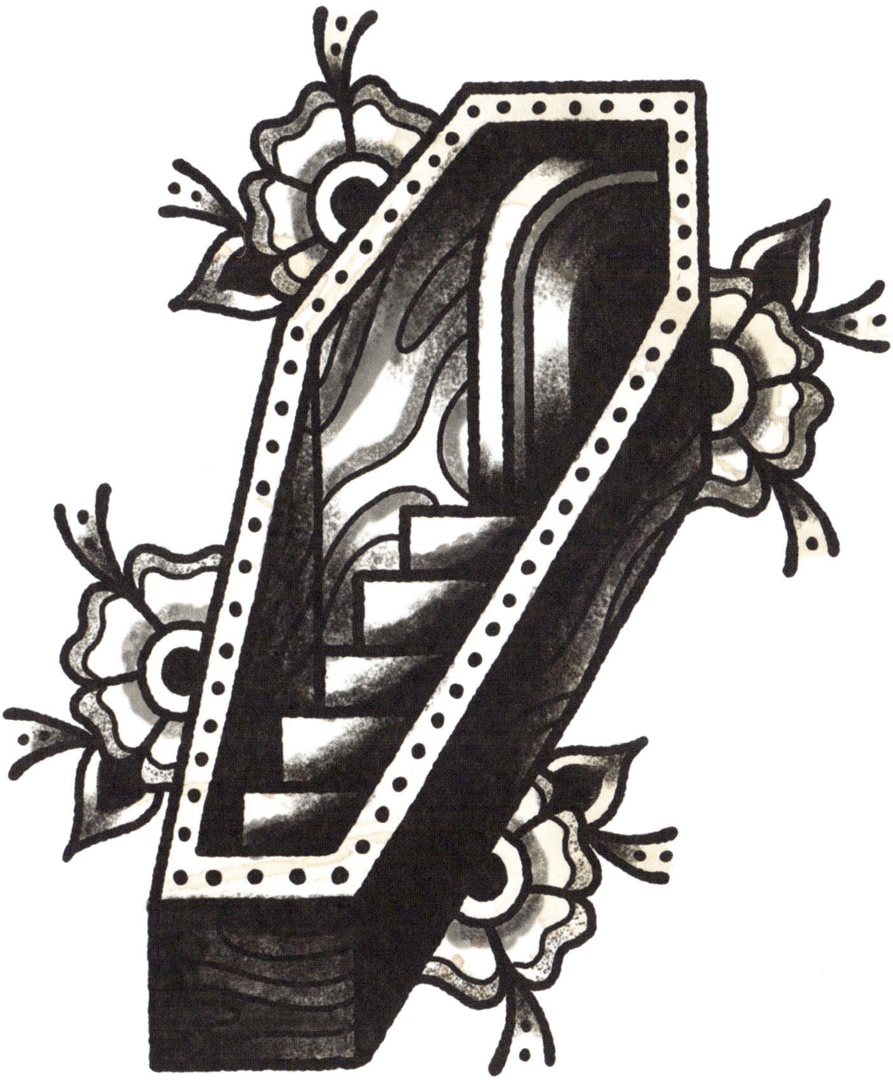

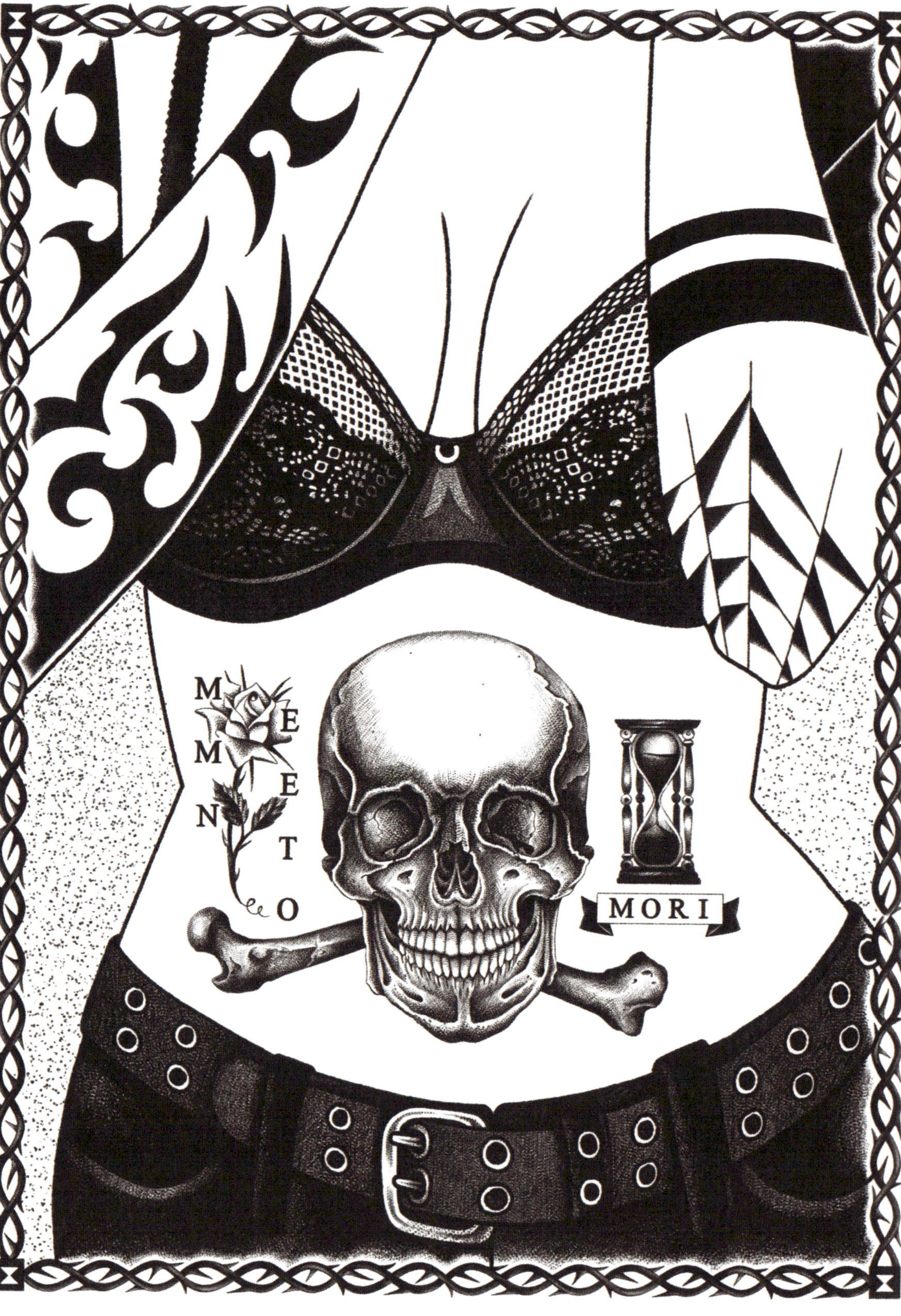
MEMENTO
MORI

Memento Mori

'Remember you must die'. In both direct translation and visual articulation, memento mori articulates the impermanence of life. Popular compositions include skull, candle, hourglass, fruit and more as representations of decay and mortality.

However, it is also common, and has been since the 1700s, to balance these elements with suggestions of earthly pleasure. In this, one may capture the vanities (or interests) of the deceased honouring a life lived and pursuits followed. Seen in this light, the memento mori becomes a sort of vanitas still life, symbolizing the specific character and culture of a given individual.

Namakubi

These severed and pierced heads, undoubtedly gruesome in composition, have origins in samurai tradition, particularly in the Edo period, when there was staunch belief in death with honour. Rather than die a shameful death, they chose *seppuku* – a two-part ritual in which the samurai stabbed themselves while another swung a sword to decapitate them.

Generally, the namakubi design conveys a dedication to ideas. The tattooers of New York's Kings Ave Tattoo refer to it as 'a more romantic take on the impermanence of life'.

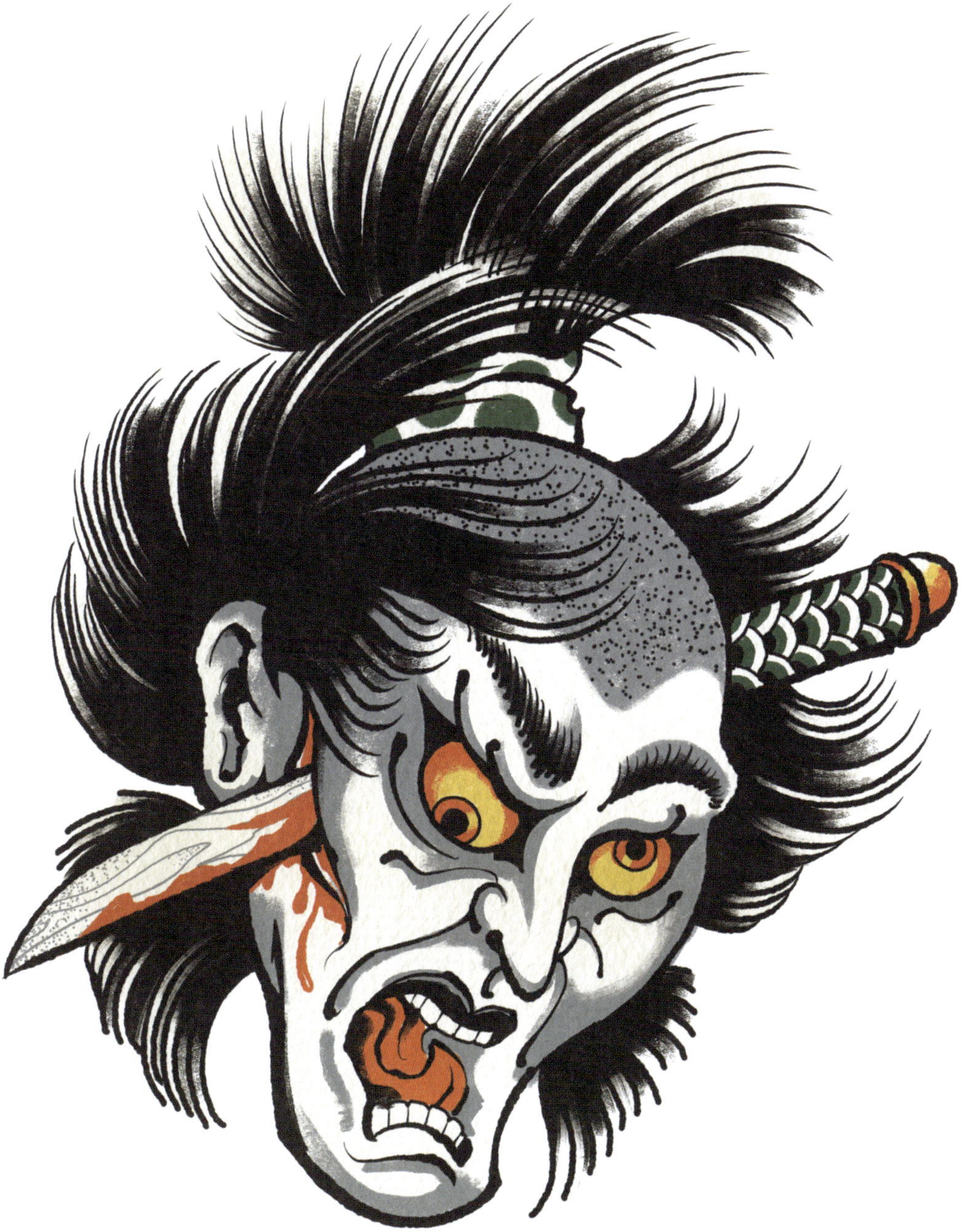

Index

Quarto

First published in 2022
by Frances Lincoln,
an imprint of The Quarto Group.
1 Triptych Place, 2nd Floor,
London, SE1 9SH,
United Kingdom
T (0)20 7700 9000
www.Quarto.com

EEA Representation, WTS Tax d.o.o.,
Žanova ulica 3, 4000 KranJ, Slovenia.
www.wts-tax.si

A catalogue record for this book is available from the British Library.

ISBN 978-0-7112-6786-2
Ebook ISBN 978-0-7112-6787-9

10 9

Illustrations by Oliver Munden
Design by Eleanor Ridsdale Colussi

Printed in Huizhou, Guangdong, China, TT042026

MIX
Paper | Supporting responsible forestry
FSC® C016973
FSC www.fsc.org

ABOUT THE ARTIST

Artist Oliver Munden has turned his hand to all manner of styles and applications for what is fast approaching two decades. Whether it be large scale murals, retail interiors, record covers, custom products, paper or skin, another surface is just another challenge.

Vintage skate art, psychedelia, renaissance art and, most notably, European, American and Japanese tattoo aesthetics are combined to create a recognisable signature style which has attracted many commercial clients as well as private clients in his work as a tattooist.

Oliver works at Rock Steady Tattoo located on the south coast of England as well as taking on commercial artwork projects.

THANKS

Oliver would like to thank his family; Vanessa, David and Joshua Munden, as well as his friends, for their support and motivation during the creation of this book.

INFO

Website - www.olivermunden.com
Instagram - @olivermunden

MUNDEN